A GUIDE TO LIFE

By the same author

The Will and Testament of the Biala Rabbi
A Guide to Hasidism
The Slave Who Saved the City
The Jewish Literary Treasures of England and America
The Legacy of Polish Jewry
The World of Hasidism
Treasures of Judaica
Hasidism and the State of Israel
Hasidism: The Movement and Its Masters
Hasidic Rebbes

A Gift

A GUIDE TO LIFE

Jewish Laws and

Customs of Mourning

Rabbi Tzvi Rabinowicz

JASON ARONSON INC.
Northvale, New Jersey
London

First softcover edition—1994

Library of Congress Cataloging-in-Publication Data

Rabinowicz, Tzvi. 1919–
    A guide to life : Jewish laws and customs of mourning / by Tzvi
Rabinowicz.
        p. cm.
    Bibliography: p.
    Includes index.
    ISBN 0-87668-833-4 (hb)
    ISBN 1-56821-143-0 (pb)
    1. Mourning customs, Jewish. I. Title.
BM712.R3   1989
296.4′45 – dc20   89-35085

Manufactured in the United States of America. Jason Aronson Inc. offers books and
cassettes. For information and catalog write to Jason Aronson Inc., 230 Livingston
Street, Northvale, New Jersey 07647.

Contents

Introduction

Judaism, we are constantly reminded, is more than a creed; it is a way of life. Its doctrines and teachings are given practical expression in our daily actions, so that the difficult journey through life is eased and ennobled. Our sages emphasize that it is the sacred duty of the Jew to conduct his life as to make it a continuous act of service to God and to man.

The real purpose of religion is to open the heart to true joy and to strengthen the spirit in those inevitable moments of darkness and despair.

Over the centuries the rabbis have evolved a pattern of practices and rites that are concerned with every aspect of death, and these include tender regard for the dying and deep concern for the sorrowing family. The ritual of burial and the manner of mourning are prescribed to preserve, *inter alia*, the qualities of taste and moderation. Moreover, the sages endeavored to reconcile the natural and spontaneous expression of profound grief with the reasoned and resigned self-control that the believing Jew is enjoined to practice. Jewish laws of mourning are many and detailed, but they are always inspired with a warm humanity. This is in pursuance of the guiding principles of the rabbis to always adopt the "lenient view" when questions arose in connection with the laws of mourning.

A vast Hebrew literature on the subject of mourning has evolved, beginning with the post-talmudical minor tractate *Evel Rabbati* or *Semachot,* continuing with *Torat Ha-Adam* by Rabbi Moses ben Nachman (1194–1270), and the publication of *Maavar Yabok* by the Italian Kabbalist Berachiah ben Moses of Modena (d. 1638), culminating with Rabbi Leopold Greenwald's *Kol Bo Al Avelut* (On Laws of Mourning), published between 1947 and 1952. Yet apart from the translation of Rabbi Simon Frankforter's *Sefer Chayyim* (The Book of Life) by the Rev. Benjamin Chayyim Ascher (1812–1893) published in 1847, *The Handbook of Life,* issued by the *Chevrah Kaddisha* of London in 1909, and *Eternal Life,* by Rabbi J. S. Sperka, published in 1939, little has been written on the subject in English.

The present book is not designed to be an exhaustive compendium of the laws of mourning, nor is it intended to supplant or supersede the authorized rabbinic codes. It is merely intended as an elementary guide for the layman, who should in all cases of doubt seek the advice of competent rabbinical authorities who alone have the power to give decisions in the light of individual circumstances.

T.R. 1964

PREFATORY NOTE
TO THE PRESENT EDITION

When this book first appeared in 1964, it was something of a pioneering work. The work was originally dedicated to the memory of Eva Rosalind Sher. The third revised edition has been made possible by the generosity of the late Louis J. Mintz and Mr. Frank Green, J.P.

The reception given to this book has been most gratifying. Now that it is being issued afresh, the opportunity has been taken to make a few corrections and to bring it up to date, with additional material making it suitable for American Jewry. I am grateful to Rabbi Dr. B. Susser, Rabbi Dr. Nisson E. Shulman, Mr. Norman Cohen, and Mr. Aaron Gleiser for a number of valuable suggestions.

It is my pleasure to thank my publisher Mr. Arthur Kurzweil for his expertise. As always, however, my greatest debt is to my wife Bella for her unfailing support, forbearance, encouragement, and advice.

T.R. 27 *Nisan* 5749 — *Yom Ha-Shoah*

Chapter 1

The Way of All Flesh

VISITING THE SICK

Visiting the sick—*bikkur cholim*—is one of the many social obligations that Judaism has clothed with religious significance. Even God Himself is said to have observed this *mitzvah* (an obligation or duty ordained by God or the rabbis),[1] and man is enjoined to follow this Divine example.

Bikkur cholim is classified by the *Mishnah*[2] as one of those precepts "the fruit of which a man enjoys in this world, while the stock remains for him in the world to come." It is an act that benefits the visitor almost as much as the sick person. When a friend or neighbor is ill, a man should not be indifferent. He should regard it his duty to visit the sufferer, regardless of the invalid's age, color, or race.[3]

Thoughtless visits, however, are to be discouraged, for they may hinder rather than help the patient's progress. The visitor is, therefore, urged to disregard his personal inclinations and to consider only the patient's welfare. Visiting too early in the morning or too late at night is to be avoided.[4] "Do not fatigue him by staying too long," counsels Rabbi Eleazar ben Isaac of Worms, the eleventh-century moralist, "for his malady is heavy enough already. Enter cheerfully, for his heart and his eyes are on those who come in."[5]

1

Merely to visit a patient is not necessarily the true fulfillment of the *mitzvah*. *Bikkur cholim* was never envisaged by our sages as a mere passive and perfunctory convention.[6] If the sick person is in want, then his needs must be satisfied. "My son," advised Rabbi Eleazar, "when thou visitest a sick man who is without means, be quick to offer refreshments to him and he will esteem it as though thou didst uphold and restore his soul. The Lord will requite thee."[7] But even when a patient has ample means and is well cared for, the visitor is expected to add to his comfort by giving practical expression of his sympathy. If one cannot visit a sick person, by all means enquire, even if only by telephone, but the *mitzvah* of *bikkur cholim* cannot be fulfilled by the enquiry; only warm contact can give the patient the reassurance and the comforting knowledge he needs, in the hours of pain and weakness, that he is not left to suffer alone.

Although it is obviously important to minister to the physical needs of the patient and to relieve him of those material worries that might retard healing or even aggravate his illness, nevertheless, the best help is prayer, which is an indispensable part of *bikkur cholim*.[8] There are many references in the Bible and Talmud to prayers for the sick.[9]

Selected Psalms may be read, particularly Psalm 119, which consists of twenty-two stanzas corresponding to the letters of the Hebrew alphabet. Another appropriate prayer is Psalm 23, which is unrivaled for calm serenity and perfect faith. Under the Almighty's loving care, the Psalmist knows neither want nor fear. Even when unknown perils are thickest, where deathly gloom and horror are on every side, he knows no fear. The patient should find comfort in the immortal line: "Yea, though I walk through the valley of the shadow of death, I will fear no evil, for Thou art with me; Thy rod and Thy staff, they comfort me." Psalm 103, too, in which the Psalmist summons his soul and all his faculties to praise God for pardon, redemption, and bountiful provisions for every need, is ideal for the man on his sickbed. Man may be frail and transitory, but those who fear God can rest in His assurance of His eternal faithfulness.

Well-wishers for the good of the patient often fast or visit the graves of loved ones or give charity "which delivereth from death."[10] At the Reading of the Law, a special *Mi-Sheberach* may be recited.[11] When prayers are offered for the sick, a reference should be made to "All the sick of Israel."[12] In the words of Rabbi Simcha Bunem of Przysucha, "When a Jew lies in his sickbed, the God of Israel is in danger of losing one of His soldiers in the battle for goodness and truth."

Where the illness is grave, more serious measures should be taken. The patient may be given an additional name, such as Chayyim (or Chayah), Yechiel, Raphael, Benzion, or Alter (Alta). In the Talmud, Rabbi Isaac affirms that the changing of a name is one of the four things that cancel the doom of a man.[13] This custom, known as *shinnui ha-shem* (change of name), is mentioned by Rabbi Judah ben Samuel Ha-Chassid (d. 1217)[14] and by many medieval rabbinical authorities.[15]

When the name of the sick person is mentioned in a *Mi-Sheberach*, it is customary to refer to the name of the mother and not to that of the father. The *Zohar*[16] traces this custom to David, who prayed to God, "Save the son of Thy handmaid" (Psalm 86:16).

The Kabbalist Rabbi Isaiah Horowitz (1565–1630), the author of *Shnei Luchot Haberit*, cites the custom that, in times of sickness, graves would be visited. The grounds of the cemetery "would be encircled," i.e., relatives would walk around the cemetery perimeter, reciting *techinot* (supplicatory prayers), and give charity to the poor. This was regarded as a very effective remedy.[17]

Nothing must be allowed to stand in the way of preserving or prolonging life. "It is a religious precept," states the Talmud,[18] "to desecrate the Sabbath for any person afflicted with an illness that may prove dangerous." The rabbis give this graphic illustration: "For a day-old child (who is dangerously ill) the Sabbath may be profaned; however, for the dead, be he even David, the king of Israel, the Sabbath must not be violated."[19]

Human life is precious and its preservation takes precedence over almost every other consideration. A sick person should not be given bad news, nor should he be told of the death of a relative lest he be so distressed that his recovery is retarded.[20]

Sabbath is a good day for visiting the sick.[21] In medieval times it was customary in many communities for the worshipers to pay such visits before returning home to eat the Sabbath meal. In 1360, Rabbi Nissim ben Reuben Gerondi, the foremost halachic authority of his time, refers to a society for visiting the sick. An organized chaplaincy service is provided in the City of New York by the New York Board of Rabbis.

PHYSICIANS

God Himself is the supreme physician "who healeth the broken in heart, and bindeth up their wounds" (Psalm 147:3). Three times a day, Jews pray for heaven-sent healing: "Heal us, O Lord, and we shall be healed; save us and we shall be saved; for Thou art our praise. Grant a perfect healing to all our wounds; for Thou, almighty King, art a faithful and merciful physician. Blessed art Thou, O Lord, who healest the sick of Thy people Israel."[22]

Nevertheless, the rabbis readily conceded that the Divine Healer does His work through mortals, and thus physicians were held in high regard.[23] Joseph employed house physicians (Genesis 50:2), and a physician was in attendance in the Courts of Law.[24] This was not in any way a usurpation of Divine prerogative, since the Torah itself, the rabbis assure us, granted the physician authority to heal.[25] "Honor a physician," advises Ben Sira, "according to thy need of him, with the honors due unto him; for verily the Lord hath created him" (Ecclesiastes 38:1–2).

In medieval times many of our great rabbis were physicians. The celebrated bibliographer Moritz Steinschneider (1816–1907) listed 2,168 Jewish physicians who are known to have lived between the Dark Ages and the eighteenth century.[26]

It is the doctor's duty to prolong life as long as possible, and he or she must not allow any consideration to weaken the patient's power of resistance. "Even when the physician realizes that his patient approaches death, he should order him to eat this and not to eat that, drink this and not to drink that, but on no account should he tell him that the end is near."[27]

EUTHANASIA

Euthanasia (painless killing) for sufferers from incurable diseases is contrary to the teachings of Judaism. The account given of the burning at the stake of Rabbi Chaninah ben Tradyon (a *tanna*—teacher—of the second century) states that his disciples were anxious to save him unnecessary pain. "Open thy mouth," they pleaded, "so that the fire enter into thee." He replied: "Let Him who gave my soul take it away, but no one should injure oneself."[28] However, he permitted the executioner to remove from over his heart the tufts of wool that had been put there to increase his torture by delaying his death.

Our sages believed that a "man who destroys a single soul is regarded as having destroyed an entire world."[29] Hence no direct action to hasten death is permitted.

VIDDUI—CONFESSION

Judaism does not have the ceremony of Last Rites. A patient nearing his end should be encouraged to confess his sins before God, for such a time calls for sincere penitence and evokes God's forgiveness. The moral efficacy of confession is affirmed in the Bible: "He who confesses and forsakes his sins will obtain mercy" (Proverbs 28:13). Achan, before his death, was called upon to confess his sins (Joshua 7:19).

No confessor is needed, since only God can absolve sin. The patient is urged: "Confess your sins! Many confessed their sins and died not, and many who have not confessed died; and as a reward, should you confess, you will live; and he who confesses his sins has a portion in the world to come."[30] The Talmud does not prescribe a form of deathbed confession, but Nachmanides in his work *Torat Ha-Adam* records a form of confession that had long been in vogue. The following is a brief form of confession:

> I acknowledge unto thee, O Lord my God and God of my fathers, that both my cure and my death are in Thy hands. May it be Thy will to send me a perfect healing. Yet if my death be fully determined by Thee, I will in love accept it at Thy hand. O may my death be an atonement for all my sins, iniquities, and transgressions, of which I have been guilty against Thee. Bestow upon me the abounding happiness that is treasured up for the righteous. Make known to me the path of life: In Thy presence is fullness of joy; at Thy right hand, bliss forevermore. Thou who art the father of the fatherless and judge of the widow, protect my beloved kindred with whose soul my own is knit. Into Thy hand I commend my spirit; Thou has redeemed me, O Lord of Truth. Amen, and Amen.[31]

If one does not know that confession should be said, others should tell him to say, "May my death be an atonement." However, such things should not be said to him in the presence of women and children, for it may make them weep and cause the sick person distress.[32] This rite may be performed on the Sabbath and on Holy Days.

LAST WILL AND TESTAMENT

Our sages relate that when Jacob felt that his end was near he asked for Divine mercy: "Lord of the world!" he

prayed, "May it please Thee to grant that a man should fall
ill for two or three days and then be gathered into his people,
in order that he may have time to put his house in order and
repent of his sins." The Holy One replied: "It shall be so and
thou shalt be the first to profit by the new dispensation,"[33]
and so it happened that Jacob fell sick a short time before his
death.

Thus the blessing of Jacob,[34] the final requests of
Joseph,[35] the farewell address of Moses,[36] the advice of
David,[37] and the last exhortations of Mattathias[38] have set a
pattern that runs like a golden thread through Jewish literature. These deathbed declarations of faith are remarkable
writings that are filled with love of God and humanity,
worldly wisdom, and other-worldly visions. "The testa-
ments," writes Israel Abrahams,[39] "give an intimate insight
into the personal religion of Jews in various ages. The wills
convey much information as to social life, the position of
women, habits of dress and domestic economy, schemes of
education, and indeed, the many interests of business and
culture."

Isaiah's advice to King Hezekiah, "Set thy house in
order, for thou shalt die, and not live" (Isaiah 38:1),[40] has
always been taken literally by pious Jews. The rabbis regarded such final instructions to be of paramount importance, and they considered the oral testament of a dying
person as legally binding as if his instructions had been
written down and witnessed.[41]

LAST MOMENTS

A dying person is known as a *gosess*.[42] Despite the
talmudic dictum "Most *gosessim* die,"[43] the Sabbath may be
profaned to prolong their lives, even if it is unlikely that they
can survive much longer. Not until life has actually departed
may the services that are normally performed for a dead
person be performed for a *gosess*.[44]

Family members should consider it their duty to be

present when death is imminent, especially if the dying person is fully conscious and is aware of their presence.

Those visiting a dying man should not discuss worldly matters nor eat or drink in his presence.

A dying person should not be left alone. It is a great *mitzvah* to be present at *yetziat neshamah* (departure of the soul).[45] When the end is approaching the last paragraph of the confession should be recited, especially "Hear O Israel; the Lord our God, the Lord is One."[46]

Death is presumed to occur when breathing appears to have stopped. The body must then be left untouched for about eight minutes while a feather is laid across the lips and nose and those present watch carefully for the slightest sign of movement. When death is finally established, the eyes and mouth are gently closed by the son or the nearest relative.

Jacob was assured that Joseph would render this final filial service (Genesis 46:4).[47] Legend has it that the dying are granted a glimpse of the Divine. "Thou canst not see My face, for men shall not see Me and live" (Exodus 33:20); in other words, a man cannot see God in life but only in death.[48]

According to Jewish law, death coincides with the cessation of both cardiac and respiratory functions.[49] When life has departed and the eyes are closed, the arms and hands are extended at the sides of the body and the lower jaw is bound up before rigor mortis sets in. The body is then placed on the floor with the feet toward the door, and is finally covered with a sheet, while a lighted candle is placed close to the head.

On the Sabbath[50] or on a *Yom Tov*[51] (a holiday or Festival) the body must not be moved, although the chin may be lightly bound. If a Jew dies in a hospital or nursing home, and no fellow Jews are available to perform these services, they may be carried out by the gentile staff.[52]

The departure of life is sad but never sinister. When Rabbi Simcha Bunem of Przysucha (1765–1827) was lying on his deathbed, his wife wept bitterly, whereupon he said:

"Why dost thou weep? All my life has been given me merely that I might learn how to die!" Death should be regarded simply as a transition, a move from one home to another, from the lower world into the higher. A believing Jew echoes the words of the Psalmist, "Yea, though I walk through the valley of the shadow of death, I will fear no evil, for Thou art with me" (Psalm 23:4).

Chapter 2

Respect for the Dead

The body, the creation of God and the dwelling place of the soul, must be accorded every respect. *Kevod ha-met*, respect for the dead, is a fundamental principle of Judaism. The first mention of this concept is in the Bible: 'And Hezekiah slept with his fathers . . . and the inhabitants of Jerusalem did him honor at his death" (II Chronicles 32:33).

Judaism, always more concerned with deeds than with words, defines our duties to the living and details our obligation to the dead. The biblical heroes were demonstrative in their expressions of grief. Abraham, we are told, "came to mourn for Sarah, and to weep for her" (Genesis 23:2), and Jacob "mourned for his son (Joseph) many days" (Genesis 37:34), while Joseph "fell upon his father's face, and wept upon him, and kissed him" (Genesis 50:1). Then there is David's moving reaction to the death of Saul as we read: "And they wailed, and wept, and fasted until even, for Saul, and for Jonathan his son, and for the people of the Lord, and for the house of Israel; because they were fallen by the sword" (II Samuel 1:12).

The rabbis, although they were opposed to excessive display of grief, stressed that the dead should be mourned in a fitting manner. "If one sheds tears for a worthy person, the Holy One, Blessed be He, counts them and lays them up in

His treasure house. . . . Whoever weeps for a worthy man is forgiven all his iniquities on account of the honor which he showed him."[1] Consideration for the dead is an act of loving-kindness, devoid of the self-interest that sometimes mars human relationships.

Our rabbis forbade men to slander or speak in derogatory terms of the dead. The *Midrash* quotes God as reproving Moses for making disparaging reference to the ancestors of his generation. Among the twenty-four offenses punishable by excommunication, which in talmudic times and the Middle Ages meant social ostracism and economic ruin, was "insulting a learned man even after death."[2]

After mentioning the name of a dead person, it is customary to add the phrase "*Alav ha-shalom*" (May peace be to him) or "*Zichrono livrachah*" (May his memory be for a blessing). If the deceased was a pious man one should say, "*Zecher tzaddik livrachah*" (May the memory of the righteous be for a blessing).

In the first year of mourning, the formula used by children is "*Hareni kaparat mishkavo*"[3] (May I be his [or her] atonement).

WATCHERS

A dead body should not be left alone. It must be guarded night and day on weekdays as well as on Sabbath until the funeral. The rabbis attached so much importance to this rite that the watchers did not have to say prayers or put on *tefillin* (phylacteries) while attending to their duties.[4] The reasons that have been given for guarding the body are varied. Some have suggested that it was to keep away evil spirits, others to protect the body from rodents and body snatchers. The most probable explanation is that it is a mark of respect for the dead, since it is considered disrespectful to leave a human body in a defenseless state, unattended. "As long as man is alive, his fear lies upon dumb creatures

(Genesis 9:2); once he dies, his fear ceases. Therefore, even a mighty man like Og, King of Bashan, needs guarding once he dies."[5]

It is forbidden to have a meal in the room where a dead person is lying. No member of the *Chevrah Kaddisha* (Holy Brotherhood) may drink any alcoholic beverages during the watch. Other persons participating in the watch must also refrain from doing so. Only matters concerned with the deceased may be pursued in the presence of the corpse.

The watchers should spend the time reciting verses from the Book of Psalms,

> which contains the whole music of the heart swept by the hand of his Maker. In it are gathered the lyrical burst of his tenderness, the moan of his penitence, the pathos of his sorrow, the triumph of his victory, the despair of his defeat, the firmness of his confidence, the rapture of his assured hope. In it is presented the anatomy of all parts of the human soul. In it, as Heine says, "are collected sunrise and sunset, birth and death, promise and fulfillment—the whole drama of humanity. . . . To weary travelers of every condition and at every period of history, the Psalms, then, are a mirror in which each man sees the motions of his own soul. They express in exquisite words the kinship which every thoughtful human heart craves to find with a supreme, unchanging, loving God, who will be to him a protector, guardian and friend. . . . They translate into speech the spiritual passion of the loftiest genius; they also utter, with beauty born of truth and simplicity, and with the exact agreement between the feelings and the expressions, the inarticulate and humble longings of the unlettered peasant. . . . They alone have known no limitations to a particular age, country or form of faith. In the Psalms the vast hosts of suffering humanity have found the deepest expressions of their hopes and fears."[6]

EARLY BURIAL

It is obligatory upon Jews to bury the dead as soon as possible, and early burial has always been the Jewish practice.[7] In 1772, when the Duke of Mecklenburg-Schwerin prohibited burial before the lapse of three days, the leading rabbinical authorities protested vigorously.

Early burial was not due entirely to the exigencies of the hot climate of the Holy Land, as it is sometimes said. Rather, it was considered a humiliation of the dead to leave them unburied.

However, a delay in burial is permitted if it is "for the sake of his honor," e.g., for the purpose of making a coffin or providing shrouds, or to enable relatives and friends to pay their last respects.[8]

FUNERAL ARRANGEMENTS

After the medical practitioner has performed his statutory duties, the funeral director should be contacted as soon as possible. His professional functions are to arrange for and supervise the transportation, care, preparation, and disposition of the body and to keep the body prior to the funeral in suitable surroundings (in a mortuary, chapel, or funeral home), see to all sanitary requirements, contact cemetery authorities, arrange the funeral service, order the cleansing of the remains by a *Chevrah Kaddisha*, adhering conscientiously to religious requirements, and engage a rabbi to officiate at the burial, unless the family express a preference.

The funeral director and his staff should be sensitive to the feelings of the family, who may be especially vulnerable when faced with the trauma of bereavement. They should be competent to deal with the intense grief and distress of relatives, who are anxious to preserve the dignity of the deceased. Tact and decorum are the prerequisites of their work, and they should be aware that "with the death of a husband you lose your present; with the death of a parent your past, and with the death of a child you lose your future."[9] It is wrong for Jews under ordinary circumstances to employ a non-Jewish funeral director. The funeral director must provide an itemized statement of costs when the funeral arrangements are made. The rabbi's role is one of giving spiritual support and guidance. At this time of emotional vulnerability, when family feelings run high and when there are no easy answers to mitigate irreparable loss, great strength and comfort can be found in religious observance.

POSTMORTEM EXAMINATION

It is forbidden to carry out an autopsy to ascertain the cause of death unless the civil authorities so order. For the same reason, dissection is regarded as dishonoring the human body—an insult to the dead and an infringement of the principle that forbids any benefit to be derived from the dead. This prohibition was upheld by Rabbi Ezekiel ben Judah Landau (1713–1793)[10] and Rabbi Moses Schreiber (1763–1839).[11] Rabbi Landau permits an autopsy only if the life of another patient then "at hand" might thereby be saved.

Today in the State of Israel, the Chief Rabbinate sanctions a postmortem examination when (1) it is legally required; (2) in the opinion of three doctors, the cause of death cannot otherwise be ascertained; (3) it might help to save the lives of others suffering from maladies similar to that from which the patient died; or (4) in cases of certain hereditary diseases, when it safeguards surviving relatives.[12]

Moreover, "The Plenary Council of the Chief Rabbinate of Israel . . . does not object to the use of bodies of persons who gave their consent in writing of their own free will during their lifetime for anatomical dissections as required for medical studies, provided the dissected parts are carefully preserved so as to be eventually buried with due respect according to Jewish law."[13]

When a person dies of unnatural causes, or the cause of death is uncertain, the coroner or public examiner may insist that an autopsy be performed. The conditions under which an official autopsy is demanded without the consent of the family are generally prescribed by the state. If necessary, the coroner may call an inquest to determine the cause of death.

TRANSPLANTS

Although a number of rabbinic authorities forbid the transplanting of the cornea from a dead person on account of the inevitable mutilation, most rabbinic scholars permit it under certain safeguards, since it will help to restore sight to the living.[14] Where a person expressly bequeaths his eyes for the benefit of another, irrespective of the consequent mutilation to his own body, such instructions may be obeyed. Laws that may appear stringent are interpreted leniently when life is at stake.

With regard to the hair of the dead, the consensus is to permit its use for the living.[15]

EMBALMING

Embalming was specifically an Egyptian rite and the Bible records only two cases, those of Jacob and Joseph (Genesis 50:2 and 50:26). In later times, the body of Aristobulus II, King of Judea (67–63 B.C.E.),[16] was also embalmed. This practice, however, was contrary to Jewish custom.[17]

If transportation to another city or country should be necessary, ecclesiastical authorities should be consulted. During the summer months, refrigeration may be used before the *taharah* (ritual of cleansing the corpse), if necessary.[18]

CREMATION

Judaism is unequivocally opposed to cremation for a number of reasons, principally because it is, like embalming, contrary to Jewish custom. From earliest recorded times,

Jews have invariably buried their dead in the earth, for it is written, "Dust thou art and to dust thou shalt return" (Genesis 3:19). Our sages[19] trace the rite of burial to the beginning of mankind and relate that Adam and Eve were greatly distressed when they saw the dead body of Abel, their son, and they did not know how to dispose of it. Then a raven took pity on them. The grief-stricken parents observed how it scratched the earth away in one spot and then hid a dead bird of its own kind in the ground. In like manner Adam dealt with his son.[19] Subsequently the heroes of the Bible from Abraham to the kings of Israel were interred in the ground.

Additional evidence that burial was the traditional Jewish method is provided by the Roman historian Tacitus (120–55 B.C.E.) who writes: "They [the Jews] bury rather than burn their dead."[20]

"Burning" was one of the "four deaths" imposed by the biblical penal code for a number of offenses.[21] "Bring her forth and let her be burnt" (Genesis 38:25), Judah said when told of Tamar's unchastity. "Achan and his family were stoned, and their bodies were burnt" (Joshua 7:25). These are but two examples of this penalty being carried out. Yet so abhorrent was burning to the rabbis that, unlike the Sadducees, they did not take it literally.[22] The act of reducing the human body to ashes was to them unthinkable.

Our sages teach that cremation is an indignity, an affront to man as the highest form of creation. The body, the temple and the servant of the soul, must be guarded against sacrilegious desecration.

In rabbinic writings, burning was described as an idolatrous practice. "Every death which is accompanied by burning," say the rabbis, "is looked upon as idolatry."[23] The record of the idolatrous kings who caused their children to pass "through the fire to Molech in the valley of the Children of Hinnom"[24] associated burning with paganism. Legend has it that in order to avoid Divine judgment, Titus, who destroyed the Second Temple in the year 70 C.E., instructed his descendants to burn his body and scatter the ashes over the seven seas "so that the God of the Jews should not find me and bring me to trial."[25] The Roman practice of cremation and their worship of ancestral ashes as household gods were additional reasons for classifying cremation as *chukkat ha-goy* (pagan custom).

Maimonides considers burial a scriptural injunction and rules that if one leaves a testamentary injunction not to be buried, his wishes are ignored in this matter.[26]

Nevertheless, there are a number of references in the Bible sufficiently interesting and unusual to merit careful study. In the First Book of Samuel (31:12) we read that "when the inhabitants of Jabesh Gilead heard concerning him that which the Philistines had done to Saul, all the valiant men arose, and went all night and took the body of Saul and the bodies of his sons from the wall of Beth-Shan; and they came to Jabesh, and burnt them there." This was surely an extraordinary incident, a desperate action designed to save the corpses from further indignity at the enemy's hands. Yet even in this instance, the parallel passage in Chronicles merely states that "their bones were buried" (I Chronicles 10:12).[27]

The passage applied to King Asa, "And they buried him in his own sepulchres which he had hewn out for himself in the city of David, and laid him in the bed which was filled with sweet odors and divers kinds (of spices) prepared by the perfumers' art; and they made a very great burning for him" (II Chronicles 16:14), clearly refers to the burning not of the body but of spices and plants.

Evidence that such was the practice may be found in the talmudic passage that states that when Patriarch Gamaliel II (c. 80–110 C.E.) died, Onkelos—commonly called the Proselyte Onkelos,[28] author of the best-known Aramaic translation of the Pentateuch (*Targum*)—"burned in his honor articles worth seventy Tyrian *maneh*."[29] It was evidently the practice to honor the dead by burning spices and other materials.

RESURRECTION AND CREMATION

Belief in resurrection is a principle of Judaism, as can be seen from our liturgy. When Maimonides said, "There are no material bodies in the future world,"[30] he was referring to life after death. But he himself believed that there would be a resurrection for the righteous in this world, and this tradition of a physical[31] as well as a spiritual resurrection has persisted and has been accepted throughout the ages.

Ezekiel's vision of the dry bones (Chapter 37) is taken by our sages to imply that the "righteous are destined to arise (from the dead) clothed in all their garments."[32] This physical resurrection, our sages tell us,[33] will begin from a bone called *Luz*, the base of the spinal column (*Os Coccyx*).

Cremation is thus a denial of the belief in bodily resurrection.

BURIAL OF THE ASHES

In November 1887, the British Chief Rabbi, Nathan Marcus Adler (1803–1890), wrote to Nathaniel Mayer, the first Lord Rothschild (1840–1915), President of the United Synagogue of London:

> With reference to the religious bearings on the question, I beg to state that whilst there does not exist any precept prohibiting the interment in a Jewish cemetery of the ashes of a person who has already been cremated, our law is decidedly and emphatically opposed to the practice of cremation. Both Jewish law and usage require the interment of the bodies of the dead and view the reduction of a corpse to ashes by fire as an indignity and an outrage. This can be proved by several passages in the Holy Scriptures, e.g., Amos 2:1 where punishment is pronounced upon Moab "because he burned the bones of the King of Edom into lime."[34]

Four years later (September 27, 1891) the wife of Dr. Maurice Davis was cremated, and Chief Rabbi Dr. Hermann Adler, the son of Nathan Marcus Adler, was asked for a ruling on the interment of the ashes. "I have given this request my full consideration in concert with the members of the *Bet Din*," he wrote in reply:

We subscribe to the opinion stated by my venerated Predecessor, that there does not exist any precept prohibiting the interment in a Jewish cemetery of the ashes of a person who has already been cremated, an opinion supported by other eminent rabbis including the Chief Rabbi of Kovno (Rabbi Isaac Elchanan Spector, 1817–1896). We accordingly permit such a burial. At the same time we earnestly beg you and the members of the community not to construe this permission into a sanction of the practice of cremation. We ardently hope that no brother or sister in faith will make a similar testamentary disposition, involving, as it does, a grave breach of Jewish law.[35]

A bylaw of the Burial Society of the United Synagogue of London states: "The society shall not make any arrangements whatever for cremation. Where cremation is nevertheless to take place a Service may be held at the house prior to the removal of the body, and if the ashes be encoffined then interment may take place at a Cemetery of the United Synagogue and the Burial Service shall be conducted there at the time of the interment."[36]

On the other hand, the other London Orthodox Synagogal bodies, the Federation of Synagogues and the Union of Orthodox Hebrew Congregations, do not permit the ashes of cremated persons to be buried in their cemeteries.

Chapter 3

The Period of Aninut: The Interval between Death and Burial

Until the burial of the deceased, the mourner is known as an *onen*.[1] The interval between death and burial is called *aninut*. After the interment, these two terms are superseded by the words *avel* (*avelim*) and *avelut*, respectively.

While having to abide by the negative precepts of the Torah, the *onen* is absolved from the performance of all the religious duties enjoined therein[2] such as the recital of prayers or the putting on of *tefillin*. There are two reasons for this: (1) to enable him to attend without distraction to the needs of the dead, since nothing must interfere with the preparations for burial—"he who is engaged in a religious act is exempt from performing other religious duties";[3] and (2) there must be no lessening of the honor and respect accorded to the deceased.[4]

The Jerusalem Talmud derives this law from Deuteronomy 16:3, "so that you may remember the day of your departure from the land of Egypt as long as you live." The commitment accepted in Egypt is applicable to one who is preoccupied with life and not to one who has encountered death.[5]

"What is the reason behind this law exempting the mourner from the performance of *mitzvot*? Because our commitment to God is rooted in the awareness of human dignity and sanctity. Once the perplexed, despairing individual begins to question whether or not such distinctiveness or choiceness exists, the whole commitment expires. Man, who has faith in himself, who is aware of his charisma, was chosen and burdened with obligations and commandments. Despairing, skeptical man was not elected. How can man pray and address himself to God if he doubts his very humanity, if speech is stripped by his doubts of its human characteristics and turned into mere physical sound? How can the mourner pronounce a benediction or say amen if he is speechless? He is still capable of producing sounds, but a benediction consists of spiritual words and not just of physical sounds. In a word, the motto of *aninut* is to be found in the old pessimistic verse in the Book of Ecclesiastes: 'So that man has no pre-eminence over the beast for all is vanity.' "[6]

THE ONEN

Although today in most communities there are well-organized burial societies that efficiently carry out all the detailed duties, the *onenim* still have the responsibility of approaching and making arrangements with the burial society as well as obtaining death certificates and other certificates that may be required before the funeral can take place. They must also inform relatives and friends so as to ensure that all honor and respect are paid to the deceased.[7]

The *onen*, as has been mentioned, does not recite prayers or put on *tefillin*,[8] and he is forbidden to eat meat, drink wine,[9] or overindulge in food.[10] When he eats bread, he must wash his hands, but he is not required to recite the benediction thereof. He must not be gainfully occupied. Only in cases where great hardship might be incurred may he complete his unfinished tasks, provided they do not interfere with or in any way delay the funeral arrangements. A minor is not subject to the laws of *aninut*.

If death occurs on the Sabbath, or if the Sabbath is part

of the *aninut* period, the *onen* must perform the same *mitzvot* as anyone else.[11] He may also eat meat and drink wine on that day.[12] However, he is not to study the Torah or be called up to the Reading of the Law in the synagogue.[13] The same rulings that apply to the Sabbath apply to the Festivals.

A *Kohen* who is an *onen* may not recite the *Duchaning* (priestly blessings) during *Musaf* (the Additional Service) on a Festival. Only if no other *Kohen* is available may he officiate at the *pidyon ha-ben* (redemption of the firstborn), a ceremony that must take place on the thirty-first day after birth. If the *onen* officiates, the benediction over the wine is recited by another person. On *Yom Kippur* (the Day of Atonement), the *onen* must obey every requirement of the fast day. However, the duties to the dead take precedence over the *mitzvah* of building a *sukkah* (festive booth for tabernacles),[14] and the *onen* is not required to *bensch lulav* (pronounce the blessing over the four species) on *Chol Ha-Moed* (the secular days of Passover and *Sukkot*).

On Passover he must eat *matzah* (unleavened bread) and drink the four cups of wine during the *seder* service. However, he is not required to recite the *Haggadah* (story of Passover)[15] nor to count the *omer* (the seven weeks between Passover and Pentecost).[16] He should delegate to another person the ceremony of *bedikat chametz* (search for the leaven) on the eve of the fourteenth day of *Nisan*. He may, however, recite the declaration *Kol Chamira*[17] (all manner of leaven). On *Chanukah*, he should not kindle the lights if it is possible to delegate this to another member of the household. On *Purim* he may go to the synagogue to hear the *Megillah* (Book of Esther),[18] and it is permitted to eat meat and drink wine during the day.[19] Yet on the ninth of *Av* he may not go to the synagogue to hear the Book of Lamentations and *kinot* (dirges and lamentations).[20]

If the only rabbi in the town becomes an *onen*, he may decide ritual questions,[21] but a Torah reader who is an *onen* may not officiate in the synagogue.[22] An *onen* who is a *shochet* (ritual slaughterer) may slaughter during the period of *aninut*,[23] and a *shammash* (beadle) may attend to his duties on the Sabbath and on the Festivals. An *onen* who is a *mohel* (circumciser) may circumcise his own and other children if there is no other *mohel* available. The *brit milah* (covenant of circumcision) may take place before the burial, and the benedictions can be recited by others. A circumcision generally takes precedence over the interment of the dead.[24]

If a person receives news of the death of a relative in another city, he becomes subject to the laws of *aninut* if there are no other relatives residing in the town where the deceased lived. However, if he is notified that the burial will take place on a certain day, and distance makes it impossible for him to attend, then he is not subject to the laws of *aninut*.

Even if a man leaves directions that only one of his children should occupy himself with the burial arrangements, nevertheless the status of *aninut* falls on all the children. If the *onen* is already a mourner for his father or his mother or if he has a *yahrzeit* (anniversary of death), he may recite the *Kaddish* (doxology recited by mourners).[25]

Aninut does not apply in cases of an infant dying within thirty days of birth.[26] In the case of a stillbirth or if the infant died before being circumcised, the operation is performed before the burial.[27]

POURING AWAY WATER

"It is a custom," states the Code *Yoreh Deah* (the section of *Shulchan Aruch* dealing with dietary and ritual laws),[28] "to pour out all drawn water[29] in the neighborhood[30] of the corpse." Explanations of this practice range from the crude suggestion that the Angel of Death cleans his knife in water to the metaphorical concept of the pouring out of the soul before God. The custom has also been ascribed to the primitive practice of providing food for the departed spirit and to the superstitious belief that thus the spirit can be saved from drowning.

There are more rational interpretations. It is suggested that the practice was a means of announcing a death, since

Jews have always been reluctant to be the bearers of evil tidings. Hence, the pouring away of the water also served to remind the neighbors of their duty to the deceased and to the mourners. Again, water stands for life and fertility. Note the passage in the Book of Psalms (22:15), "I am poured out like water," meaning that life is drawing to an end. The pouring out of water symbolizes the extinction of life. Some scholars claim that this custom goes back to biblical times and in support of this theory quote: "And Miriam died there and was buried there. And there was no water for the congregation" (Numbers 20:1–2).

MIRRORS

It is customary to cover mirrors or to turn them to the wall in the house of mourning. This custom is not mentioned in medieval sources. Some hold that this is done to prevent the soul of the departed from being reflected in the glass; others say that it is done simply to prevent the mourner from seeing his own sad countenance, thus adding to his grief. Another view is that mirrors, so often associated with vanity, are out of place at such a time. The most rational explanation is the rule that forbids prayer in front of a mirror, since the reflection distracts the attention of worshipers,[31] and prayers are normally recited in the house of the mourner.

THE RENDING OF GARMENTS

"One who has suffered a bereavement for which mourning has to be observed must rend his garments."[32] The origin of this practice of *keriah* (rending) is found in the Divine Command, given expressly to the priests Aaron, Eleazar, and Ithamar after the death of Nadab and Abihu: "Let not the hair of your heads go loose, neither rend your clothes" (Leviticus 10:6).[33] From this explicit prohibition, it is inferred that everyone else must perform *keriah*.

From earliest times the rending of garments has been regarded as a sign of grief. When his sons brought him Joseph's bloodstained coat, "Jacob rent his garments" (Genesis 37:34). When the goblet was found in Benjamin's sack, his brothers "rent their clothes" (Genesis 44:13). When David heard of the death of Saul, "he took hold of his clothes, and rent them; and likewise all the men that were with him" (II Samuel 1:10).

The Talmud lays it down that "one who is present at the time of the departure of the soul of a Jewish man or woman is in duty bound to rend his garments."[34] This ritual is not enforced today, since it might have the effect of deterring people from attending a dying person.

Nowadays, *keriah* is only compulsory when the loss is that of a father, mother, wife, husband, brother, sister, son or daughter, or half-brother or half-sister.

The rending of the garments must be done either in the house before the funeral or at the cemetery before the interment. The mourner should stand when the rite is performed.[35] "Then Job stood up and rent his mantle" (Job 1:20).

The custom of standing has been homiletically explained by the former Chief Rabbi Dr. J. H. Hertz: "Meet all sorrow standing upright. The future may be dark, veiled from the eye of mortals—but not the manner in which we are to meet the future. To rail at life, to rebel against a destiny that has cast our lines in unpleasant places, is of little avail. We cannot lay down terms to life. Life must be accepted on its own terms. But hard as life's terms may be, life (it has been finely said) never dictates unrighteousness, unholiness, dishonor."[36]

For men, the jacket, sweater, or vest is used, and for women, either the dress, blouse, or sweater. The use of a black ribbon for *keriah* is not permitted. One may intentionally for this purpose wear an old jacket, cardigan, or dress.

The regulations governing *keriah* are that a small cut should be made in the garment with a knife, and the tear extended by hand to at least one hand-breadth. In support of this the Talmud quotes: "Then David took hold on his clothes, and rent them" (II Samuel 1:10), since it has been established that the measure of a garment that man can seize in his hand is a hand-breadth.[37]

The following blessing is recited: "Blessed art Thou, O Lord our king, King of the Universe, the true Judge."

בָּרוּךְ אַתָּה יְיָ אֱלֹהֵינוּ מֶלֶךְ הָעוֹלָם, דַּיַּן הָאֱמֶת:

Baruch Attah Adonai Elohaynu Melech Ha-Olam Dayan Ha-Emet.

For parents, one rends his or her garment on the left side (close to the heart) and for other relatives on the right side. The rent should be made from above downward and not from side to side.

Keriah is forbidden on the Sabbath or on the Festivals, and many ecclesiastical authorities do not permit rending on Chol Ha-Moed, insisting that the rite be delayed until the Festival is ended.

In the case of relatives other than a parent, keriah takes place only if the news has come within thirty days of death; in the case of a parent, keriah is always obligatory.

The tear for relatives other than parents may be loosely stitched together after seven days, and the edges resewn after thirty days. The tear for a parent, however, may only be stitched together after thirty days but must never be thoroughly repaired. It is likewise forbidden to cut out the part that was rent and to mend the torn part with another piece of material.

The rites of keriah do not apply when the deceased is an infant less than thirty days old.[38]

If the mourner forgets to rend the garments at the proper time but remembers or is reminded during the shivah days (seven days of mourning), he must perform the keriah just the same. "For all other dead," states the Code, "if he has occasion to change his garments during the shivah, he does not again rend them; for one's father and mother, if one changes his garments during the shivah period, he must perform keriah on the fresh garments."[39]

In honor of the Sabbath, he should change his garments and not wear torn clothes.

If a relative dies and the mourner in his distress does not perform *keriah* and then another of his relatives dies, he must perform two separate *keriot:* The first rent must be a hand-breadth and then, at a distance of three finger-breadths, he should make the second rent. One who had simultaneously heard "of the death of his father and his mother or of the death of two other relatives, should rend his garments once for his double loss."[40]

A minor who has reached the age of instruction becomes subject to the laws of mourning and must perform *keriah* in the same way that he must perform all other *mitzvot.* The garment of a child "should be slightly rent for him to manifest his grief and to mark his mourning."[41] *Keriah* is thus obligatory for children under thirteen years of age.

NO MUTILATION

The holiness of Israel is to be maintained by abstention from cuttings for the dead. "Ye shall not cut yourselves, nor make any baldness between your eyes for the dead" (Deuteronomy 14:1). Such mutilations occur among many primitive peoples, and their object appears to be to maintain blood communion, or a blood covenant, with the dead. Similar cuttings were made by the heathen priests opposed by Elijah (I Kings 18:28) to establish the blood bond with their deity. Although the prohibition against cutting the flesh was addressed only to the priests, the law was extended to all Israel as God's children. "If a man made any cuttings for the dead," says the *Mishnah*, "he is liable to forty stripes."[42]

CHEVRAH KADDISHA

The *Chevrah Kaddisha* is the organization that concerns itself with the burial of the dead. It was already known in talmudic times. Once, when Rabbi Hamnuna, a fourth-century-C.E. Babylonian teacher, came to Daru-Mata (North of Nisibis), he heard the sound of the funerary bugle, and seeing some people carrying on with their work, he said: "Let the people be under the *shammeta* [ban]. Is there not a person dead in the town?" They told him that there was a *Chevrah Kaddisha* in the town. "If so," he replied "you are allowed to work."[43]

The *Chevrah Kaddisha* carry out a sacred task and even scholars and sages did not consider it beneath their dignity to attend to the dead. Rabbi Eliezer Ashkenazi in 1564 in Prague laid the foundations of an efficient burial society that became the model of all similar bodies. Their *vade mecum* was *Maavar Yabok* (Ford of Yabok)[44] of Aaron Berachiah of Modena (Venice, 1626).

During the Middle Ages, it became customary for the *Chevrah Kaddisha* to devote one day each year to fasting and prayer. At the close of this day, which was usually held on the seventh of *Adar*[45] (the date of Moses' death), a *seudah* (festive meal) was organized for them.

In many large communities the members of the *Chevrah Kaddisha* are paid officials of the community. Many Orthodox synagogues in New York and in other large Jewish centers have their own voluntary *Chevrah Kaddisha* societies that cooperate with the funeral directors.

Today, as in ancient times, it is essential that the members of the *Chevrah Kaddisha* be observant Jews.

TAHARAH–RITES OF PURIFICATION

The rite of the ritual washing of a corpse before burial is derived from the biblical injunction: "As he came so shall he go" (Ecclesiastes 5:5). When man is born he is washed and when he dies he is washed.[46] The *Mishnah* mentions the practice of washing the body.[47]

A separate building, the *bet taharah*, in the cemetery,

was used for this purpose, but nowadays the rite is usually carried out in the funeral parlor. A candle is kept burning during the ceremony. Among the *Sephardim* (Spanish Jews) it was customary to blow the *shofar* (ram's horn) during the *taharah* or the funeral.[48]

The utmost respect must be shown to the body during the *taharah,* and at least two persons should be employed in moving or changing the position of the body. No person assisting at a *taharah* shall smoke "while so engaged."[49]

The purification rite is as follows: The body is laid on the *taharah* board in the sheet in which it lies. Warm water (about three gallons) must then be poured down the body from the head to the feet. The mouth is covered so that no water should trickle down it. The body is then turned slightly, first on the right side and then on the left, the warm water being poured down on each side as before. The sheet is used to dry each side so that the hands do not touch the body. The nails of the hands and feet are then cleansed. The hair, too, is washed and combed. A further three gallons must be poured over the head so that it should run down over the entire body. The body is then wrapped in clean sheets and properly dried.[50]

Where death is due to infectious or contagious diseases, the *taharah* must be dispensed with. If a woman dies in confinement, no *taharah* is carried out. Similarly, if "they find a slain Israelite they must bury him in the same condition as they find him."[51]

TACHRICHIM—SHROUDS

The garments in which the dead are clothed are known as *tachrichim,*[52] from the Hebrew root meaning "to wrap up." The shrouds should be made from fine white linen. Neither a hem nor a knot of any sort should be made in the shrouds. No corpse must be shrouded in less than three garments. Some pious people even prepare their shrouds during their lifetime, basing the practice on the verse from Amos: "Prepare to meet thy God, O Israel" (Amos 4:12).

After the *taharah*, the *halbashah* (dressing) commences. The cap is placed on the head. The breeches are put on, then the shirt and neckcloth, then the robe and girdle. It is a custom dating from talmudic times to bury a dead man in the woollen *tallit* (prayer shawl) that he used during his lifetime, with the fringes deliberately rendered ritually unfit. The *tallit* is then spread out in the coffin and the body is carefully transferred there with the face upward, the legs extended and the arms at the side.[53]

A man distinguished for his piety may also be clad in his *kittel*.[54] Earth from the Holy Land is often placed in the coffin.

Of the many references in the Talmud to shrouds, one states: "Formerly the expenses of taking the dead out to his burial fell harder on his near-of-kin than his death, so that the dead man's near-of-kin abandoned him and fled. This continued until the time of Rabban Gamaliel,[55] who disregarding his own dignity, left instructions that he should come out to his burial in flaxen vestments and thereafter the people followed."[56] Rabbi Papa, who lived in the fourth century, declared that the dead were buried in a garb worth only one *zuz* (a small Palestinian coin).[56]

The *tachrichim* used to be of different colors such as white or black. Rabbi Jannai, a Palestinian *amora* (rabbinic authority) of the third century, said to his sons: "My sons, bury me neither in white shrouds nor in black shrouds. Not in white, lest I do not merit (to be amongst the righteous) and am like a bridegroom among mourners; not in black, in case I have merit and am like a mourner among bridegrooms. But bury me in court garments (mixed colors) that come from overseas."[57] Rabbi Josiah, on the other hand, gave different instructions: "Clothe me in white shrouds."[58] No firm rule concerning shrouds was laid down in early times, but from the sixteenth century C.E. it became the general practice to use white shrouds.

THE COFFIN

Coffins used for Jewish funerals must be made of plain unpolished boards without any ornamentation. No metal nails may be used, nor may there be any inside or outside lining. The cover must consist of a single flat board. It is wrong to encase the remains in a sealed container made of stainless steel or other metal. The casket should be made of wood so that the body will decompose in a natural way.

The Hebrew word for coffin is *aron*, and although this word occurs many times in the Bible, only in one instance is it used to mean a coffin (Genesis 50:26). In biblical times coffins were not generally used. Instead, the dead were carried to the burial place upon a *mittah* (bed or bier).

Both in the *Mishnah*[59] and the *Gemara*[60] there are a number of references to the use of coffins. Rabbi Levi, commenting on the verse, "And Adam and his wife hid themselves from the presence of the Lord God amongst the trees of the garden" (Genesis 3:8), said, "This was a sign for his descendants that they would be placed within wooden coffins."[61]

In medieval France it was the practice to use as coffin boards the table upon which food for the poor had been served.

The Kabbalists, on the other hand, took the phrase "for dust thou art and unto dust shalt thou return" (Genesis 3:19) literally and therefore did not use coffins for burial. This was also the general custom in Eastern Europe before the Nazi Holocaust.

In some communities it was customary to place small sticks in the dead person's hands. This custom can be traced to the Jerusalem Talmud, in which it is recorded that Rabbi Jeremiah requested that a staff be put into his hand when lowered into the grave so that he would be ready to march at the announcement of the coming of the Messiah.[62]

It is forbidden to gain any benefit from either a dead body or the shrouds.[63] Objects that are attached to the body, such as a wig or artificial teeth, must be interred with the body. However, articles such as ornaments and clothes that are not attached to the body may be removed and used by others.

Beautification of the body with cosmetics is not allowed; nor is it permitted to put the body on view. In fact, the casket should remain closed at all times.

FUNERALS ON A HOLY DAY

Funerals may not take place on the Sabbath or on the Day of Atonement. On the first day of a Festival[64] it was at one time permitted to hold funerals, provided that certain functions were performed by gentiles. On the second day of a Festival, including the second day of *Rosh Hashanah* (New Year), funerals are permitted, but only those whose services are essential for the burial[65] may ride to the cemetery. The rabbis regarded the second day of *Yom Tov* "as a weekday as far as the dead are concerned."[66] It is an accepted custom in the Anglo-Jewish community not to arrange any funerals on the first or second days of *Yom Tov*. In the United States, too, when cemeteries are beyond city limits, funerals are not allowed on the second day of a Festival.

SERVICE PRIOR TO THE FUNERAL

The rabbi should make a prefuneral pastoral call on the bereaved family to take time to get to know the family, should they not be members of his congregation.

At Orthodox funerals, there are slight variations in procedure and in the choice of Psalms and scriptural verses. It is usual to have a brief service in the mortuary chapel or funeral home before the leaving for the cemetery. This service includes a Psalm (Psalm 16, 23, or 130), scriptural verses, a eulogy of the deceased, and *El Malay Rachamim* (memorial prayer) with the plea to God: "Open unto him (her) gates of righteousness and light, the gates of pity and grace. O shelter him (her) for evermore under the cover of Thy wings; and let his (her) soul be bound up in the bond of eternal life. The Lord is his (her) inheritance; may he (she) rest in peace. And let us say, Amen."

Chapter 4

The Bet Olam: The Jewish Cemetery

The Jewish cemetery has many euphemistic names such as
Bet Olam (the House of Eternity), "Long Home,"[1] "House of
the Living,"[2] "the Pure Place," *Guter Ort* (the Good Place).
These names spring from the rabbinic belief that "this world
is the temporary lodging place; the world to come is a
home."[3]

BIBLE TIMES

It is difficult to ascertain from the Bible whether there
was a generally accepted place of burial. Phrases such as "He
lay with his fathers" or "He was gathered unto his fathers,"
indicate a preference for burial in family plots or caves.
Abraham bought the Cave of Machpelah for 400 shekels of
silver, and it became his family sepulcher (Genesis 23:20).
There were, however, other types of resting places in biblical
times. Manasseh, for instance, "was buried in the garden of
his own house" (II Kings 21:18); Amon in the garden of Uzza
(II Kings 21:26); Deborah, Rebecca's nurse, under an oak tree
(Genesis 35:8); Saul under a terebinth tree (I Chronicles
10:12); and Rachel on the road near Bethlehem (Genesis
35:19).

Special sepulchers were constructed for the kings of Judah (II Chronicles 21:20). There were also communal burial places, "the graves of the common people" (II Kings 23:6; Jeremiah 26:23).

There are several biblical references to a desire to be buried together with one's family. Ruth, for example, affirmed: "Where thou diest, will I die, and there will I be buried" (Ruth 1:17), and Barzillai declined King David's invitation to remain with him at court, saying: "Let thy servant, I pray thee, turn back, that I may die in mine own city by the grave of my father and my mother" (II Samuel 19:38). Finally, Nehemiah, six centuries later, requested King Artaxerxes to allow him to return from Mesopotamia to the city of his "father's sepulchers" (Nehemiah 2:5).

In talmudic times, burial took place in caves, hewn tombs, stone tombs, sarcophagi, and catacombs. Great care was lavished on the cemetery, and there was a saying, "The Jewish graveyards are fairer than royal palaces."[4]

With the Dispersion, Jewish communities prepared communal cemeteries. Several of these ancient burial places have survived, as for instance the "Garden Cemetery" of Mainz that dates back to the eleventh century.

It was often difficult for the Jews to obtain their own cemeteries. Until the reign of Henry II, there was only one Jewish cemetery in the whole of England, and it was only in 1177 that each Jewish community was permitted to purchase a place for interring its dead outside the city walls.[5]

Wherever possible, the cemetery was situated outside the Jewish quarter, yet near enough to avoid carrying the dead over long distances. Thus, in December 1656, within two or three months of renting a house in Creechurch Lane (in the City of London) for a synagogue, the tiny local Jewish community leased a piece of ground in nearby Mile End as a cemetery.[6]

Where Jews were unable to acquire their own exclusive cemetery, they would lease a burial plot from the non-Jewish authorities, and wherever possible they would erect a partition that separated the Jewish graves from the others. The

Jews planted trees[7] and took so much care of their cemeteries
that a Jewish graveyard often became known as *Hortus
Judaeorum* (Garden of the Jews).[8]

Even disused cemeteries were carefully preserved and
maintained.

DESECRATIONS

It is one of the sad features of Jewish history that not
only were Jewish lives always in jeopardy, but even the dead
were not allowed to rest in peace. There are innumerable
records of Jewish cemeteries being desecrated. Pope Calixtus
II (1119–1124), Pope Eugenius III (1145), and Pope Innocent
III (1199) all issued solemn warnings: "To counteract the
wickedness and avarice of evil men in this respect we decree
that no one shall dare to desecrate or reduce a Jewish
cemetery, or for the sake of gain to exhume human bodies."[9]
Equally stern was the law enacted by Duke Frederick II of
Austria on July 1, 1244: "If a Christian attempts to destroy a
Jewish cemetery or to break into it, he shall be put to death
after the manner of the law, and all his property, no matter
what it may be, shall be confiscated by the Duke."

During the eighteenth century, when the Resurrection-
ists plundered graveyards, synagogues instituted a system
that ensured regular guards.

Abraham de Mattos Mocatta (1733–1800) left 200
guineas to have his grave in the burial ground of the Spanish
and Portuguese Jews watched for twelve months.[10]

The medieval acts of desecration pale into insignificance
when compared with the wholesale systematic destruction
of Jewish cemeteries in Europe by the Nazis and the desecration by Jordan of the ancient Jewish cemetery on the
Mount of Olives in Jerusalem.

SACRED PLACE

Cemeteries must be treated with respect,[11] and be-
havior in them must always be decorous. People must wear

suitable head coverings. They may not eat, drink, or smoke in a cemetery. Care must be taken not to tread on a grave or lean on a gravestone. It is forbidden to use a path through a cemetery as a short cut. Cattle are not permitted to graze there.[12]

THE MITZVAH OF BURIAL

It was fervently believed that, as an act of atonement, the body should be returned as soon as possible to the earth from which it came. Josephus (the Jewish historian of the first century) records that it was forbidden to let anyone lie unburied,[13] and thus the burial of a corpse was a sacred duty of every Jew. Even the body of a criminal could not be left exposed overnight but had to be buried on the day of death for the "body left hanging brings down the curse of God" (Deuteronomy 21:23).

Even the high priest, who was forbidden to incur uncleanliness even for his closest relatives, was obliged to attend to a *met mitzvah*[14] (a corpse that had no one to attend to its burial). In the words of the sages, "For his father and mother he may not defile himself" (Leviticus 21:11), but for a *met mitzvah*, he may defile himself.[15] Joshua, when he partitioned Canaan to the tribes of Israel, stipulated that a *met mitzvah* should be buried in whatever spot he may be discovered.[16]

Consideration for the dead is one of the central features of the Book of Tobit, and whenever Tobit found an unburied Israelite, he buried him at the peril of his own life (Tobit 2:8).

Where the primary duty of burial is involved, no distinction may be made between saint and sinner. If there are two bodies to bury, the first to have died must be buried first.[17]

The child of a Jewish mother and a non-Jewish father may be buried in a Jewish cemetery, but Jewish burial is not permitted if the mother is not Jewish, even though the father is Jewish. Non-Jews who have married Jewish women but have not been converted by a recognized *Bet Din* (Jewish court of law) are denied burial in an Orthodox Jewish cemetery.

ESCORTING THE DEAD

It is a great *mitzvah* to escort the dead to their last resting place. The *Mishnah*[18] lists "escorting the dead" among the deeds "the fruit of which a man enjoys in this world while the stock remains for him in the world to come." So important was this *mitzvah* considered that our sages permitted a man to suspend the study of the Torah in order to fulfill it.[19]

"One who sees a funeral procession and does not accompany it," states the Talmud,[20] "transgresses thereby." "Whoso mocketh the poor [i.e., the dead] blasphemeth his Maker" (Proverbs 27:5) and "should be placed under a ban."[21]

Where the dead man is not distinguished for saintliness or scholarship or where there is a great crowd present at the funeral, one may fulfill one's obligation by rising as the funeral cortege passes[22] and by accompanying it at least four cubits (four paces). In the case of a scholar, however, every effort should be made to accompany the cortege to the cemetery. This old Jewish custom is supported by Josephus, who writes: "All who pass by when a corpse is buried must accompany the funeral and join in the lamentations."[23]

It is customary for the funeral cortege of a devout and important member of a congregation to pass by the synagogue on the way to the cemetery.

Even nonmourners who have not visited the burial ground for thirty days say the following: "Blessed be the Lord our God, King of the Universe, who formed you in judgment, who nourished and sustained you in judgment, who brought death on you in judgment, who knoweth the number of you in judgment, and will hereafter restore you to

life in judgment. Blessed art Thou, O Lord who quickenest
the dead.

"Thou, O Lord, art mighty for ever, Thou revivest the
dead, Thou art mighty to save.

"Thou sustainest the living with loving kindness,
revivest the dead with great mercy, supportest the falling,
healest the sick, loosest the bound, and keepest thy faith to
them that sleep in the dust. Who is like unto Thee, Lord of
mighty acts and who resembleth Thee, O King, who causeth
death and revivest and causeth salvation to spring forth?
Yea, faithful art Thou to revive the dead."[24]

OBSOLETE RITES

With the passage of time, funeral rites have changed
considerably. The practice ordered in the *Mishnah*, "Even the
poorest man must provide no less than two flute players and
one lamenting woman,"[25] has been discontinued, as have
the use of musical instruments (pipes, harps, tambourines)
and the employment of torch bearers and barefoot mourners.

BURIAL SERVICE

The coffin is borne from the hearse to the grave. It is
customary to pause during the recital of Psalm 91. This
exquisite Psalm describes the security of the Godly man
under God's protection amid the perils of his journey
through life. Whoever takes refuge with God will find
himself under the protection of the Almighty. In talmudic
times during the funeral procession it was the custom to stop
seven times and make lamentations over the dead.[26] It is still
customary to halt several times[27] (at least three times) on the
way to the grave, when Psalm 91 is recited.[28] The customary
halts are not made at the cemetery on days when *Tzidduk
Ha-Din* (acknowledgment of Divine Judgment—part of the
burial service) is not recited.

The seven halts are symbolic of the seven times the word *hevel* (vanity) occurs in the Book of Ecclesiastes.[29] The number seven, too, corresponds to the days of the world's creation and also to the seven stages that man experiences in his lifetime.[30]

The body is lowered into the grave with the head facing toward the west and the feet toward the east, and all those who are present say: "May he (or she) come to his (or her) place in peace."[31]

It is a *mitzvah* to fill the grave. Three spadesful[32] of earth are dropped into the grave by each of those present as a symbol of the threefold composition of man: soul, spirit, and breath. After the spade has been used, it must not be passed to the next man but is to be replaced on the ground so that one man should not appear to be passing on trouble to another. Moreover, the passing of the spade from hand to hand would indicate a relationship of overlordship and servitude, but in the presence of death all are equal. "Neither hath he power over the day of death" (Ecclesiastes 8:8).

When the grave is completely filled, the prayer *Tzidduk Ha-Din* is recited. The *Tzidduk Ha-Din* begins with the affirmation, "The Rock, His work is perfect for all His ways are judgment."[33]

The prayer originated in talmudic times[34] and was completed in the geonic period. Its themes are resignation and submission to the inscrutable will of God, belief in the immortality of the soul, and the affirmation of the principle that there is a Heavenly Judge who will recompense everyone "according to his ways and according to the fruit of his doings."

The *Tzidduk Ha-Din* concludes with the words: "The Lord gave and the Lord hath taken away; Blessed be the Name of the Lord. And He, being merciful, forgiveth iniquity and destroyeth not; Yea, many a time He turneth His anger away, and doth not stir up all His wrath."

On those days on which *Tachanun* (supplicating prayers) are not said, Psalm 16 is read instead of this prayer.[35] *Tzidduk Ha-Din* is not recited on Friday afternoon or on the eve of a

Festival. It is, however, recited on the eve of the New Moon, on the eve of *Purim,* and on the eve of *Chanukah.*[36] On the days after the New Moon of *Sivan* (ninth month) until Pentecost, on the ninth of *Av,* and on the eve of *Rosh Hashanah,* it should be said before noon.[37] *Tzidduk Ha-Din* is followed by the recitation of Psalm 23, followed by the mourner's *Kaddish* and the Memorial Prayer. Two rows are formed between which the mourners pass, and those present say to the mourners: "May the Almighty comfort you among the other mourners for Zion and Jerusalem." The custom of passing through two parallel rows of friends is also of talmudic origin.[38] Formerly, the mourners used to stand still while people passed by.[39] But there were families in Jerusalem that contended with one another, each maintaining, "We shall pass first," so the rabbis established the rule that the public should remain standing and the mourners pass by.

To lower the coffin into the grave and to cover it temporarily with a rug of simulated grass later to be filled by the hands of hired grave diggers is not acceptable. In case of a cemetery strike or labor dispute when immediate interment is not possible, the laws of mourning apply after the mourner has completed all funeral arrangements. Rabbi Asher ben Jehiel records that when Rabbi Kalonymous died during a siege, the body could not be taken to the cemetery outside the city, so the coffin was placed in a ritualarium for the duration of the hostilities.[40]

WASHING THE HANDS

Before leaving the cemetery, the mourners and all those present at the funeral wash their hands[41] and say: "He maketh death to vanish in life eternal; and the Lord God wipeth away tears from off all faces; and the reproach of His people shall He take away from off all the earth: for the Lord hath spoken it."[42]

One of the many reasons given for this custom is that it

may be a symbolic demonstration that there is no responsibility for the death of the deceased.[43] Normally, hand-washing facilities are provided at the cemetery. In the event of there being no such provisions, the mourner should wash his hands prior to entering his house.

PLUCKING GRASS

On leaving the burial ground it is customary to pluck a few blades of grass[44] and say: "And may they blossom out of the city like grass of the earth" (Psalm 52:16), for "He remembereth that we are dust" (Psalm 103:14). This custom is an allusion to the resurrection of the dead.

There is no *din* (law) governing the attendance of women at funerals. It is a question of local custom as to whether or not they attend.

FLOWERS

Flowers played an important part in the idolatrous rites of many ancient peoples. They were spread on the marriage bed, on the altar, and on the grave. The placing of flowers on the grave is therefore regarded as *chukkat ha-goy*, and it is discouraged by Orthodox rabbinic authorities. Yet there are many references in the Talmud[45] to spices for the dead. Rabbi Jannai commanded his sons to place myrtle twigs on his body, and it was even permitted to cut myrtle twigs on the second day of the Festival for this purpose.[46]

MEMORIAL ADDRESS

It is regarded as unnatural not to weep for the dead. "My son," says Ben Sira, "let thy tears fall over the dead, and as one that suffereth grievously begin lamentation. . . . Make bitter weeping and make passionate wailing, and let thy mourning be according to his desert, for one day or two, lest thou be evil spoken of; and so be comforted for thy sorrow" (Ecclesiastes 38:16–18). The Bible also records David's moving eulogies when he mourned over Saul, Jonathan, and Abner. There were even professional mourners[47] whose bitter lamentations were an example for the other mourners. "Call for the mourning women, that they may come; and send for the wise women, that they may come" (Jeremiah 9:16). Often they used a set refrain: "Alas, my brother!" or "Ah Lord!" (I Kings 12:30; Jeremiah 34:5).

Our sages, too, stress the importance of lamentation at funerals.[48] The Talmud records twenty-nine funeral dirges.[49] It is forbidden to praise the dead too highly or attribute to them qualities that they did not possess. A body should not be taken into the synagogue for the *hesped* (eulogy),[50] except in the case of a noted rabbinical scholar or a man of exemplary piety.

FASTING

In biblical times fasting was a sign of mourning. The inhabitants of Jabesh Gilead "fasted seven days" after the burial of Saul (I Samuel 31:13). David and his men fasted until nightfall when they heard of the deaths of Saul and Jonathan (II Samuel 1:12). David would not eat during his mourning for Abner (II Samuel 3:35). Daniel fasted as a sign of mourning, with the accompaniment of prayer, penitence, and confession (Daniel 9:3). The Jewish community of Elephantine fasted as a sign of mourning.[51]

EXHUMATION

Jewish tradition forbids exhumation, because this is considered disrespectful. Exception is made, however, in certain circumstances,[52] such as when the remains are to be transported to the Holy Land. For "whoever is buried in the land of Israel," says the Talmud,[53] "is deemed to be buried under the Altar."

The earth of the Holy Land was credited with having the power of atonement,[54] and burial there was a sure means of expiation. It is often customary to place earth of the Holy Land in the coffins of people buried outside the Holy Land. Moreover, the resurrection is expected to take place in the Holy Land. Those who have died in the Diaspora, runs the legend, will roll across the earth through cavities until they reach the Holy Land,[55] where they will be brought back to life. In the words of the sages,[56] "Why did the Patriarchs deserve to be buried in *Eretz Yisrael* (land of Israel)? Because the dead of *Eretz Yisrael* will be the first to be revived in the Messianic period and to enter the year of Messianic splendor."

There is no objection in Jewish law for a woman who married another after the death of her first husband to be buried next to her first husband when she dies.

A Jewish body buried in a non-Jewish cemetery may be exhumed in order to be reinterred in a Jewish cemetery.

Chapter 5

The Shivah—A Unique Institution

Immediately after the funeral the bereaved family gather together preferably in the house of the deceased to sit *shivah*. During this period they sit on low stools and are prohibited from performing manual labor, conducting business transactions, bathing or anointing the body, cohabitation, washing and preparing garments, or cutting their hair. Torah study, excepting that of certain portions of the Scriptures and of other sacred works, is also forbidden.

Shacharit (Morning Services), *Minchah* (Afternoon Services), and *Maariv* (Evening Services) are held in the house.[1]

The *shivah* is a unique institution. For seven days, the mourners, irrespective of status or disposition, are united in their common sorrow. Daily routine and work cease. Death, with its awesome majesty, casts its shadow on the mourners.

Most of the *shivah* customs that developed in talmudic times have been retained, although a number of them, such as wearing sackcloth and sitting in ashes, have been discarded.

The sages offer a number of reasons why seven days has been chosen as the period of mourning. One teacher, commenting on the verse "I will turn your feasts into mourning" (Amos 8:10), says, "Just as the days of the Feasts (Passover and Tabernacles) are seven, so are the days of mourning."[1]

45

Another teacher traces it back to the verse: "Let her not, I pray, be as one dead. . . . And Miriam was shut up without the camp seven days" (Numbers 12:12–15); the days of isolation (for leprosy) are seven (Leviticus 13:31); finally, the *Zohar* gives a mystical reason: "For seven days the soul goes to and fro, from the house to the grave and from the grave to the house, mourning for the body."[2]

The antiquity of the *shivah* is unquestioned. Our sages, in fact, maintain that this institution is even older than the Flood. "And it came to pass after the seven days, that the waters of the flood were upon the earth" (Genesis 7:10). "What was the nature of these seven days?" asks the Talmud.[3] "These were the days of mourning for Methuselah, thus teaching that the lamentation for the righteous postpones retribution." "God Himself," attests Rabbi Joshua ben Levi (a third-century *amora*), "mourned seven days for the destruction of the world."

In patriarchal times the seven days[4] are first mentioned in connection with Jacob, when it is stated that Joseph "made a mourning for his father seven days" (Genesis 50:10). According to the Jerusalem Talmud, it was Moses who appointed seven days of mourning.[5] The Apocrypha is very explicit on this point. Ben Sira declares: "Seven days are the days of mourning for the dead" (Ben Sira 22:12).

The day of burial counts as the first day of the *shivah*, provided the interment was completed before sunset, and the *shivah* ends on the morning of the seventh day. On that day the mourners fulfill their obligations by sitting for a short while (one hour). When the seventh day falls on the Sabbath, the mourner does not resume his *shivah*, which in this case ends with the conclusion of the morning service. The Sabbath is included in the seven days of mourning, although no outward sign of mourning is permitted on that day.

On Friday, or on the eve of a Festival (unless it is on the seventh day when one hour suffices), mourning is observed until two-and-a-half hours prior to nightfall. An exception is made on Passover Eve, when mourning ends at noon.

Shivah must be observed for father, mother, wife,

husband, son, daughter, brother, and sister (including half-brother and half-sister), but not for an infant less than thirty days old. A child that dies after thirty days is no longer regarded as having been born prematurely or as not having been viable at birth. From the age of 13 and one day (in the case of boys) and 12 and one day (in the case of girls), children must observe the laws of mourning for their relatives.

A mourner who has been prevented by sickness from observing *shivah* must do so on his recovery, if by then the thirty days of mourning have not elapsed since death.

Because of the injunction: "And thou shalt rejoice in thy Feast" (Deuteronomy 16:14), our rabbis deduced that a Festival annuls the *shivah*, provided that the mourner has been able to observe the *shivah* one hour before the commencement of the festival.[6] *Rosh Hashanah* and *Yom Kippur*, although not characterized by rejoicing, terminate the *shivah*,[7] since these two Festivals are included in the "appointed season" mentioned in Leviticus 23:4, "These are the appointed seasons of the Lord, even holy convocations, which ye shall proclaim in their appointed season."

If the deceased leaves instructions that his relatives should not observe *shivah*, his wishes must be disregarded.

A telegram may be accepted as a bona fide evidence of death, thus requiring the relative to observe *shivah*. In the case of a missing person or one presumed drowned, the relatives do not observe mourning unless there is evidence of death.

SEUDAT HAVRAAH (MEAL OF CONSOLATION)

The mourner's first meal after the funeral is known as *seudat havraah* (meal of consolation). This meal is invariably provided by friends and neighbors in obedience to the talmudic injunction, "A mourner is forbidden to eat of his own food at the first meal after the burial."[8] Reference to this custom is made by both Jeremiah and Ezekiel. "Neither shall men break bread for them in mourning, to comfort for the dead; neither shall men give them the cup of consolation to drink for their father or for their mother" (Jeremiah 16:7). Ezekiel was told by God, "Sigh in silence; make no mourning for the dead, bind thy headtire upon thee, and put thy shoes upon thy feet, and cover not thine upper lip, and eat not the bread of men" (Ezekiel 24:17). Ezekiel was forbidden to observe the practices of mourning. We see, therefore, that one of the rites of mourning was not to eat of one's own food but to allow others to provide food. This custom gives friends and neighbors the opportunity to express in a practical form their solicitude and sympathy.

The Talmud[9] tells how, in ancient times, it was the custom to take food to a house of mourning. For the rich, food was conveyed in baskets of gold and silver; for the poor, food was brought in baskets of osier willows. As this made the poor feel ashamed, the rabbis ruled that willow baskets should be used to convey the food to all mourners, rich and poor alike.

The menu of this meal has changed from that of talmudic times,[10] and according to the tradition followed nowadays, it consists of hard-boiled eggs and rolls of bread. These have a special symbolism. In ancient times, the egg was regarded as a symbol of life and resurrection. Moreover, because the egg is completely sealed inside its shell, it serves as a reminder to the mourners to remain silent and refrain from casual talk. Bread is the staple food, for it "stayeth man's heart" (Psalm 104:15).[11]

It was also customary to provide the mourners with lentils because, the rabbis said, they were made into a broth by Jacob to comfort his father when Abraham died.[12] Our sages gave an additional reason: "Lentils are round like a wheel, and mourning is a revolving wheel that touches everyone sooner or later." Yet a further reason is that just as lentils have no mouths, so too must mourners "have no mouth," for they are forbidden to greet people.[13]

Salt is not placed on the table. It is usual to dip bread in salt because the table is compared to a sacrificial altar, and the Bible says of sacrifice: "And every meal offering of thine shalt thou season with salt" (Leviticus 2:13). Since a mourner may not offer a sacrifice, there can be no place for salt on his table. If burial takes place late on Friday afternoon or late on the eve of a Festival, the mourner should not be served with a meal of condolence,[14] nor is it obligatory for the meal to be served at the termination of the Sabbath. On *Chol Ha-Moed*[15] (the semi-festive days intervening between the first and last days of Passover and Tabernacles), *Purim, Chanukah,* and *Rosh Chodesh* (New Moon), it is prepared, but not on the eve of Passover in order that the mourner's relish for the unleavened bread at the *seder* should not be diminished. The *seudat havraah* is not served if the news of a death arrives after thirty days.[16] Nor is the meal served if the mourner wishes to fast after the funeral until nightfall.

Candles must burn continuously for the entire seven days.[17] Before his death, Rabbi Judah Hanasi (135–219) instructed that a light should be kept burning in his home,[18] and the custom was widely practiced as early as the thirteenth century.

LOW STOOLS

In earlier times people normally sat on couches or beds. During the period of mourning they were required to overturn them[19] and sit on the ground. There is biblical authority for this. When King David became a mourner, he "lay on the earth" (II Samuel 13:31). And it states in the Book of Job: "So they sat down with him upon the ground seven days and seven nights" (Job 2:13). Nowadays, it is customary for the mourners to sit on low stools.

The mourner is not allowed to put on leather footwear;[20] he must wear slippers of cloth, felt, or rubber. This does not apply to a woman after confinement,[21] an expectant mother, or someone with an injured foot.[22] An invalid whose health may be injured by going without shoes is permitted to wear them. When the mourner leaves the house (for instance, to attend the synagogue on the Sabbath), he may wear leather shoes. A mourner who walks out-of-doors is permitted to wear boots. He should, however, sprinkle a little earth therein.

BATHING

The mourner is forbidden to bathe all over even in cold water.[23] This prohibition is based on the verse "And Joab sent to Tekoa, and fetched thence a wise woman, and said to her, 'I pray thee, feign thyself to be a mourner, and put on mourning apparel, I pray thee, and anoint not thyself with oil' " (II Samuel 16:2).

Bathing, like anointing, is included among the pleasures forbidden to mourners, who may, however, wash their face, hands, and feet in cold water.[24] The prohibition against bathing is waived for a man covered with mud, a woman after childbirth, or a delicate person[25] who must bathe himself for reasons of health.

A woman should not use any cosmetics during the *shivah* period.[26] A more lenient attitude in this respect is adopted toward a bride or a young girl.

The Talmud relates that services were held in the house of the mourner.[27] When a neighbor of Rabbi Judah died without there being any surviving children to be comforted, the rabbi assembled a *minyan* (ten men above the age of 13) daily and offered prayers in his memory. The dead man appeared to the rabbi in a dream and said: "Thy mind be at rest, for thou hast set my mind at rest."

Praying in the house of mourners so as to show respect for both the dead and the living was a well-established custom in the Middle Ages. One of the functions of the *Chevrah Maariv be-Zemanah Ohev Shalom* (Society for Praying the Evening Service at the Nighttime with Loving Peace), founded in 1790 in London, was to provide a *minyan* during the *shivah*.[28]

In 1853 *Chevrat Menachem Avelim Chesed Ve-Emet* (Society of Kindness and for Comforting the Mourners) was formed in London. In return for a weekly contribution of two pence, the friendly society undertook to provide: (1) a *shivah* benefit of ten shillings during the week of confined mourning; (2) *minyan* during *shivah;* and (3) payment of a rabbi to speak at morning and evening service at *shivah* and on the Sabbath during the *sheloshim.*[29]

A *Sefer Torah* (Torah scroll) for the Reading of the Law during the services should be loaned by the community if proper facilities for its care are available, and also providing it is to be read on three occasions.

If it is not possible to obtain a *minyan* in the home, the mourner in certain circumstances may go to the synagogue for services.

LITURGY

In the house of mourning, the normal order of the daily services is subject to variations. The additions, substitutions, and omissions are as follows:

Psalm 49,[30] which expresses firm belief in the Redemption of the Soul, is read.

The talmudic passage *Pitum Ha-Ketoret*[31] (the compound forming incense) is omitted.

Tachanun (petitions of grace), also known as *Nefilat Appayim* (falling on the face),[32] are omitted. The theme of *Tachanun* is "I have sinned before Thee" and is deemed inappropriate to a mourner.

On those days on which *Tachanun* is not said, Psalm 16,[33] which praises complete submission to the Divine Will, is substituted for Psalm 44.

Psalm 20[34] is omitted.

The Priestly Benediction[35] (Numbers 6:24–26) is omitted.

The mourner omits the six Psalms (Psalms 95–99 and 29) recited before the evening service on Friday night. At the synagogue on Friday evening mourners remain in the anteroom until the conclusion of *Lechah Dodi* (a hymn sung during Friday evening services).

The beadle then announces: "Comfort the mourners," and the congregation rises and greets them with the words: "May the Almighty comfort you among the other mourners for Zion and Jerusalem."[36]

The verse (Psalm 90:17), "And let the graciousness of the Lord our God be upon us: establish thou also upon us the work of our hands, yea, the work of our hands establish thou it," is omitted.[37]

Spices are not used for the *Havdalah* service (the benedictions recited at the termination of the Sabbath) in the house of a mourner.[38]

In the Grace After Meals, the passage: "Comfort, O Lord our God, the mourners of Jerusalem" is substituted for the verse, "And rebuild Jerusalem, the holy city, speedily in our days."[39]

Hallel ("Hymns of Praise," Psalms 113–118) is not said in the house of a mourner on *Rosh Chodesh* and *Chanukah*[40] because they contain sentiments that might sadden mourners, such as, "The dead praise not the Lord, neither any that go down into silence" (Psalm 115:17), and, "This is the day which the Lord hath made, we will rejoice and be glad in it" (Psalm 118:24). If possible, the mourner should go into another room while the congregation recites the *Hallel*. If *Rosh Chodesh* occurs on the Sabbath, *Hallel* should be recited with the congregation even in the house of a mourner, for on the Sabbath there is no outward mourning.

The mourner is not called up to the Reading of the Law during the week of *shivah*, even if he is the only *Kohen* or *Levi* (special priestly classes entitled to the first and second *aliyot*—blessing before and after reading the Torah) in the congregation.

In the *Kaddish Shalem*, the words, "May the prayers of all Israel be accepted by their Father who is in heaven,"[42] are not said by the mourner; they are generally recited by the officiating reader in the house of mourning.

TEFILLIN ON THE FIRST DAY

The Code states:[43] "On the first day of the *shivah*, mourners do not put on *tefillin*".[44] This is deduced from the Divine command to Ezekiel who, when he became a mourner, was instructed "to bind thy headtire upon thee" (Ezekiel 24:17), i.e., *tefillin*, the implication being that all other mourners are exempt from putting on *tefillin* on the first day, as they must not indulge in any personal adornment. This view has been endorsed by many leading rabbinical authorities, among them Rabbi David ben Samuel Halevi, the *Taz*, Joseph ben Meir Teomin (1727–1793), and Rabbi Akiva Eger (1761–1837).

The custom nowadays is to put on *tefillin* on the first day of the *shivah*, although some authorities maintain that the mourner need not make the usual benedictions.

If, however, burial took place at twilight, and the mourner immediately commenced his *shivah*, the authorities hold that he should put on the *tefillin* the following day, since this was considered as the second day of mourning. A man bereaved on *Chol Ha-Moed* should put on *tefillin* provided that it is his custom to put on *tefillin* on those days.

A mourner is permitted to conduct services in his own house since he is bound to observe all the *mitzvot*. If a person mourning for his parents officiates in the synagogue, he complies with the usual order of the service,[45] including the recital of the Priestly Benediction, but he omits *Tachanun*. He should not officiate on *Rosh Chodesh* nor on days when *Tachanun* is not said. He may go to the synagogue to hear the *Megillah* on *Purim* but must not himself recite the *Megillah* for the congregation. From *Rosh Chodesh Elul* until after *Yom Kippur* and during the Ten Days of Penitence, the mourner may officiate and may even recite *Selichot* (penitential prayers).

During the *shivah* week a mourner should not officiate as reader on the Sabbath and Festivals unless there is no one else to do so.

A mourner during the *shivah* period should not go from

his house to the synagogue to recite *Selichot*, except on the eve of *Rosh Hashanah*, when many *Selichot* are said.[46]

In times of pestilence, one does not observe mourning rites;[47] "I have heard," confirms Rabbi Moses Isserles, "that some have adopted this practice."[48]

If a mourner is prevented through illness from commencing the period of the *shivah* at the time of the interment, he is not required to observe the full seven days on his recovery, but must observe the remaining days of the *shivah*.

Chapter 6

The Manner of Mourning

Judaism makes many demands on mourners, all with good reason. The mourning period is ordered, not to enforce idleness or encourage morbid thought, but for reflection and self-examination. During these few brief days, all normal activities are suspended.

For the period of the *shivah*, as has already been mentioned, the mourner is forbidden to do any work or even to supervise work that is performed by others, whether they be fellow-Jews or gentiles.

In certain exceptional circumstances, such as poverty or where irreparable loss is probable, the mourner, after consulting a rabbi, may be permitted to carry on his usual work after the third day of the *shivah*. Nevertheless, our sages say: "May a curse come upon his neighbors who [by not providing for his maintenance] force the mourner to work."[1]

It is regarded as a great *mitzvah* to give alms to poor people during the *shivah*.

Although the law in general requires total cessation from any gainful occupation by a mourner during the *shivah*, it makes a number of important concessions. It is permitted to delegate to others the execution of transactions that, if postponed, would entail irretrievable loss. Such transactions

55

include the recovery of debts, receiving commissions for work to be executed later, and the writing of urgent letters.[2]

If two individuals own a shop in partnership and one of them becomes a mourner, the shop should be closed.[3] Where, however, great loss may result, rabbinical authorities should be consulted as to whether it may be opened after three days.

It is permissible for a woman in mourning to bake and cook and attend to all her domestic duties.[4] Sweeping the house, washing up, and making the beds are not considered forbidden work for the mourner.[5] A domestic servant may carry out her normal duties during the period of the *shivah*. She must not, however, leave the house during the *shivah*.

STUDY

The Psalmist says: "The precepts of the Lord are right, rejoicing the heart" (Psalm 19:9). Our rabbis have therefore forbidden a mourner to study or even to meditate on the Pentateuch, Prophets, Hagiographa, *Mishnah*, Talmud, *halachot* (laws), or *aggadot* (tales).[6] Both Ezekiel and Job throw light on this command. "Sigh in silence" (Ezekiel 24:17) and "None spoke a word" (Job 2:13) have been homiletically explained as "Torah Study."[7]

However, the mourner may spend his time reading the following works: the Book of Job, Lamentations, the sad parts of Jeremiah,[8] the chapter *Eilu Megalchin*[9] (which deals with the laws concerning mourning and excommunication), *Semachot*,[10] and *Menorat Ha-Maor* (Candelabrum of Light) by Rabbi Isaac Aboab the Elder, a religioethical writer of the fourteenth century.

GREETINGS

During the first three days of the *shivah*, the mourner does not greet people or reply to them,[11] as this period is devoted to strict mourning. After the third day, the mourner may reply to those who greet him. This custom, too, like so many of the mourning rites, is derived from Ezekiel, who was told, "Sigh in silence" (Ezekiel 24:17).

After the *shivah*, but before the end of the *sheloshim*, the mourner may greet others, but these do not return the greeting of peace.[12] According to Rabbi Zechariah Mendel (the *Beer Hetev*), conventional salutations like "Good morning" and "Good day" are not included in the prohibition that is confined to the *Shalom Aleichem* (Peace be unto you) formula.

The phrase, which is popular in the English-speaking world, "I wish you long life," can be traced back to the *Midrash*. "In ordinary cases," states the *Midrash*, "where a man's son dies, people say to him, to comfort him, 'May your other son who is left you live;' and if he has no other son they say 'We wish you long life.' "[13]

It is customary among very observant Jews not to shake hands with the mourners.

It is permissible to greet mourners on Sabbath.[14] The Talmud relates that on one occasion Rabbi Hoshaya the Elder went to a certain place and met mourners on the Sabbath. He greeted them by saying: "I know not what is the custom of your place [with regard to greeting on the Sabbath]; however, peace be unto you in accordance with the custom of your place."[15]

COMFORTING THE MOURNERS

It is a great *mitzvah* to comfort the mourners. "It is one of those things," say the rabbis, "that bring good to the world."[16] God Himself comforted the mourners in one instance:[17] "And it came to pass after the death of Abraham, that God blessed Isaac his son" (Genesis 25:11). According to Ecclesiastes (7:2), "It is better to go to the house of mourning, than to go to the house of feasting." The *Midrash* illustrates this idea with the parable: "It is as if there were two ocean-going ships, one leaving the harbor and the other entering it. As the one sailed out of the harbor the by-standers all rejoiced, but none displayed any joy over the one that was entering the harbor. A wise man was there and he said to the people: 'I take the opposite view to you. There is no cause to rejoice over the ship that is leaving the harbor because nobody knows what will be its plight, what seas and storms it may encounter; but when it enters the harbor all have occasion to rejoice since it has come in safely.' Similarly when a person dies all should rejoice and offer thanks that he departed from the world with a good name and in peace."[18]

In both the Bible and rabbinic literature there are many references to visiting the bereaved. We read in the Bible how Jacob was consoled by his children: "And all his sons and all his daughters rose up to comfort him" (Genesis 37:35). According to the Talmud both Ahab and Elijah went to comfort Hiel, the Bethelite, when his sons died (I Kings 16:34).[19] Similarly, the *tannaim* (teachers)[20] and the *amoraim* (interpreters)[21] visited bereaved teachers, colleagues, and disciples to console them.[22]

The manner of visiting a mourner is as important as the visit itself. Respect should be shown for the mourner's grief and bitterness. Indeed, the danger of converting the *shivah* visit into a social occasion was not unknown to the rabbis. "The merit of attending a house of mourning," says the Talmud, "lies in the silence observed."[23]

Throughout the ages discreet men, like Job's comfort-ers, paid their visits of condolence in sympathetic silence. "So they sat down with him upon the ground seven days and seven nights, and none spoke a word unto him; for they saw that his grief was very great" (Job 2:13). Also, when Aaron was bereaved, he "held his peace" (Leviticus 10:3). In general, visitors are advised not to speak until the mourner has spoken.

The present-day practice of sending or bringing gifts of food to the mourner during the *shivah* is frowned on by many rabbinical authorities, since this is regarded as copying the gentiles. A distinction, however, is made between necessities, which may be sent, and luxuries, such as cakes and sweets, which should not be sent. Basically, gifts are not approved of because they might bring joy and thus lessen the natural sorrow that the mourner feels.

The *mitzvah* of comforting the mourner cannot be fulfilled by telephone, since the would-be comforter cannot be deemed to have participated physically in the act.

Upon leaving, the visitor should approach the mourners and say:

הַמָּקוֹם יְנַחֵם אֶתְכֶם בְּתוֹךְ שְׁאָר אֲבֵלֵי צִיּוֹן וִירוּשָׁלָיִם׃

Ha-Makom Yenachem Etchem Betoch She'ar Avelay Tziyyon Verushalayim. "May the Almighty comfort you among the other mourners for Zion and Jerusalem."

Most of the laws and rituals of mourning are developed around a communal or social structure. Since the key to the therapeutic efficacy of mourning is the ability of the mourner to transfer his dependency, needs, and love impulses to other persons and objects, the Jewish sociocultural system gives him abundant opportunity to accomplish this. The mourner does not perform the mourning rites in isolation but as an active member of the group.[24]

In the words of Rabbi Samson Raphael Hirsch, "Be with him from whom God has taken a member of his family . . . stay by him that he is not forsaken . . . sit silently by the mourner until he himself gives vent to his sorrow in words."[25]

LAUNDERED GARMENTS

The mourner is not allowed to wash his garments during the *shivah*, because this involves work, which is forbidden.[26] Furthermore, he must wear only garments that were worn prior to the *shivah*. A reference to this is found in the Second Book of Samuel (14:2): "I pray thee, feign thyself to be a mourner, and put on mourning apparel, I pray thee, and anoint not thyself with oil, but be as a woman that had a long time mourned for the dead."

It is likewise forbidden to wash household linen.[27] Diapers and essential clothing for small children may be washed. On the Sabbath the tables may be covered with clean tablecloths provided that they were washed before the *shivah*.

A mourner may not have his hair cut, shave his beard,[28] or cut his fingernails. "Let not the hair of your heads go loose" (Leviticus 10:6), the priests who were mourning were commanded in the tabernacle. The interpretation of this is that all other mourners must let their hair grow long during the *shivah*. Mourners are, however, permitted to comb their hair.[29]

There is "a time to weep, and a time to laugh," says Ecclesiastes (3:4). But although only the first three days are designated as "days of weeping," any kind of entertainment is strictly forbidden during the *shivah*.

If the mourner celebrates a *brit milah* during the *shivah*, he may change his clothes and go to the synagogue but may not cut his hair. Neither may he provide a festive meal,[30] although he may invite ten people in order to recite the special Grace After Meals. If there is no one else available, he may act as the *mohel*.[31] After the third day he may also act as *gevater* (one who carries the infant) or *sandek* (the man who holds the baby on his knees during the circumcision), but he must not participate in the *seudah* afterward. Nor may he join in a *seudah* on the occasion of the redemption of a first-born or the conclusion of a talmudic tractate. He may not in any circumstances attend a wedding feast, even if it takes place in his own house, nor may he leave his home to hear the seven marriage benedictions.[32]

It is forbidden to have marital intercourse during the *shivah*,[33] nor is it permitted to kiss and embrace,[34] because such demonstrations are unseemly during the week of mourning.

SABBATH

Although the mourner does not observe public mourning at all on the Sabbath, this is nevertheless counted as a full day of *shivah*.[35] Support for this is found in the Jerusalem Talmud[36] in the commentary on the verse: "The blessing of the Lord, it maketh rich, and toil addeth nothing thereto" (Proverbs 10:22). Here the Talmud says that "the blessing of the Lord maketh rich" refers to the blessing of the Sabbath, and the second part of the verse, "And toil addeth nothing thereto," implies that there is no public mourning on the Sabbath.

While mourners are forbidden to study, bathe, or cohabit on the Sabbath,[37] they do not have to sit on low stools and may change their clothes.[38] If the Sabbath is the seventh day when the funeral took place on the previous Sunday, the *shivah* terminates after the Sabbath morning service.

SYNAGOGUE

In the synagogue the mourner does not occupy his usual seat. This custom goes back to talmudic times. Our rabbis taught: "When a *chacham* (sage) dies, his *bet ha-midrash* (house of study) closes; when the *Av Bet Din* (Vice-President of the Supreme Court) dies, all the colleges in the city are closed, and the people enter the synagogues and change their usual places; those that usually sit in the north sit in the south, and those that usually sit in the south sit in the north."[39]

Originally, this practice was followed only on the death of the Vice-President of the Court to indicate that his death had disrupted their lives. Nowadays, however, it is practiced by all mourners.[40] A man mourning his parents should change his place for the whole year. His new place should be at least four cubits from his accustomed seat.

A mourner during the *shivah* is not called up to the Torah, even if he is the only *Kohen* or *Levi* in the congregation. If he is a *Kohen* or a *Levi*, it is advisable for him to leave the synagogue just before the Reading of the Law in order to avoid embarrassment both to himself and the congregation. If, however, he is inadvertently called up to the Torah, he should not decline the *mitzvah,* and the usual *Mi-Sheberach* is made for him.

Rabbi Jacob b. Meir Tam[41] was regularly called up to the reading of the third portion of the *Sidra* (weekly Torah portion) every Sabbath. On the Sabbath of his bereavement he would not forgo his *aliyah* (when one is called to the Reading of the Law). His argument was that any departure from the established practice would amount to a public demonstration of *avelut* (mourning), which is forbidden on the Sabbath.[42]

A mourner who normally participates in the *seudah shelishit*[43] in the synagogue may do so during the *shivah*. He may ask for a memorial prayer to be said in memory of the deceased on Sabbath.[44] A grandfather who is sitting *shivah* may attend his grandson's *bar mitzvah* service, but he should not be called to the Reading of the Law.

GREETING THE MOURNERS

After *Minchah* on Friday afternoon, the mourner, during the week of the *shivah* retires to the annex or anteroom of the synagogue. On his re-entry after *Lechah Dodi* and before the recitation of Psalm 92, the congregation recites the traditional formula, *Ha-Makom Yenachem Etchem Betoch She'ar Avelay Tziyyon Verushalayim* (see p. 59).

"This humane custom," writes Dr. Hertz, "is not as well known and fully understood as its touching beauty and sublimity warrants. For if the Sabbath-psalms prove the interpretation of Nature and the Divine, Greeting the Mourners is eloquent testimony that in Judaism, the whole of life—all its joys and sorrows, its sunshine and sorrow—is interpenetrated with Religion."[45]

FESTIVALS

There is no mourning on *Yom Tov*[46] so that if a death occurs during a Festival, mourning does not begin until the Festival is ended. A *Kohen* who is a mourner should not pronounce the priestly blessings on *Yom Tov*. It is preferable for him to leave the synagogue before the beginning of the priestly benedictions.[47] If, however, only one other *Kohen* is present in the congregation, he may officiate during the twelve-month period of mourning for his parents or during the *sheloshim* for any other relative, but not during the *shivah*.

A mourner is forbidden, during the *shivah*, to attend the synagogue on the Eve of Passover to hear the *siyyum*[48] that exempts the firstborn from fasting that day.

One who becomes a mourner during *Sukkot* (the Feast of Tabernacles) may be called up to the Torah on *Simchat Torah* (Rejoicing of the Law) but he may not be one of the Bridegrooms of the Law.[49] According to *Sephardi* (Spanish Jews) custom[50] a mourner takes part in the *hakkafot* (processional circuits during *sukkot*).[51] *Ashkenazim* (German Jews) do not participate in the *hakkafot* when mourning the loss of father or mother.[52]

It is customary for mourners to attend the synagogue on the night of the ninth of *Av* to hear *Echah* (the Book of Lamentations) and in the daytime to recite the *Kinot* (Prayers of Lamentations).[53] It is also permissible for them to be called up to the Reading of the Law.[54]

The authorities are divided on the subject of mourning on *Purim*. Rabbi Joseph Caro[55] states that during the *shivah* a mourner should observe all the laws of mourning. Rabbi

Moses Isserles, on the other hand, quotes a number of authorities who maintained that "outward" mourning is not observed on *Purim* or *Shushan Purim* (the day after *Purim*).[56] The mourner is forbidden "to witness any manner of festivity" but may put on his shoes and sit on a chair.[57] At night he can gather a *minyan* to his house to hear the *Megillah*. If it is not possible to obtain a quorum he may go to the synagogue.[58]

If *Purim* occurs at the termination of the Sabbath, the mourner should go to the synagogue after the Third Meal while it is still Sabbath. A mourner during the *shivah* period is permitted to send gifts to the needy and *mishloach manot* (gifts to friends and neighbors).[59] He should not, however, send anything of a joyous nature. It is, moreover, forbidden to send gifts during the entire twelve months[60] to one who is mourning for a parent.

The mourner is obliged to kindle lights during the festival of *Chanukah*, and on the first night he recites the benediction, *Shehecheyanu* ("Who hast kept us alive").[61]

HEAD OF THE HOUSE

There are times when members of a family observing *shivah* have to follow the lead of the head of the family. If a person comes from a nearby town (within a day's walking distance) and finds his relatives sitting *shivah*, he should count the days of mourning with them. Even if he comes on the seventh day, he should still go according to their reckoning, and consequently he will himself not need to observe *shivah* again. This applies only where the head of the family (*gedol ha-bayit*)[62] is present; all other mourners follow the head of the family with regard to the *shivah*.

If, however, the chief mourner comes from another town and finds members of the household sitting *shivah*, he should begin to count for himself; in this case, those who are already in mourning do not follow his lead.

SUICIDE

Although suicide is not regarded in the Mishnaic Code as a felony, nevertheless, where it is committed with full deliberation and by somebody unquestionably of sound mind, it is regarded as a usurpation of the Divine prerogative and a trespass against both God and man. Despite all his suffering, even Job did not attempt to end his life: "What? shall we receive good at the hand of God," he reasoned, "and shall we not receive evil?" (Job 2:10).

In many cases, however, suicide is not an act of wanton self-destruction but a manifestation of intense despair. In the whole of the Bible there is mention of only a few people who took their lives, and in each case the circumstances were exceptional. Each incident took place in a time of despair or when death by hostile hands was imminent. So it was with Ahithophel, Privy Councillor to David (II Samuel 17:23), Zimri (I Kings 16:18), Samson (Judges 16:28–30), and Saul (I Samuel 31:4).

Josephus had strong views on suicide. "Is it noble to destroy oneself?" he demanded with forceful rhetoric. "Not so, but most ignoble; in my opinion there could be no worse coward than the pilot who, for fear of a tempest, deliberately sinks his ship before the storm. No! Suicide is alike repugnant to the nature which all creatures share and an act of impiety towards God who created us."[63]

Here Josephus is in complete accord with rabbinical teachings. The verse "And surely your blood of your lives will I require" (Genesis 9:5) is interpreted by the *tanna* Rabbi Eleazar as: "I will require your blood if shed by the hands of yourselves."[64]

A suicide is called in Hebrew *me'abed atzmo ladaat* (one who knowingly destroys himself).[65] The rabbis have never shared the opinion of Seneca (31 B.C.E.–30 C.E.) that the "eternal law that has assigned a single entrance to this life has mercifully allowed many exits. Any death is preferable to servitude."

The Jew is bidden to take great care of valuables,

whether they are natural objects or human possessions. The special law of *Bal Tashchit* (warning not to destroy something of value)[66] is derived from the verse in Deuteronomy (20:19): "When thou shalt besiege a city a long time, in making war against it to take it, thou shalt not destroy the trees thereof by wielding an axe against them; for thou mayest eat of them but thou shalt not cut them down; for is the tree of the field man that it should be besieged of thee?"

"He who in anger tears his clothes," say the rabbis,[67] "and breaks crockery or throws away his money, is to be accounted as one who worships idols." If this applies to inanimate objects, how much more serious it is for a man to extinguish his own life; for man created "in the image of God" is deemed to be the center of the creation, the glory of the world.

MARTYRDOM

It is a man's sacred duty to prolong and to preserve life by all the means within his power. "Ye shall therefore keep My statutes, and Mine ordinances, which if man do, he shall live by them; I am the Lord" (Leviticus 18:5). From this verse our rabbis deduced that all negative commandments in the Torah, except those with regard to idolatry, immorality, and murder, may be transgressed if life is in danger.[68] Yet the phenomenon of Jewish martyrdom, manifested in *Kiddush Ha-Shem* (the sanctification of God's name) has few parallels in other cultures.

When the First Temple was destroyed, the priests leaped into the flames and died in their holy home.[69] Three years after the destruction of the Second Temple, many of the heroes of Masada[70] killed themselves rather than submit to their cruel conquerors.[71] Jewish history is filled with accounts of similar sacrifices.

The most famous martyr was Rabbi Akiva ben Joseph (c. 50–135 C.E.) When Rabbi Akiva was taken out for execution, it was the hour for the recital of the *Shema* (section of the scripture recited every morning and evening), and while they combed his flesh with iron combs, he was accepting upon himself the kingship of heaven. His disciples said to him: "Our Master, even to this point?" He said to them: "All my days I have been troubled by this verse 'with all my soul,' which I interpret as 'even if He takes thy soul.' I said 'When shall I have the opportunity of fulfilling this?' Now I have the opportunity; shall I not fulfill it?" He prolonged the word "one." A *Bat Kol* (a voice descending from heaven) went forth and proclaimed: "Happy art thou, Akiva, that thy soul has departed with the word *Echad*" (literally, One—the last word of the *Shema*).[72]

PROCEDURE FOR SUICIDES

The second chapter of *Semachot* and the Code *Yoreh Deah*[73] deal with the procedure to be adopted in the case of a suicide. "One who commits suicide willfully is not attended to at all; and one does not mourn for him and no lamentation is made for him, nor does one rend garments." He is regarded as one who dies in a state of excommunication.[74] The rabbis consider only a premeditated and deliberate act of self-destruction to be suicide; but when there is an act of aberration or sudden impulse, or where there is a doubt, a more lenient view is generally taken and the deceased is given "the benefit of the doubt." An instance is recorded in the Talmud. Threatened by his father with punishment, the young son of a citizen of Lydda ran away and killed himself. When the case was brought before Rabbi Tarfon (late first century C.E.), he decided that it was not suicide, saying that the boy was moved by fear of his father.[75]

According to the majority of rabbinic authorities, in most cases of suicide one may assume that the balance of the person's mind was disturbed. It was thought to be inconceivable that a person with a sound mind would commit such an abominable act. Many rabbinic authorities, therefore, permit surviving members of the family of a suicide to observe mourning and to recite *Kaddish* in the synagogue for the soul of the deceased. In this way they would be spared further humiliation and grief.[76]

If a minor commits suicide, it is regarded as if he had done the deed unintentionally.[77]

Mourning rites are not observed for apostates or for those who "cast off the precepts from their necks and are not included among Israelites as regards the performance of the precepts."[78] But a person who has been executed, even if he were an apostate, should be mourned.[79]

Chapter 7

The Kaddish

When death visits a household, the whole house, indeed life itself, appears empty and the future bleak. At such a time, the son of the house rises in prayer and proclaims: "Magnified and sanctified be His great Name in the world which He hath created according to His will. May He establish His kingdom during your life and during your days, and during the life of all the house of Israel, even speedily and at a near time, and say ye, Amen."[1]

Thus, the *Kaddish* is a paean of praise, an affirmation of faith for all the world to hear. Three times a day, during the eleven-month period of the year of mourning, and on every *yahrzeit* (anniversary of a death), a bereaved son affirms the greatness of God and honors his father's memory. His father is dead, but his spirit lives forever. This is the fundamental meaning of the *Kaddish*, a prayer of almost mystical force, for it has bound successive generations together and it transcends the barriers of death.

When the mourner recites: "Glorified and sanctified be the great Name," he declares: No matter how powerful death is, notwithstanding the ugly end of man, however terrifying the grave is, however nonsensical and absurd everything appears, no matter how black one's

69

despair is and how nauseating an affair life is, we declare and profess publicly and solemnly that we are not giving up, that we are not surrendering, that we will carry on the work of our ancestors as though nothing has happened, that we will not be satisfied with less than the full realization of the ultimate goal—the establishment of God's kingdom, the resurrection of the dead and eternal life for man.[2]

Kaddish means sanctification, and the practice of saying *Kaddish* has become an integral part of Jewish life, since paradoxically it is connected with life and not with death.

The stress of modern living may have led to the nonobservance of many religious rites, but it has not devalued the *Kaddish*, which is deeply ingrained in the minds and hearts of the people. It is a matter of honor with the majority of mourners not to miss a *Kaddish*, no matter what hardship or inconvenience may be incurred in carrying out this act of filial duty and reverence. Jewish custom and usage may vary, but the familiar words of the *Kaddish* are heard wherever ten Jews join together for worship. The compulsive urge to say *Kaddish* is often a means of return to the synagogue for many who have been totally or partially estranged from it. "Help to make up a *minyan* for *Kaddish*" is a plea that few ignore.

HISTORY

Although verses of the *Kaddish* prayer are said to date from Patriarchal times,[3] the present text dates from the geonic period.[4] The geonic period is the post-talmudic period from the sixth to the eleventh centuries C.E. involving the intellectual leaders of the Babylonian Jewish community. The prayer had its origin in the schoolhouse in the Holy Land, where it was recited by the teacher or preacher as a doxology at the conclusion of a talmudic discourse. Later, the practice was continued in Babylon. The responses of the

congregation were regarded as being of the utmost importance, and according to the *Targum* (Aramaic translation of
the Bible) (Deuteronomy 6:4), Jacob made these responses.
"Joining loudly in unison in the congregational chorus of
Yehay Shemay Rabbah ["May His great Name be blessed"–
part of *Kaddish* said by the entire congregation]," say the
rabbis, "has the power of influencing the heavenly decree in
one's favor, or of obtaining forgiveness."[5] Similarly, Rabbi
Jose b. Chalafta, a second-century teacher, affirms: "Whenever the Israelites go into the synagogues and schoolhouses
and respond: 'May His great Name be blessed,' the Holy
One, blessed be He, as it were, shakes his head and says,
'Happy is the King who is thus praised in His house. Woe to
the father who banished his children, and woe to the
children who had to be banished from the table of their
father.' "[6] Again and again the rabbis emphasize the importance of these verses. Rabbi Joshua ben Levi says that the evil
decree is annulled for the man who makes the responses
with complete devotion, and Rabbi Chiyyah bar Abba, in the
name of Rabbi Jochanan, goes even further. "Even if he has
a taint of idolatry, he is forgiven . . . and the gates of
Paradise are open to him."[7]

Later the schoolhouse doxology became part of the
liturgy of the synagogue. It is clear from the tractate *Soferim*
(of the geonic period) that the synagogue services at that
time began with *Barechu* ("Bless ye the Lord Who is to be
blessed") and the *Kaddish* and concluded with the Reading of
the Law and a second recital of the *Kaddish*.

MOURNER'S PRAYER

Perhaps the earliest reference to the *Kaddish* as a
"Mourner's Prayer" was made in the thirteenth century by
Rabbi Isaac ben Moses of Vienna (ca. 1180–1260) in his book
Or Zarua,[8] and it has been the practice ever since for both
Sephardi and Ashkenazi mourners to recite the *Kaddish*,
with minor textual variants. True, objections were occasion-

ally made by leading authorities who were afraid that the
Kaddish might become the center of Judaic worship. "They
buoy themselves up with vain hope," writes Rabbi Abraham
b. Chiyya Hanasi (twelfth century), "when they reckon that
the actions and prayers of their sons would benefit them
after death."[9] The same sentiment was expressed by Rabbi
Abraham Hurwitz in the sixteenth century:

> Let the son keep a particular precept given him by his
> father, and it would be of greater worth than the
> recitation of the *Kaddish*. The same is true also of
> daughters, for the *Kaddish* is not a prayer by the son that
> the father may be brought up from *Sheol* [the nether
> world of the grave], but a recognition of the parent's
> merit, since through its recital the child best vindicates
> the memory of his parent by causing the congregation
> to respond to him with the praise *Amen, Yehay Shemay
> Rabba*.

REDEEMING QUALITY OF PATRIARCHS

Zechut Avot (the merit of the fathers) plays a great part
in Jewish theology. "For the merits of the fathers," the rabbis
say, "was Israel redeemed from Egypt."[11]

The Patriarchs, as well as other personages of the Bible,
accomplished or came near to perfection by their faith
and love, unselfishness and charity, observances and
performances, studies and works—those ideals for
which alone the world was worthy to be called into
existence, and for which it deserves to continue. Thus
they gathered treasures in heaven not for themselves
but for others. By their works and charity their descendants experienced miracles and wonders in the course
of their historical life. By their merits Israel escaped
thousands of perils and dangers. For their sake Israel's
immortality and eternity are assured.[12]

Paradoxically, just as a father can intercede for his children, so children can be of service to their parents, for the dead need to be forgiven, and a man's son is his best advocate. There is an old Jewish belief that "the son confers privileges on his father."[13] Rabbi Akiva once saw in a vision the shadowy figure of a man carrying a load of wood upon his shoulders. "What aileth thee?" asked the Rabbi. "I am one of those forlorn souls condemned for his sins to the agony of hellfire," replied the shadow. "And there is no hope for you?" enquired the Rabbi further in great compassion. "If my little son, who was a mere infant when I died, could be taught to recite the *Kaddish*, then and only then would I be absolved." The rabbi took the boy under his care and taught him to lisp the *Kaddish*. He was then assured that the father had been released from *Gehinnom* (hell).

By piety and devotion men can intercede successfully for those who have sinned during their lifetime. For example, when David heard of Absalom's death, he uttered the cry, "My son, Absalom," eight times and with each heart-rending cry, say the rabbis, raised his son up by stages out of his misery.[15] The righteousness of a living child favorably affects the destiny of a dead parent.

The old Jewish doctrine of the merit of the fathers has a counterpart—the idea that the righteousness of the living child favorably affects the fate of the dead father. This might be called the doctrine of the "merit of the children." In this way the living and the dead hold converse. The real message of the dead is their virtue. The response of the living is again their virtue. Thus is a bridge built over the chasm of the tomb. Thus do the hearts of fathers and children beat in eternal unison.[16]

SUBMISSION TO GOD'S WILL

The *Kaddish* further declares man's submission to the will of God. Although there is no reference to death in the

Kaddish, its clear implication is, "His will, not ours, be done." When a man's grief is almost unbearable and his heart is full of sorrow, the *Kaddish* prayer, "Magnified and hallowed be His great Name," is a wonderful way for him proudly and publicly to proclaim his unshakable faith that "whatever the Merciful One does, it is for good."[17]

The *Kaddish*

possesses wonderful power. Truly, if there is any bond strong and indissoluble enough to chain heaven to earth, it is this prayer. It keeps the living together and forms the bridge to the mysterious realm of the dead. One might almost say that this prayer is the watchman and the guardian of the people by whom alone it is uttered; therein lies the warrant of its continuance. Can a people disappear and be annihilated so long as a child remembers its parents? It may sound strange: In the midst of the wildest dissipation has this prayer recalled to his better self many a dissolute character, so that he has bethought himself and for a time at least purified himself by honoring the memory of his parents.

Because this prayer is a resurrection in the spirit of the perishable in man, because it does not acknowledge death, because it permits the blossom that, withered, has fallen from the tree of mankind to flower and develop again in the human heart, therefore it possesses sanctifying power.[18]

RESURRECTION AND KADDISH

Judaism stresses the "immortality of the soul" and the "revival of the dead." True, the *Kaddish,* apart from the burial *Kaddish,* makes no reference to the resurrection, but it does refer (more markedly so in the Sephardi version) to the messianic vision.[19] The resurrection is closely interwoven with the coming of the Messiah and the universal acknowledgment of the Unity of God. In the *Kaddish*, the mourner reaffirms his conviction in the hereafter. "The dust returneth to the earth as it was; but the spirit returneth unto God who gave it" (Ecclesiastes 12:7).

THE LANGUAGE

Apart from the closing verse, "He Who maketh peace in His high places, may He make peace for us and for all Israel, and say ye Amen," the original language of the *Kaddish* was Aramaic. For nearly a thousand years (from the time of Ezra to well after the end of the talmudic period), Aramaic was the vernacular of the Jewish masses in Babylon and Palestine. Several passages and sections of the Bible[20] were written in Aramaic, as were the *Targumim*, much of the *Talmud Yerushalmi* (Jerusalem Talmud), the *Talmud Bavli* (Babylonian Talmud), *Midrashim*, the *Masorah*, the geonic writings, liturgical works, and Kabbalistic literature. Although the sacred liturgy is for most part in *Leshon Ha-Kodesh* (the holy tongue), the Hebrew prayer book still retains a number of Aramaic prayers,[21] including the *Kaddish*.[22]

DURATION

At first the *Kaddish* was recited during the whole twelve months of mourning.[23] "The memory of the dead," says the Talmud,[24] "begins to grow dim in the heart when twelve months have passed away." But as twelve months were regarded as the maximum period of punishment accorded to the wicked in *Gehinnom*,[25] Rabbi Moses b. Israel Isserles (c. 1525–1572) of Cracow, limited the recital of the *Kaddish* to eleven months[26] (even in a leap year), for it would be unfilial for a man to assume that his parent had deserved the maximum penalty. Thus the *Kaddish* is recited for eleven months less one day.

Originally a son recited the *Kaddish* in memory of

parents only. Gradually the practice was extended, and other relatives also joined in this prayer. Nowadays, *Kaddish* is recited by close relatives: for a wife, sister, brother, son, or daughter when they have no son of their own to recite the *Kaddish*.[27] Grandchildren may say *Kaddish* for their grandparents, and pupils for their teachers. If the mourner's parents are living, he should not recite *Kaddish* for another relative. "It is the adopted usage to recite *Kaddish* for one's mother even when the father is still living, and the latter has no right to prevent his son from reciting *Kaddish* for his mother."[28]

When there are no children or relatives, a stranger, provided that he is a pious man, may be deputed to recite *Kaddish* for the deceased.[29] A man should not undertake to recite *Kaddish* for two people at the same time.

It is the general view of rabbinic authorities that daughters, even in the absence of sons, do not recite *Kaddish* in the synagogue.[30] If, however, the daughter wishes to honor her departed father, she should listen attentively to the recitation of the *Kaddish* and respond "Amen" with devotion, in which case it is regarded as if she herself had said *Kaddish* and fulfilled the precept.

It is worth noting that several rabbinic authorities saw no objection to daughters saying the *Kaddish* prayer. For example, the famous chasidic woman—Channah Rachel (1815-1892), the Maid of Ludomir, an only daughter—recited *Kaddish* in memory of her father, Monesh Werbermacher.

CONGREGATIONAL PRAYER

The *Kaddish* can only be recited if there is a *minyan*.[31] This conforms with the liturgical maxim in the Talmud:[32] "Words of holiness and sanctification need a religious quorum of ten males for their recitation." Whoever recites *Kaddish* must do so standing. In some communities it is general practice for the congregation also to stand; in Eastern Europe the congregation remained seated.

Worshipers must maintain strictest decorum during the *Kaddish*. According to Rabbi Chezekiah de Silva (d. 1698), author of *Pri Chadash*, it is even forbidden to meditate upon the words of the Torah during this prayer, for attention must be paid to every single word of the *Kaddish* and its responses. The *Zohar* states that "whosoever talks in the synagogue while the congregation is occupied in the praise of God, shows that he has no portion in the God of Israel and his sin is very grievous." It is also strictly forbidden to pass in front of a man reciting the *Kaddish*.

RECITATION

The custom today is for every mourner to recite *Kaddish*. Among the Sephardim, the *minhag* (custom) is for mourners to recite the *Kaddish* in unison.

The mourner's *Kaddish* is recited at certain points in the service: after the *Alenu* ("It is our duty")[33] at the end of the statutory services; after the Daily Psalm;[34] after the *Anim Zemirot* (Hymn of Glory);[35] and after Psalm 30 in the Morning Service.[36]

At the end of the *Kaddish*, as at the end of the *Amidah* (Prayer of the Eighteen Blessings), the worshiper takes three steps backward, as would a person withdrawing from the presence of a king.

During the Ten Days of Penitence, as a reminder that God reigns supreme above all creatures, the word *Le'eyla* ("though He be high above") is added, and the two words *min kol* are contracted into one word, *mikol*. The sentence from *Yehay Shemay Rabba* to *Olmaya* (last word of the line) contains twenty-eight letters, equaling the numerical value of the word *koah* (power), and mystics point out that both by their meaning and by the number of letters, that sentence represents our acknowledgment of the power of God, and by reciting this declaration Israel clothes itself with strength.

LAWS OF PRECEDENCE

Leading rabbinical authorities in the past such as Rabbi Shabbethai ben Meir Ha-Kohen (*Shach*) and Rabbi David ben Samuel Halevi (*Taz*)[37] set down a rigid order of precedence. In saying *Kaddish*, a resident takes precedence over a stranger. If several *yahrzeit* mourners are present, the *kaddishim* are divided among them to the exclusion of others. A mourner who is sitting *shivah* takes precedence over a stranger, as well as over one observing a *yahrzeit*. If there were more *yahrzeit* mourners than there were *kaddishim* in the service, lots were drawn. As these rules frequently lead to contention, modern Ashkenazi practice is that all mourners recite the *Kaddish*.

RABBINICAL KADDISH

Kaddish De-Rabbanan[38] (scholar's *Kaddish*) was so named because it was recited upon the completion of a division of the *Mishnah* or of a tractate of the Talmud or after a discourse; the reciter should, if possible, take part in the study course.

It is also recited after the *Beraita*[39] (of Rabbi Ishmael) in the Morning Service,[40] after the quotation at the conclusion of *Bameh Madlikin* on Friday night,[41] from *Berachot* ("Rabbi Eleazar said in the name of Rabbi Chaninah") and at the conclusion of the Sabbath *Musaf* service if the talmudic reading *Pitum Ha-Ketoret* is recited.[42]

BURIAL KADDISH

Apart from the *Chatzi Kaddish* (half *Kaddish*), which marks the end of certain sections of the service, as well as the *Kaddish Shalem* (full *Kaddish*), the *Kaddish Yatom* (mourner's *Kaddish*), and the *Kaddish De-Rabbanan*[43] (rabbinical *Kaddish*), there is also the *Kaddish leithudata* (*Kaddish* of renewal),[44] which is recited by sons at the interment of parents. It is omitted on those days when *Tachanun*[45] is not said. The theme of the burial *Kaddish* is, "God will revive the dead and raise them up into life eternal. He will rebuild the City of Jerusalem and establish His Temple in the midst thereof."

This prayer was also originally used as a doxology by the scholars after a homiletical discourse in rabbinical colleges. Today, however, the burial *Kaddish* is recited by all mourners at funerals. It may be truly said that the *Kaddish* has become a link between the generations, between man and God, and between man and man.

It possesses wonderful power. Truly, if there is any bond, strong and indissoluble enough to chain heaven to earth, it is this prayer. It keeps the living together, and forms a bridge to the mysterious realms of the dead. . . . Can a people disappear and be annihilated, so long as a child remembers its parents? . . . To know that when you die, the earth falling on your head will not cover you entirely; to know that there remain behind those who, wherever they may be on the wide earth, whether they may be poor or rich, will send this prayer after you; to know that you leave them no house, no estate, no field by which they must remember you and that yet they will cherish your memory as their dearest inheritance—what more satisfying knowledge can you ever hope for? And such is the knowledge bequeathed to us all by the *Kaddish*.[46]

Chapter 8

The Period of Mourning

Judaism disagrees with the philosophy of life of the eminent humanist, Dr. Albert Schweitzer, who said, "Unrest, disappointment, and pain are our lot. . . . All life is suffering." The Jew believes that his religion gives him guidance at all times; it upholds him in times of gladness and of sorrow, in moments of exaltation and of deep despair. For every aspect of life, Judaism has its counsel. In bereavement, when man's mind and emotions are so powerfully challenged, Judaism teaches how to give expression to one's sense of loss, how to regain one's composure, one's zest, indeed, inspiration for one's own life and that of future generations.

The rabbis discourage excessive mourning; "Weep ye not for the dead," says Jeremiah, "neither bemoan him" (Jeremiah 22:10). This has been interpreted by the sages as "weep not in excess, nor bemoan too much." This concept should, according to the Talmud, be carried out in the following way: "Three days are set aside for weeping and seven days for lamentation and thirty days to refrain from cutting the hair and donning pressed clothes; thereafter, the Holy One, Blessed be He, says: 'Ye are not more compassionate toward him (the departed) than I.' "[1]

During the thirty days (the *sheloshim*), the change from the sadness of bereavement to normal life gradually takes place. There are several references in the Torah to this thirty-day period of mourning. For instance, "The whole House of Israel wept for Aaron for thirty days" (Numbers 20:29), and for Moses, too, the children of Israel wept "for thirty days, so that the days of weeping for Moses were ended" (Deuteronomy 34:8). A female captive was made a concubine only after an interval of a month. "She shall bewail her father and mother a full month" (Deuteronomy 21:13). Similarly in *mishnaic* times, Rabbi Judah Hanasi, before he died, gave instructions that the "assembly for study should be reconstituted after the lapse of thirty days from the day of his death."[2]

The relatives for whom the period of *sheloshim* is observed are: father, mother, husband, wife, brother, sister, son, and daughter, and brother and sister of the same father or mother.[3]

The period of the *sheloshim* starts on the day of the funeral and ends on the morning of the thirtieth day. If this should fall on a Sabbath, a mourner may wear his Sabbath clothes and bathe in warm water before the Sabbath, but he must not cut his hair on the Friday before.[4]

TIMELY OR DISTANT NEWS

If a mourner learns of the death of a relative within thirty days, the news is regarded as "timely" (*shemuah kerovah*).[5]

The mourner must then sit *shivah*, rend his clothes, and count the period of *sheloshim* from the day of the report. If, however, he receives news of a death more than thirty days after it has taken place, the news is regarded as "delayed" or "distant" (*shemuah rechokah*), and mourning need only be observed for one hour.

In the latter event he need only remove his shoes and sit on a low stool. He is not required to tear his clothes unless the death is that of a parent.[6] The remainder of the twelve months of mourning must be observed by commencing counting from the day of death.

One who has received "timely" news on the Sabbath should count the Sabbath as one day, and at the termination of the Sabbath he should rend his garments and observe six days of mourning thereafter.[7]

During the *sheloshim*, a mourner must not take part in any festivity or attend any place of entertainment whether on the Sabbath, Festival, or a weekday. If he mourns a parent, this period of abstinence should continue for the full twelve months.[8] He should not listen to instrumental music or play any musical instruments himself during the whole period of mourning.

Some authorities differentiate between a "feast," which is of a purely secular or social nature, and a *seudat mitzvah*, a meal that is primarily of a religious significance.[9] Generally, "a mourner is forbidden to join in the circumcision feast, or in the feast to celebrate the redemption of the firstborn, or on the occasion of the conclusion of a tractate of the *Mishnah* or Talmud, and more especially a wedding feast, during the thirty days of his mourning for one's relatives and during the year for one's parents."[10]

It is permissible for the mourner after the seven days of mourning to enter the synagogue where they recite the betrothal and wedding benedictions and where there is no joyous entertainment.[11] Some authorities prohibit this until after the *sheloshim* and, "This seems to me," writes Rabbi Moses Isserles, "to be the correct view."[12]

A mourner for a parent may act as *Unterfuhrer*[13] provided it is after the period of *sheloshim*. A mourner for other near-of-kin is permitted to be an *Unterfuhrer* even during the *sheloshim*.[14] If a mourner for a parent gives in marriage an orphan, he may attend the wedding ceremony and participate in the festivities.[15] Some authorities permit a mourner to eat at a wedding banquet or a circumcision "with those who wait upon the guests, provided it is not in a place of joyous entertainment."[16]

A rabbi or a reader in mourning for a parent is permitted

by some authorities to attend a wedding celebration even within the *sheloshim*, if it is a question of losing a livelihood.[17] For example, a musician is permitted to play music during the twelve months of mourning for a parent or within the *sheloshim* for other relatives.[18] Parents who are in mourning may participate in the wedding celebration of their son or daughter.

NO SHELOSHIM

If burial takes place before a Festival, and the mourner observes the mourning rites even for one hour prior to the Festival, the *Yom Tov* annuls the entire *shivah* period.[19] If the *shivah* is completed prior to the Festival, then the incoming Festival cancels the *sheloshim* period in its entirety.[20] The *sheloshim* are not suspended when mourning for one's father or mother. The mourner is not allowed to "cut his hair until he is reproved by his friends."

If the mourner observes the *shivah* prior to the commencement of *Rosh Hashanah*, the *sheloshim* come to an end with the advent of *Yom Kippur*. Similarly, if the *shivah* terminates during the Ten Days of Penitence, the *sheloshim* come to an end with the commencement of *Yom Kippur*.[21]

If the mourner observes *shivah* even for a short time prior to the Festival of Passover, it is regarded as if he had observed seven days of *shivah*, and with the "eight days" of Passover added we have fifteen days. The *sheloshim* are thus terminated fifteen days after Passover.[22] Similarly, if he has observed one hour of *shivah* prior to the Festival of Pentecost, only fifteen days are observed after the Festival.

If he has observed *shivah* prior to the Festival of Tabernacles, he need only observe eight days after the Festival to complete the period of *sheloshim*.[23] If, however, the funeral takes place on *Chol Ha-Moed*, the *shivah* is observed at the termination of the Festival and the *sheloshim* follows suit.[24] The last day of the Festival counts as one of the days of the *shivah* and *sheloshim*.[25]

HAIRCUT

The mourner for relatives other than parents should not cut his hair or beard during the *sheloshim*. However, if he is mourning for his father or his mother, he should let his hair grow until his friends remark on its untidiness. "The common practice," says Rabbi Moses Isserles, "is to wait three months. But in some localities it is the adopted practice not to cut one's hair when in mourning for a father or mother during the entire twelve months of mourning, unless the need is great, e.g., if his hair is too heavy upon him or he goes among gentiles and appears repulsive to them with his hair, in which case he is permitted to cut his hair."[26]

Rabbi Moses Schreiber (1763–1839), the *Chatam Sofer*, regarded as the foremost rabbinical authority of his time, reports that his teachers once permitted an individual, even during the seven days of mourning for his father, to cut his hair, wash, and put on pressed garments in order to see a royal personage with whom he had an appointment, the postponement of which would have entailed great loss to the individual.[27]

Just as it is forbidden to cut hair during the entire thirty days of mourning, so also is it forbidden to cut one's nails with scissors.[28] Combing the hair is allowed even during the first seven days of mourning.[29]

MOURNING CLOTHES

It used to be the custom for mourners to wear black throughout the *sheloshim*, since black was regarded as the symbol of death. The *aggadah* quotes Moses as saying: "Joshua, put on black clothes after my death." Simeon the Just (end of the fourth century B.C.E.) predicted his approaching death. When he was asked how he knew this, he replied: "On every Day of Atonement an old man, dressed in white . . . would join me entering the Holy of Holies. . . . But today I was joined by an old man dressed in black."[30]

Jews would normally wear dark clothes, as Israel Abrahams writes,[31] "The Jews of all countries wore black; in Spain, Germany, and Italy the phenomenon was equally marked. Black being the color of grief the Jews – 'mourners of Zion' as they were called – were no doubt strengthened in their predilection for black on the score of modesty, by its applicability to their persecuted state."

In mourning for Jerusalem, the Talmud records[32] that the Jews wore black shoes. In the Middle Ages there was a sect of Jews who always deliberately wore black as a sign of perpetual mourning.[33]

In London, until the second half of the nineteenth century, all the principal mourners attending a funeral were given black "mourners' cloaks" that were worn throughout the week of the *shivah*.[34] In Amsterdam it was the custom among the Sephardim for mourners who attended the synagogue on Sabbath afternoon to be dressed in black.

Nowadays, however, Orthodox Jews do not wear black for mourning, and the wearing of a black arm band is regarded as *chukkat ha-goy*.

A woman in mourning who has given birth to a child and who wishes to go to the synagogue on a Sabbath may wear her best garments and jewelry.

MOURNING AND MARRIAGE LAWS

"The mourner is forbidden to take a wife during the entire thirty days of mourning, even without making a wedding feast, but after the *sheloshim* he is permitted, even if he is mourning for his father or mother, to marry and to make a wedding feast."[35] He is permitted to betroth a wife prior to the termination of the *sheloshim*. Many rabbinic authorities, however, assert that "betrothal is forbidden during the entire thirty days of mourning," and this is the view that Rabbi Moses Isserles follows.[36]

A man whose wife has died should wait until at least three Festivals have elapsed before he remarries.[37] In this connection *Rosh Hashanah, Yom Kippur,* and *Shemini Atzeret* (The Feast of the Eighth Day) are not regarded as Festivals.[38] In exceptional cases, such as that of a widower with very young children and with no one to look after them, the marriage may be allowed earlier.

The period of waiting serves a double purpose: A man ought not to forget his first wife too quickly; and he will better appreciate his new wife after a period of loneliness.

A widow is forbidden to remarry until ninety days have elapsed after the death of her husband.

If one of the immediate relatives of the bride or bridegroom dies, the wedding should be deferred until after the *shivah.*[39]

THE YEAR OF MOURNING

Various reasons are given for the twelve-month period of mourning. According to the *Zohar,*[40] the soul clings to the body for twelve months. The Talmud, on the other hand, says: "For twelve months the body is in existence and the soul ascends and descends; after twelve months the body ceases to exist and the soul ascends but descends no more."[41] It was furthermore believed that purification in afterlife takes place in the first twelve months and that after a year the memory wanes.

VISITING THE CEMETERY

There is no uniform custom with regard to visiting the grave during the first year of mourning. Some people purposely refrain from visiting it during this year. Others visit the cemetery frequently, and some do so on the last day of the *shivah.* In Spain it was customary to visit the grave during the first week of mourning.[42]

The popular idea that the grave must not be visited during the first twelve months after death has little support in Jewish teachings. Indeed, it was believed that the dead take an interest in the living and intercede for them,[43] and visits for the purpose of beseeching such intercessions were not discouraged. Jacob buried Rachel near Efrat at Bethlehem (Genesis 35:19) so that she might pray for her children as they passed by her grave on their way to the Babylonian exile. "Rachel weeping for her children, she refuseth to be comforted for her children because they are not" (Jeremiah 31:15). And Caleb, one of the twelve spies[44] who went to explore the land of Canaan, is reported to have gone to the graves of the Patriarchs and prayed: "My fathers, pray on my behalf that I may be delivered from the plans of the spies."[45]

It has always been regarded as a *mitzvah* to visit the graves of saintly people and beseech their aid—a common practice among the *tannaim* and *amoraim*. The Talmud records that "it is the custom of the people to take earth from the grave of the Babylonian *amora* Rav[46] and apply it as a remedy on the first day of an attack of fever."[47] During the fast days they would go to the cemetery "in order that the departed ones should pray for mercy on our behalf."[48]

However, visiting the grave too often was discouraged, as it might lead to attempts to communicate with the dead by spiritualistic means, and this was forbidden in the Torah. "There shall not be found among you . . . a charmer or one that consulteth a ghost or a familiar spirit or a necromancer" (Deuteronomy 18:10–12). Necromancy was classified with idolatry and magic, and "those that dig up the dead" and "those who predict by means of the bones of the dead" have no place in Judaism. Sleeping in cemeteries was considered one of the signs of insanity.[49] The Talmud enumerates five things that "cause the man who does them to forfeit his life and his blood is upon his own head." One of these is sleeping in a cemetery in order to obtain an "unclean spirit."[50]

It is traditional to visit the cemetery on the ninth of *Av*,[51] during the month of *Elul*,[52] during the Ten Days of Penitence and on the eve of New Year, and particularly on the eve of the Day of Atonement[53] and on a parent's *yahrzeit* or on the day before.[54] Special prayers (*techinot*) in books known as *Maane Loshon* (The Answer of the Tongue)[55] were recited. Rabbi Judah the Pious (d. 1217), however, prohibited visits to a grave twice in one day.[56]

It is a common practice among those who accept the mystical way of life to "invite" dead parents to take part at a *simchah* (a joyous occasion), for the mystics believe that even in the world of eternity the souls of the departed derive pleasure on hearing good news.

Those Orthodox Jewish authorities who do not approve of decorating graves with flowers believe that it constitutes *chukkat ha-goy*.

ADDITIONAL CUSTOMS

A mourner must not officiate as a reader on Sabbath, Festivals,[57] *Rosh Chodesh, Purim,* or on the first night of *Chanukah* during the entire year unless there be no other reader. However, if prior to his having become a mourner he had been accustomed to act as reader on the Sabbaths and Festivals, he may also act as such during the mourning period.[58] A professional reader may conduct services in the synagogue during the period of mourning.

A mourner should not light the *Chanukah* lights in the synagogue on the first night, as he is required to say the benediction *Shehecheyanu,* but he may recite the blessing in his own home.

A mourner, even in the first seven days of mourning, is obliged to send gifts to the needy on *Purim*. Gifts, however, are not sent to a mourner for the entire twelve months of mourning.

A minor need not observe any of the laws of mourning.

The clothing of a deceased person who did not die of a contagious disease should not be destroyed. It should be given to the poor.

THE KOHEN AND MOURNING RITES

A *Kohen* is forbidden to enter a house where there is a corpse. He is even forbidden to enter a house where a person is dying, as death may occur at any moment and thus cause his defilement. Nor may he go within four cubits[59] of a grave.[60] However, these prohibitions do not apply when he has lost a father, mother, son, daughter, wife, brother, or unmarried sister on his father's side.[61] The reason for these prohibitions is that a high standard of purity was demanded of the priests, "the emissaries not of the people but of God."

Chapter 9

The Yahrzeit

Like the *Kaddish*, the *yahrzeit* (anniversary of a death) is a powerful magnet, drawing a man back to the synagogue and back to his people with regular and incessant rhythm. Even those whose synagogue affiliations are slender make new contact on this memory-hallowed day. Even in small communities, where there is no regular *minyan* and where the house of prayer is closed the entire week, even there the doors of the synagogue are opened and arrangements are made for a service to take place when a Jew has a *yahrzeit* to observe. For the observance of the *yahrzeit* is one of the honors that a man can pay his departed parents, and it is a duty that his heart, mind, and conscience bid him pay with scrupulous care. As the strains of the *yahrzeit Kaddish* reverberate through the soul, they reawaken with indescribable poignancy the faded memories of past years.

"And it was a custom in Israel, that the daughters of Israel went yearly to lament the daughter of Jephthah, the Gileadite, four days in a year" (Judges 11:40). This is the first scriptural reference to *yahrzeit*, which was widely observed in talmudic times,[1] when many people fasted on the anniversary of a parent's death. The traditional date of the death of Moses is observed on the seventh of *Adar* (the twelfth month). Natronai Gaon, head of the academy of Sura

90

(second half of the ninth century), states that at the end of the year of mourning they were accustomed to say *Hashkavah* (memorial prayer).

Although the anniversary of a death is known to have been observed in biblical times, the term by which the institution is now widely known is medieval and was first used by Rabbi Moses Minz, a fifteenth-century scholar.[2] The Ashkenazim call it *yahrzeit*, whereas among the Sephardim it is called *nachalah meldado* or *Annos*.

Yahrzeit is observed on the Jewish date on which the parent died. If death took place after dark, it must be dated from the next day, as the day is reckoned among Jews from sunset to sunset.[3] According to some rabbinic authorities, if three or more days elapse between death and burial, the first *yahrzeit* is observed on the date of burial. Subsequently, *yahrzeit* is observed on the anniversary of the day of death. If death took place during *Adar* 1 or *Adar* 2, i.e., in a leap year, *yahrzeit* is observed in a leap year in the same *Adar* in which the death took place. If death occurred in the month of *Adar* in an ordinary year, the *yahrzeit* is observed on the first *Adar* of a leap year, but *Kaddish* may be recited in *Adar Sheni*.

A difficulty arises in connection with a death occurring on the last day of the months of *Cheshvan* (second month) or *Kislev* (ninth month) in the years when they have thirty days. In some years these months contain only twenty-nine days, and in such circumstances, the *yahrzeit* for a person who died on the thirtieth of *Cheshvan* or *Kislev* is observed on the first of *Kislev* or first of *Tevet* (tenth month) as the case may be.[4]

In cases of doubt as to the exact day of death—for example, in the case of relatives of the six million Jews murdered by the Nazis—the bereaved may select an appropriate day of the Jewish calendar and observe it as the *yahrzeit* in all successive years.

If one knows only the month of death of a parent, one should observe the *yahrzeit* on the last day of the month.

The mourner's *Kaddish* should be recited at every service during the day, a custom that is mentioned by Rabbi Isaac b. Moses of Vienna (c. 1250) in his ritual code *Or*

Zarua: "For the recital of *Kaddish,*" say the Kabbalists, "elevates the soul every year to a higher sphere in Paradise."[5]

Normally the mourner conducts the service if he is able to and if circumstances permit. On the Sabbath before the *yahrzeit* he should be called up to the Reading of the Law and if possible should recite *Haftarah* (conclusion to the reading of the Torah).[6] This practice is derived from an ancient synagogue ritual when the words "O, faithful God who sayest and doest, who speaketh and fulfillest all whose words are truth and righteousness"[7] were chanted by the one who read the *Haftarah,* and the congregation responded, "Faithful art Thou, O Lord our God."

A memorial prayer is offered on the Sabbath before the *yahrzeit* in memory of the deceased, and the mourner in some congregations officiates at the evening service at the end of the Sabbath.

It is a well-established custom to visit the grave on the *yahrzeit.* "I have seen in the *responsa* [written replies to questions on all aspects of Jewish law] of the *geonim,*" writes Rashi,[8] "that on the anniversary of the death people assemble around the grave and hold a discourse and offer a prayer."

MEMORIAL LIGHT

It was a well-established practice to have a candle or lamp burning in the home throughout the twenty-four hours of the anniversary of the death of a departed parent or relative,[9] although no authority for this is found in the Talmud or *Midrash.*

Many reasons for this custom have been suggested. Light, for instance, symbolizes the soul and suggests immortality. "The soul of man," says the Book of Proverbs, "is the lamp of the Lord" (Proverbs 20:27). Also, the mystics have pointed out that the numerical value of the letters of the Hebrew phrase *ner daluk* (a kindled light) and the Hebrew word *Ha-Shechinah* (the Divine Presence) add up to 390.[11]

Others give a different reason. In the Torah portion *Tetzaveh* (Exodus 27:20–30:10), which is read during the week of the seventh of *Adar* (the traditional date for commemorating Moses's death), the opening verse states that the children of Israel were commanded "to bring pure olive oil beaten for the light to cause a lamp to burn continually" (Exodus 27:20).

Oil, candles, or even an electric light may be used for this purpose.

FASTING

Fasting was closely associated with mourning in the Bible[12] and also in the Apocrypha, where we read that Judith fasted every day except Friday and Saturday while she was mourning. The Talmud considers the validity of a vow by a man who says: "I am not to eat meat or drink wine on the day that my father or teacher died."[13] From this we gather that it was the custom to fast on the anniversary of the death of a parent. But this was not done if it was a day on which *Tachanun* is not said. The *Kol Bo*[14] cites the authority of Rabbi Meir b. Baruch of Rothenburg (a thirteenth-century scholar) for the antiquity of this custom. "It is a religious duty to fast on the day that one's father or mother died."

Rabbi Israel Baal Shem Tov (1700–1760) maintains that on the day of the *yahrzeit* God judges the soul that is in the upper world and so, when a son fasts, he brings honor to his departed parent. Fasting is an expression of repentance and atonement, a mark of reverence for the departed and an act of humiliation before God.

If the *yahrzeit* falls on the day before or after a public fast, and the mourner is unable to fast on two consecutive days, he should observe the public fast and fast only until noon on the day of the *yahrzeit*.

If the *sandek* or the *mohel* should happen to have *yahrzeit* for a parent on the day of a *brit milah*, he may not fast. Nor does the father of a firstborn or the *Kohen* from whom the latter is redeemed fast if he observes *yahrzeit* on the day of the redemption of the firstborn.[15] A bride or bridegroom does not fast if *yahrzeit* occurs during the seven days of marriage festivities.[16] If a man has fasted once on a *yahrzeit*, he should fast every year.[17]

STUDY AND CHARITY

On *yahrzeit* a man ought to set aside a certain time for study and should also distribute money to worthy causes. "Forgive, O Lord, Thy people Israel, whom Thou hast redeemed, and suffer not innocent blood to remain in the midst of Thy people Israel" (Deuteronomy 21:8), pleaded the Elders of Israel. This is interpreted to mean that the dead need atonement, and the living can atone for them by means of charity. "Such is the power of charity that it can deliver a sinner from the punishment of *Gehinnom*."[18]

It is customary to study parts of the *Mishnah*, for the Hebrew word for soul (*neshamah*) has the same letters as *Mishnah*. The passages chosen are the twenty-fourth chapter of *Kelim*[19] and the seventh chapter of *Mikvaot* (immersion pools)[20] from *Tohorot*,[21] the sixth and last order (*seder*) of the *Mishnah*. Rabbi Yitzchak Isaac of Komarna prefers *Mikvaot* because the initial letters of its final four *mishnayot* spell the Hebrew word *neshamah*.

If one has been unable to recite *Kaddish* on the *yahrzeit* day, then he may say *Kaddish* at the *Maariv* (evening) service following the day of the *yahrzeit*.

Amusements should be avoided on the day of the *yahrzeit*. One may not, on the evening when the *yahrzeit* is observed, eat at a marriage feast that has musical entertainment. One may, however, eat at a feast held in connection with a circumcision or a redemption of a firstborn or at the conclusion of a talmudic tractate.[22]

KABBALISTIC CUSTOMS

Among the Kabbalists, the day of the *yahrzeit* is regarded as a "marriage," a blissful reunion of the soul with the *Shechinah* (Divine Presence). One outstanding celebration is the *yahrzeit* of the *tanna* and mystic Rabbi Simon bar Yochai (c. 130–160). On *Lag B'Omer*,[23] thousands of Israelis converge on the white tomb at Meron (Upper Galilee) when at midnight the *hadlakah* (bonfire) is lit, as a sign for the celebrations to begin. This pilgrimage to Meron is an old tradition that Rabbi Isaac ben Solomon Luria (1534–1572) observed. His disciple, Rabbi Chayyim Vital (1543–1620), wrote: "In these last eight years my teacher, his wife and family have gone there and they stay for three days."[24] Ashkenazim and Sephardim, Chasidim and *Mitnaggdim*, *Sabras* (Israeli-born Jews), and Yemenites all go to Meron, where they recite Psalms and quote passages from the *Zohar*.

This holy place attracts the mystic, the pious, the poor, the sick, and the anxious and, on arrival, these spectators become participants and all share in a moving experience. The pilgrims dance and pray at the same time, inspired with *hitlahavut*—religious ecstasy (not riotous revelry), a spirit of awe (not lighthearted gaiety). As the flames mount higher, the words of the song can be heard: *"Bar Yochai, bar Yochai,* happy one, anointed with oil of joy, blessed by the mouth of God, blessed from the day of Creation."

Although Rabbi Israel Baal Shem Tov instructed his followers to fast on a *yahrzeit*, most Chasidim follow the tradition of Rabbi Dov Baer, the Maggid of Messeritz (d. 1772), who advised his Chasidim "not to fast but to make a *seudah* and distribute money to charity." It is customary among the Chasidim, inspired by their enthusiasm and ecstasy, to sing and even to dance at such a *seudah* and say "The soul should have an *aliyah"* ("May the soul of the deceased be raised to a still higher level of purity").

MEMORIAL SERVICES

It is customary to recite *Yizkor* ("May God remember the soul of my revered . . .")[25] four times during the year: on the Day of Atonement, on the eighth day of Tabernacles (*Shemini*

Atzeret), on the last day of Passover, and on the second day of Pentecost. *Yizkor* is generally not recited during the first twelve months after the death of parents.

In some congregations, those whose parents are alive leave the synagogue during *Yizkor*. The object of this may be either to leave the mourners undisturbed during this moving prayer, or to spare those who have not been bereaved any unnecessary grief. All too often this results in an untidy and indecorous general exit that lowers the dignity of the service.

It is difficult to establish with any degree of certainty when *Yizkor* became customary in the synagogue.

In the Second Book of Maccabees we read that Judas collected 2,000 drachmas of silver and sent them to Jerusalem as a sin-offering for those who had died

> in that he was mindful of the resurrection. For if he had not hoped that they that were slain should have risen again, it had been superfluous and vain to pray for the dead. And also in that he perceived that there was great favor laid up for those that died godly, it was an holy and good thought. Whereupon he made a reconciliation for the dead, that they might be delivered from sin. [II Maccabees 12:43–45]

Rabbi Joseph Caro,[26] Rabbi Moses Isserles, and Rabbi Simchah ben Samuel of Vitry (d. 1105) in his liturgical work *Machzor Vitry*, all refer to the practice of pledging alms on *Yom Kippur*. "On *Yom Kippur* the names of the dead should be mentioned, for they too may obtain atonement." Some explained the plural term *Kippurim* as denoting atonement for the living and the dead.[27] Furthermore, mention of the departed makes man humble and subdues his evil impulses.

Later, *Yizkor* was also recited on the last day of Passover, the second day of Pentecost, and on the eighth day of Tabernacles, appropriate days on which to give charity on behalf of the living and in memory of the departed. For on these three Festivals, the Reading of the Law (Deuteronomy 14:22–16:17) includes the verse: "Every man shall give as he is able, according to the blessing of the Lord thy God which He hath given thee."

The recital of the names of the dead in the synagogue probably began at the time of the Crusades, which brought death and desolation to the flourishing and ancient Jewish communities on the Rhine and the Moselle. The names of the martyrs who died for the "Sanctification of God's Name" were inscribed in special books known as *Memorbuecher* (Memorial Books) or *Sefer Zikaron* (Book of Remembrance), or *Sefer Zikronot Neshamot* (Memorial Book of the Souls).[28] One of the earliest of these books was begun at Nuremberg in 1296 and served as a model for other communities. The martyrs' names were read during the *omer* period, on the Sabbath before Pentecost, and on the Sabbath preceding the ninth of *Av*.

AV HA-RACHAMIM—FATHER OF MERCIES

Av Ha-Rachamim —requiem for the martyrs—was probably composed in the Rhineland after the First Crusade in 1096, when large numbers of Jewish communities in Germany were annihilated. This prayer by an anonymous author was originally said twice a year (on the Sabbath before Pentecost and before the ninth of *Av*), but later it became the custom in some communities to recite it every Sabbath except on a Sabbath that coincides with the New Moon, *Chanukah*, and on the intermediate days of a Festival. It is also omitted in *Nisan*, on the fifteenth of *Av*, the fifteenth of *Shevat*, and *Shushan Purim*. (In many communities, *Av Ha-Rachamim* is recited every Sabbath during the *sefirah* on the Sabbaths between Passover and Pentecost— the anniversary of the massacres.) In the words of Leopold Zunz (1794–1886),[30] "If there exists a ladder in suffering, Israel has reached the highest rung. If the duration of sorrows and the patience with which they are borne ennoble, the Jews may challenge the aristocracy of every land. If a literature is called rich which possesses a few

classical tragedies, what place then is due to a Tragedy
lasting 1,500 years written and acted by the heroes themselves."

EL MALAY RACHAMIM

The prayer, "O God who art full of compassion, who
dwellest on high,"[31] is not found in the Codes or in the
works of Rabbi Jacob b. Asher (1269–1343), author of the
Arbaah Turim. Probably seventeenth-century in origin, it is
mentioned by Rabbi Naphtali Hertz in his work *Bet Hillel* and
by Rabbi Joseph ben Meir Teomim and is recited on Sabbaths
and Festivals.

There is no basis for the idea that one should not offer
prayers for the dead on the Sabbath. The *Midrash* states:
"Therefore, it is a custom to mention the dead on Sabbath in
order that they should not return to *Gehenna.*"[32] Rabbi Moses
Isserles quotes Zedekiah b. Abraham Anav (thirteenth century), author of *Shibbolay Haleket* as follows: "After the
reading of the Torah, it is customary to recite Memorial
Prayers."[33] This is not regarded as lamentation, which is
forbidden on a Sabbath. In his ethical will, Rabbi Nathaniel,
son of Benjamin Trabotti (1576–1658), writes: "Moreover, I
entreat you to offer up a memorial for my soul every Sabbath
day and I from my grave will always be mindful of you,
praying to God on your behalf."[34]

The Sephardim recite *Hashkavah* (laying to rest) on
Sabbaths, Festivals, and on Mondays and Thursdays. The
prayer is as follows:

A good name is more fragrant than rich perfume; and
the day of death better than the day of one's birth. The
sum of the matter, after all hath been heard, is to fear
God and keep His commandments, for this is the whole
of man. Let the pious be joyful in glory; let them sing
aloud upon their couches. May the repose which is
prepared in the celestial abode, under the wings of the

Divine Presence in the high places of the holy and pure—that shine and are resplendent as the brightness of the firmament—with a renewal of strength, a forgiveness of trespasses, a removal of transgressions, an approach of salvation, compassion, and favor from Him that sitteth enthroned on high, and also a goodly portion in the life to come, be the lot, dwelling, and the resting place of the soul of our deceased brother. . . .[35]

The *El Malay Rachamim*[36] (O Lord who art full of compassion) may also be said several times at the cemetery, provided that each time it is accompanied by almsgiving, for "Charity delivereth from death." "Unless we are prepared to maintain," wrote the Rev. Simeon Singer (1846–1906) "that at his death the fate of man is fixed irretrievably and forever; that, therefore, the sinner who rejected much of God's love during a brief lifetime, has lost all of it eternally—prayer for the peace and salvation of the departed soul commends itself as one of the highest religious obligations."[37]

The Memorial Service is primarily dedicated to those of our own family who have been called to life eternal; but it also recalls those countless Jews who were murderously cut down because they were Jews. Aspects of the *Yizkor* service can be traced to the days of the torturing martyrdom suffered by our forefathers in the time of the Crusades. In our own generation these memorial prayers have all too tragically become prayers through which anyone who bears the name Jew can pour out his soul in lamentation for the millions of his fellow Jews who, after foulest torture, met their end in death chambers and organized massacre. Each of us standing in the synagogue can and should passionately exclaim: "In their memory I offer charity and would do good."[38]

YOM HA-SHOAH

Our six million brethren who met a martyr's death at the hands of Jewry's most notorious oppressors have no known graves and met their death in the crematoria of Auschwitz, Treblinka, Sobibor, Belsen, and all the other death camps established by the Nazis in order to exterminate European Jewry. The dates of their death cannot be accurately calculated. No *shivah* can be observed. Only their memory and their sacrifice remain to haunt those who survived the horror, and their martyrdom serves as a warning to future generations.

One day in the year has, however, been set aside for special remembrance. In Israel it has been declared that each year *Yom Ha-Shoah* (Holocaust Remembrance Day) shall be observed on the twenty-seventh of *Nisan* (first month). In spite of the fact that *Nisan* is normally deemed a festive month commemorating, as it does, the Passover and the birth of our nationhood, on this one day a cloud of gloom hovers over our celebrations as an apt reminder of the most tragic event in our history.

Our brethren in Israel mark this day with due solemnity. It is also world Jewry's *yahrzeit* and therefore deserves to be commemorated with no less regard than that paid to a personal *yahrzeit* for a departed relative.

Just as it is an accepted practice to burn a memorial light in the home for a personal *yahrzeit*, so an anniversary memorial light should burn in every Jewish home throughout the Jewish world on *Yom Ha-Shoah*. By this simple ceremony world Jewry unites in affirming that the memory of our millions of martyrs are not, and shall not be, forgotten. It would also serve as an inducement to our children and grandchildren to enquire its meaning and for the older generation to inform them of the significance of this tragic chapter in Jewish history.

Chapter 10

Matzevah: The Tombstone

It is customary to erect a *matzevah* (tombstone) on the grave of the departed. In modern times, the ceremony of consecrating the tombstone is the climax of the year of mourning and has great significance for the mourners. A special consecration service is held at which suitable Psalms are recited and a memorial address is often given. The inscription is read, and *Kaddish* is recited.

The Bible relates that Jacob "set up a pillar upon her grave; the same is the pillar of Rachel's grave unto this day" (Genesis 35:20). Later it is stated that Absalom, too, built a monument in the valley of Kidron "to keep his name in remembrance" (II Samuel 18:18). In the Book of Ezekiel we read, "And those that thus travel will pass through the land and when anyone sees a human bone he will set up a sign by it" (Ezekiel 39:15). Many such memorials have survived, notably the tomb of King David in Jerusalem, the tomb of Rachel at Bethlehem, the tombs of the Patriarchs in Hebron, as well as the resting places of many famous rabbis in Israel.

From the biblical period and until erecting tombstones became a common practice, it was the custom simply to pile up stones, or place a distinctive sign on the site of a grave, or set up pillars as memorials.[1] This served the twofold purpose of protecting the body from wild beasts and of indicating to

101

passersby and especially *Kohanim* that a grave was there. The *Mishnah* reports that on the fifteenth of *Adar* the graves were painted white to warn people of the existence of a grave so that they might avoid becoming unclean from contact with it.[2] Rabbi Nathan lays down that "the surplus of any money collected to pay for the burial of the dead should be used to build a monument over the grave."[3]

Yet it was not until the Greek period that we begin to find evidence of the erection of lavish monuments. Simon Maccabeus (d. 135 B.C.E.), son of Mattathias the Hasmonean and brother of Judah, put up a most elaborate mausoleum for his father and his brothers at Modin.

Simon built a monument upon the sepulchre of his father and his brethren, and raised it aloft to the sight with polished stone behind and before. And he set up seven pyramids, one over against another, for his father, and his mother, and his four brethren. And for these he made cunning devices setting about them great pillars, and upon the pillars he fashioned all manner of arms for a perpetual memory, and beside the arms carved ships, that they should be seen of all that sail on the sea. [I Maccabees 13:27-29]

Josephus, too, mentions the monuments on the graves of John Hyrcanus, Alexander Janneus, and Queen Helena of Adiabene.[4]

SECOND BURIAL

In talmudic times often when the burial chamber became crowded, the relatives removed the decomposed body and placed the bones in a stone coffin known as an ossuary. The Talmud and Codes lay down minute regulations for the one "who collects bones for final burial."[5] The late Professor Eliezer Lipa Sukenik (1889-1953) excavated a number of these ossuaries in Israel. Many bore inscriptions in Hebrew, Aramaic, or Greek. Among the engravings were the *menorah* (candelabrum),[6] the *shofar*,[7] and the phrase "Peace upon Israel."

The Jews in Rome had their renowned catacombs.[8] Of the many inscriptions that have so far been deciphered, one is in Aramaic, another in both Greek and Aramaic, ten contain the Hebrew word *shalom*, and the rest are entirely in Greek or in Latin. There, too, we find familiar symbols: the *shofar*, the *etrog* (citron), the *menorah*, the trumpets, and the scroll, as well as the unfamiliar pictorial representation of human figures.

It is clear that, apart from isolated instances, the Jews in the first eight or nine centuries of the Common Era used the dominant language, Greek or Latin, for their funerary inscriptions. Hebrew gradually superseded them, and in the tenth century inscriptions written entirely in Hebrew are found in Spain, France, and many other countries.

ANCIENT TOMBSTONES

Rabbi Moses ben Nachman (1194–1270) relates that in Spain the graves were protected by heaps of stones, although these failed to prevent frequent desecrations. Menachem (Immanuel) Azariah da Fano (1548–1620) complains that "we are persecuted by men bent on stealing the stones and using them in the construction of their theaters (churches) or for sepulchers for their own dead."[9] Few of the ancient graves remained intact or preserved. Among the oldest tombstones extant is one in Prague, going back to 606, one in Breslau dated 1044, and one in Mainz, on the tomb of Rabbi Kalonymos ben Meshullam, dated 1096. Today, few ancient graves remain intact in Europe, mainly because during the Nazi Holocaust most of the historic Jewish cemeteries were wantonly destroyed. Only a few stones miraculously survived the barbaric vandalism.

TIME FOR CONSECRATION

It was formerly the practice for the tombstone to be erected as soon as possible after the *shivah*. In Israel a tombstone is usually erected after thirty days. More recently it has become the custom to allow a year to elapse and not to erect the stone until the first *yahrzeit* or during the week of the *yahrzeit*.

The stone should be simple to emphasize that in death "rich and poor meet together" (Proverbs 22:2). Many scholars left precise instructions for simple gravestones to be erected. Expensive tombstones have always been considered ostentatious. In Orthodox circles it is felt that they may undermine belief in the coming of the Messiah and the resurrection.

The Ashkenazim place their tombstones upright while the Sephardim lay them horizontally on the graves. The reason for this difference is obscure. According to one view the Sephardi custom originated in the desire to deviate from the non-Jewish practice of putting the stone in an upright position. A Levite's gravestone often bears a ewer as a symbol of his office in the Temple, that of serving the Priests. The tombs of *Kohanim* are marked by a carving of the hands raised in the Priestly Benediction. In some continental communities various emblems representing the professions of the deceased and family coats of arms were carved on the stone. It is customary in many communities, especially among the Chasidim, to construct an *ohel* (sepulcher), which often becomes a place of pilgrimage, over the grave of a *tzaddik* (a righteous man). The materials used for tombstones were generally stone, marble, or granite.

INSCRIPTIONS

There is no uniform practice with regard to the inscription on a stone. No inscriptions existed in biblical times. In the first century of the Common Era, the epitaph had the words *berabbi* or *beribbi* (Son of the teacher), *zichrono* (*zichronah*) *livrachah, zachur letov* (May he be remembered for good), *shalom*, and *noach nefesh* (Repose to his soul).

In medieval times long eulogies or laments were often added to the name of the deceased, as well as details of his character, his deeds, and his life. Elaborate inscriptions were usual for the tombs of scholars and rabbis. Many rabbis composed in advance the epitaphs that they desired to be put on their tombstones. The inscription on the stone of the talmudist and Kabbalist Rabbi Jonathan Eibeschutz (c. 1690–1764) reads as follows:

Every passerby should see what is engraved on these tablets. The man who stood as a model, who flourished like a lily, returned to dust, and his visage became marred more than any man's. Pray, take it to heart to repent sincerely and to offer for him many prayers to the Lord of spirits that He should gather to Him his soul and not cast it away. The merit of your deeds will be a protection, for all the souls of Israel are one. Learn to despise honors and to flee from greatness.[10]

Of great interest is the epitaph of Urania of Worms, belonging to the thirteenth century, which reads: "This headstone commemorates the eminent and excellent Lady Urania, the daughter of R. Abraham, who was the chief of the synagogue singers. His prayer for his people rose up unto glory. And as for her she with sweet tunefulness officiated before the female worshipers, to whom she sang the hymnal portions. In devout service her memory shall be preserved."[11]

There was no uniform practice with regard to the language used on a stone. The tombstones in the Sephardi cemetery in London in the eighteenth century were inscribed partly in Hebrew and partly in Spanish or Portuguese. An eighteenth-century writer throws some light on the Ashkenazi usage. "In the cemetery belonging to the Dutch Jews, the rows are not kept so regularly, and the tombs

represent more than in our burial grounds. The inscriptions
are entirely Hebrew. . . . The Dutch Jews are equally averse
from disturbing the bones of the dead, and, if the cemetery
is full, they cover it with a stratum of earth of sufficient depth
to make fresh graves, but the Portuguese always purchase
new ground."[12]

Nowadays communities lay down their own regulations regarding the nature of the inscriptions and in some
cases even of the tombstones. In Ashkenazi cemeteries it is
customary to place the letters

פה נטמן, פ"נ

"Here lies buried" for a male and

פה טמונה, פ"ט

"Here lies hidden" for a female. The Sephardim, however,
use the letters

מ"ק מַצֶבֶת קְבוּרַת

"The tombstone of the grave" for both sexes. Some ultra-
Orthodox communities permit only Hebrew inscriptions.[13] It
is forbidden to place a likeness of the deceased on the grave.

The tendency today is for short epitaphs. All that is
generally engraved on a tombstone is the name of the
deceased both in Hebrew and English, together with the
dates of birth and death, usually also in Hebrew, with the
Hebrew consonants of

ת"נ"צ"ב"ה

Tehe nishmato tzerurah bitzror hachayyim (May his soul be
bound up in the bond of eternal life).

TOMBSTONE UNVEILING

As with the inscription, the form of consecration service tends to vary. In Eastern Europe, even in modern times, there was no special form of service. Psalms were chanted, *Kaddish* was recited, and the duty of the mourner was discharged without formula or formality.

In western lands it has become customary to follow a special order of service in which Psalms 1, 16, and 23, and other appropriate passages are read.[14] The first Psalm, "Happy is the man that walketh not in the counsel of the wicked nor standeth in the way of sinners, nor sitteth in the seat of the scornful. But his delight is in the law of the Lord; and in His law doth he meditate day and night," is an appropriate theme for the service. Sometimes verses from Psalm 119, which consists of twenty-two stanzas (corresponding to the number of letters in the Hebrew alphabet), are recited. Appropriate stanzas are chosen to correspond with the Hebrew name of the deceased. It is also usual to pay a brief tribute to the departed and to recite an *Hazkarah*, and *Kaddish* is also recited. A eulogy should not be delivered on a day when *Tachanun* is not said. Tombstones should not be consecrated on *Chol Ha-Moed, Purim,* or on *Tisha B'Av* (the fast commemorating the destruction of the Temples).

Although in some circles attendance of women at funerals is discouraged or forbidden, women do attend tombstone consecrations.

One may take a photograph of the tombstone.[15] One may not in any way make use of or derive any profit from a disused tombstone.

Tombstone inscriptions are, of course, a valuable source of sociohistorical information. They are also rich in ethical values. Particularly inspiring, for example, is the writing on the tombstone at Middleburg, Holland, of the Dutch Rabbi Manasseh ben Israel (1604–1657): "The Rabbi did not die; his light is not yet extinguished; he liveth still in the heights of the All Revered. By his pen and the sweetness of his speech his remembrance will be eternal like the days of the earth."[16]

Chapter 11

The Undiscovered Country

A work that describes the rites and customs of mourning would be incomplete without some mention of the Jewish approach to the hereafter. At the same time, it should be pointed out that Judaism does not encourage too much probing into this subject. "Such knowledge," says the Psalmist, "is too wonderful for me; too high, I cannot attain unto it" (Psalm 139:6). Judaism discourages the attempts to seek through mystical practices release from the chains of the physical world. Indeed, it proved dangerous for the four sages who penetrated the *Pardes*[1] (the realm of mysteries), since only Rabbi Akiva (c. 50–135 C.E.) entered and returned safely. Simon ben Azzai (early second century) died, Simon ben Zoma lost his senses, and Elisha ben Avuyah, the colleague of Rabbi Akiva, became an apostate. It is thus not surprising that the rabbis approved of Ben Sira's stern warning, "Seek not things that are too hard for thee and search not out things that are above thy strength."[2]

Among believers in Judaism there have always been ascetics, such as the Nazirites,[3] the Essenes, the Dead Sea Community, and all the fasting mystics, who despised the physical delights of the world. They, however, are the exception. Self-mortification, celibacy, and asceticism have never been regarded by the sages as essential to entering the

Kingdom of Heaven. "In the hereafter," warned the sages, "a man will have to give account for the permissible pleasures from which he has abstained."[4]

Judaism has never retreated from life. Indeed, even the author of Ecclesiastes, the greatest of all pessimists, conceded: "I know that there is nothing better for them than to rejoice, and to get pleasure so long as they live. But also that every man should eat and drink, and enjoy pleasure, for all his labor is the gift of God" (Ecclesiastes 3:12–13).

On the other hand, the hedonist philosophy of "eat, drink, and be merry, for tomorrow we die" is alien and abhorrent to Judaism.

Although the period of man's life on earth is limited, it has a definite part in Divine providence and the scheme of history. In the words of John Macmurray:[5] "Jewish reflection thinks of history as the act of God. Where our historians say, 'Caesar crossed the Rubicon,' or 'Nelson won the Battle of Trafalgar,' the Jewish historian says, 'God brought His people up out of the land of Egypt.' "

Judaism rejects both the Hegelian approach to history and the dialectical materialism of Karl Marx. To Jews, God is the Lord of history controlling the destiny of man from the cradle to the grave and beyond.

Unlike the ancient Egyptians, who were as much preoccupied with death as with life and therefore filled their tombs with precious stones and utensils and provisions for life after death of the departed, the Hebrews believed that "in the hour of man's departure from this world, neither silver nor gold nor precious stones nor pearls accompany him, but only Torah and good works."[6]

"While you do not know life, what can you know about death?" demanded Confucius. The rabbis, too, asked this unanswerable question, maintaining that man could not comprehend the mystery of immortality. Maimonides reasons:

Know that just as a blind man can form no idea of colors, nor a deaf man comprehend sounds . . . so the body cannot comprehend the delights of the soul. Even as fish do not know the element of fire because they exist ever in the opposite, so are the delights of the world of the spirit unknown in this world of the flesh. Indeed, we have no pleasure in any way except what is bodily and what the sense can comprehend of eating and drinking. Whatever is outside these is nonexistent to us. We do not discern it, neither do we grasp it at first thought, but only after deep penetration.

And truly, this must necessarily be the case. For we live in a material world and the only pleasure we can comprehend must be material. But the delights of the spirit are everlasting and uninterrupted, and there is no resemblance in any possible way between spiritual and bodily enjoyments.[7]

Science cannot solve the riddle of the "undiscovered country, from whose bourne no traveler returns." Judaism does not agree with the philosophy of Martin Heidegger that man is dedicated to death for which he has a genuine instinct, nor with that of Epicurus: "While we live, death is absent, and when we die we are absent, so death is simply nonexistent for us."

But Judaism, although primarily concerned with the miracle of life, does not ignore the mystery of death, and from biblical and rabbinic literature it is possible to suggest the nature of the hereafter.

THE SOUL

The soul is known as *neshamah, nefesh,* or *ruach* (breath)[8] and is the source without which there can be no life. " 'O Lord my God,' " entreated the prophet Elijah, " 'I pray Thee, let this child's soul come back into him.' And the Lord hearkened unto the voice of Elijah; and the soul of the child came back into him and he revived" (I Kings 17:21–22). The soul originates with God (Genesis 2:17) and is a gift to man. "It is the lamp of God which He hath breathed into man. It must thus remain in its state and cannot die . . . its continued existence being natural and enduring forever."[9]

Before the body came into being, the soul already existed[10] and has done so since the beginning of time. The souls of all men are in the hands of the Holy One, Blessed be He, and are not in any way tainted by "original sin." Every morning of the year, the faithful Jew prays: "O my God, the soul which Thou gavest me is pure; Thou didst create it, Thou didst form it, Thou didst breathe it into me; Thou preservest it within me; and Thou wilt take it from me, but wilt restore it unto me hereafter. So long as the soul is within me, I will give thanks unto Thee."[11]

Some believed that the soul is diffused throughout the body. "Just as the Holy One, Blessed be He, He sees, but is not seen, so the soul sees but is not itself seen. Just as the Holy One, Blessed be He, feeds the whole world, so the soul feeds the whole body. Just as the Holy One, Blessed be He, is pure, so the soul is pure."[12] Other sages, however, held that the exact dwelling place of the soul could not be determined. "You want to know," said Rabban Gamaliel, "the dwelling place of God who is so distant from us: Your body is very close to you, yet can you tell in what part of it is your soul?"[13]

DEATH AS HOMECOMING

Jews view death neither as an enemy nor as a friend, but as the return of all elements to their original source. In death, man no longer has a full relationship with God. "The dead praise not the Lord neither any that go down into silence" (Psalm 115:17). The dead raise no *Hallelujahs;* they are cut off from communion with God and from the power of rendering Him service of life and lip. Once a man dies, he is free from all possibility of practicing Torah and good deeds. Death is thus a separation. It separates man from God.

Death is not only an established but inevitable part of life, it is the most predictable event of life. Man is distinguished from the animals by his knowledge that he must die. Death was ordained even prior to the creation of the world.[14] In the words of our sages, "For all creatures, death has been prepared from the beginning."[15]

Death is not an unmentionable subject in Judaism. Death is not regarded merely as an end of life. It is the going home of the spirit to another stage. The spirit ascends to a higher life. "Then shall the dust return to the earth as it was, and the spirit shall return unto God who gave it" (Ecclesiastes 12:7). Death is merely moving from one home to another. Although the rabbis list a number of individuals who died without sin,[16] death is nevertheless regarded as a punishment for sinfulness. "For there is not a righteous man upon earth that doeth good and sinneth not" (Ecclesiastes 7:20). No one can claim exemption from chastisement. Even Moses and Aaron died through their sin, as it is said, "Because ye believed not in Me" (Numbers 20:12).

When Israel Baal Shem Tov (1700–1760) was dying, his son Zevi cried bitterly at the deathbed. Rabbi Israel consoled his son saying, "Do not cry, my son, for I am passing through one door in order to enter another." Death to him was the entry to eternal life. In the words of the Ethics of the Fathers, "This world is like a vestibule that thou mayest enter into the banquet hall." In a similar vein Rabbi Menachem Mendel Morgenstern of Kotzk (c. 1787–1859) used to say, "Death is merely moving from one home to another. If we are wise we will make the latter the more beautiful home."[17]

"Judgment for an evil thing," says Carlyle, "is many times delayed, sometimes a day or two, sometimes a century or two, but it is as sure as life, it is as sure as death." This is also one of the beliefs of Judaism, where not only is it laid down that "the wicked shall die in his iniquity" (Ezekiel 3:18), but also that "with what measure a man metes it shall be measured to him again."[18]

Every human being is called to account. A record is kept

of all that a human being does while on earth. "All your deeds are written in a Heavenly Book of Records."[19] Some of the questions addressed to him are: "Did you transact your business honorably? Did you fix times for the study of the Torah? Did you fulfill your duty with respect to establishing a family? Did you hope for the salvation of the Messiah? Did you search for wisdom?"[20]

It is not wrong to hope for God's reward for righteous living. Nonetheless, the Law of God should be kept for its own sake. "Blessed is the man who fears the Lord and in His commandments delights greatly" (Psalm 112:1). In the words of Antigonos, who lived in the first half of the third century B.C.E., "Be not like the servants who minister to their master upon the condition of receiving a reward; but be like servants who minister to their master without the condition of receiving a reward."[21] As a chasidic master, Rabbi Shneur Zalman of Liady, stated, "I desire not thy Paradise. I desire not thy Eden, but I desire Thee only."

A man's deeds during his lifetime vindicate the saint and entitle him to enter Heaven, but they destroy the sinner so that he is rejected. For the Almighty faithfully punishes the wicked and rewards the righteous, if not in this world, then in the world to come. This belief is one of Maimonides's Thirteen Articles of Faith. "I believe with perfect faith," the Jew declares, "that the Creator, Blessed be His name, rewards those that keep His commandments, and punishes those that transgress them."[22] The rabbis stress that "it is not in our power to explain either the prosperity of the wicked or the afflictions of the righteous."[23] Belief in the existence of another world, the world of Truth, Justice, and Mercy, is the Jewish explanation of the seeming inequalities and inconsistencies of this life.

GEHENNA

Rabbi Joshua ben Levi lists seven biblical names for *Gehenna* (hell): Netherworld, Destruction, Pit, Tumultuous

Pit, Miry Clay, Shadow of Death, and the Underworld.[24]
The Bible occasionally refers to Hell, as in Job (10:22), where
it is "a land of thick darkness, as darkness itself; a land of the
shadow of death, without any order, and where the light is
as darkness." Jewish people generally call Hell *Gehinnom*
after the valley of Hinnom, a vale southwest of Jerusalem,
where Solomon erected an altar to Molech (I Kings 11:7), and
where Ahaz and Manasseh made their children "pass
through the fire."[25] Eventually, the name of this valley
became for Jewish people synonymous with the legendary
place of eternal torment.

Sheol is said to be an enormous land beneath the visible
world, the home of the dead, where God's power is effective. "But God will redeem my soul from the power of the
netherworld; for He shall receive me" (Psalm 49:16). There is
no eternal punishment there, the maximum punishment
being twelve months of penance and purification. "For I am
merciful, saith the Lord, I will not bear a grudge forever"
(Jeremiah 3:12).

Hell to the rabbis was an actual place of fire, and they
refer to its portals and even give its measurements. There are
seven habitations in Hell (*Medoray Gehinnom*),[26] each more
severe than the other. Myriads of demons under Duma
punish the sinners in Hell. The works *Reshit Chochmah* and
Shevet Musar, by medieval moralists, give a graphic description of hell.

> When Rabban Jochanan ben Zakkai fell ill, his disciples
> went in to visit him. When he saw them, he began to
> weep. His disciples said to him: "Wherefore weepest
> thou?" He replied: "If I were being taken today before a
> human king who is here today and tomorrow in the
> grave, whose anger if he is angry with me does not last
> forever, who if he imprisons me does not imprison me
> forever, and who if he puts me to death does not put me
> to everlasting death, and whom I can persuade with
> words and do bribe with money, even so I would weep.
> Now, that I am being taken before the supreme King of

Kings, who lives and endures forever and ever, whose anger, if He is angry with me, is an everlasting anger, who if he imprisons me imprisons me forever, who if He puts me to death puts me to death forever, and whom I cannot persuade with words or bribe with money—nay more, when there are two ways before me, one leading to Paradise and the other to *Gehinnom,* and I do not know by which I shall be taken, shall I not weep?"[27]

Rabbi Akiva in the *Mishnah* stated that the judgments of the unrighteous in *Gehinnom* shall endure twelve months. Rabbi Jochanan ben Nuri says, "Only as long as from Passover to Pentecost (i.e., seven weeks)."[28]

This was not the only explanation of Hell. Rabbi Jacob Joseph Ha-Kohen of Polonnoye (d. 1769) says:

No purgatory can be worse for the wicked than permission to enter the Garden of Eden. They find there no pleasure to which they were addicted in life; no eating or drinking or any other pleasures of the body. They see merely *tzaddikim* deriving great joy from the nearness of the Lord. And who are these *tzaddikim* who occupy places of prominence in Paradise? They are the very persons upon whom the wicked poured out their scorn in life, and whose learning they thoroughly despised. What, then, can these wicked persons feel in Paradise but bitterness? Can they know the joy of the *Shechinah*'s nearness, inasmuch as they never trained themselves in their lifetime for the enjoyment of the spirit?[29]

If, as the mystics say, body and soul are one, yet divisible and independent, how at the end shall man be judged? Which shall be answerable to the Divine Judge of Judges—the body, or the soul?

Antoninus (whom some identify with the Roman Emperor Marcus Aurelius)[30] once had a discussion with Rabbi Judah Hanasi:[31]

"On the great Day of Judgment, soul and body will each plead excuse for the sins that have been committed. The body will say to the Heavenly Judge, 'It is the soul, and not I, that has sinned. Without it I am as lifeless as a stone.' On the other hand, the soul will say, 'How canst Thou impute sin to me? It is the body that has dragged me down.' "

"Let me tell you a parable," answered the Rabbi. "A king once had a beautiful garden stocked with the choicest fruits. He set two men to keep guard over it— a blind man and a lame man. 'I see some fine fruit yonder,' said the lame man one day. 'Come up on my shoulder,' said the blind man. 'I will carry you to the spot, and we shall both enjoy the fruit.' The owner, missing the fruit, hauled both men before him for punishment. 'How could I have been the thief?' said the lame man, 'seeing that I cannot walk?' 'Could I have stolen the fruit?' retorted the blind man. 'I am unable to see anything.' What did the king do? He placed the lame man on the shoulders of the blind man and sentenced them both as one.' "

In the same way, the Divine Judge of the Universe will pass judgment on both body and soul together. As the body and the soul are equally concerned in the commission of a sin, they are alike penalized. The soul is rejoined to the body for the purpose of judgment.

Rabbi Israel Baal Shem Tov stated, "A *tzaddik*'s soul does not at first ascend to the upper regions of Paradise. In the beginning he resides in a lower Eden, where he is still in incomplete bliss; only by degrees is he conducted to a higher and higher realm."[32]

GAN EDEN

Many and various are the folk beliefs and poetic fancies in the rabbinic writings concerning *Gan Eden* (Heaven) and

Gehinnom (Hell). Our most authoritative religious guides, however, proclaim that "no eye hath seen, nor can any mortal fathom, what awaiteth us in the hereafter; but that even the tarnished soul will not forever be denied spiritual bliss, for Judaism rejects the doctrines of eternal damnation."[33]

Gan Eden was said to consist of seven divisions that correspond to the seven classes of righteousness. The divisions are named Presence, Courts, House, Tabernacle, Holy Hill, Hill of the Lord, and Holy Place. Each righteous person will be assigned a dwelling in accordance with the honor due to him. The Holy One will arrange a banquet for the righteous from the flesh of Leviathan.

Virtue is its own reward. Nevertheless, the righteous are constantly assured that they will be recompensed in Paradise. What is Paradise? It is known to us as *Gan Eden*, man's first home,[34] which was created even before the world came into being, and has become by tradition the eternal resting-place of the righteous.[35] "Every righteous person," says the Talmud,[36] "will be assigned a dwelling place in accordance with the honor due to him. Remember the parable of a human king who enters a city with servants. Although they all enter through one gate, when they take up their quarters each is allotted a dwelling place according to his rank."

IMMORTALITY

Throughout the ages the question has been asked: "If a man dies, will he live again?" Judaism replies emphatically that he will, and adds that this second life, the real life, will compensate for the imperfections of our brief earthly existence. "But the souls of the righteous are in the hand of God, and no evil shall touch them. . . . For though in the sight of man they are punished, their hope is full of immortality."[37]

The Jewish concept of immortality is purely spiritual, identifying the next world with the kingdom of God, the

Most High, *Malchut Shadai* or *Malchut Shamayim*. "The Day of the Lord" is the era when "the Lord shall be king over all the earth: On that day shall the Lord be One and His Name One" (Zechariah 14:9).

There are some references in rabbinic literature to the "banquet," "the huge Leviathan," and the "wine preserved since the six days of Creation"[38] for the delectation of the righteous at the end of days. These allusions are of a purely symbolic nature. "In the world to come," declares the Talmud, "there is no eating or drinking, or procreation or commerce, or jealousy, enmity, or rivalry, but the righteous sit with crowns on their heads and enjoy the radiance of the Divine Presence."[39]

Maimonides is even more explicit. "In that [messianic] era there shall be neither famine nor war, neither jealousy nor strife. Blessings will be abundant, comforts within the reach of all. The one preoccupation of the whole world will be to know the Lord . . . as it is written: 'For the earth shall be full of the knowledge of the Lord, as the waters cover the sea' " (Isaiah 11:9).[40]

OLAM HABA

Olam Haba (the world to come) and *Le'Atid Lavo* (the future that is to be) are terms that need clarification.

In the eschatological doctrine of the Talmud a clear divergence of opinion may be traced. The earlier generations of the rabbis identified the Messianic era with the World to Come. The promised Redeemer would bring the existing world-order to an end and inaugurate the timeless sphere in which the righteous would lead a purely spiritual existence freed from the trammels of the flesh. Subsequent teachers regarded the Messianic period as but a transitory stage between this world and the next.[41]

Maimonides explains: "The wise men called it 'world to come' not because it is not in existence at present, but because life in that world will come to man after the life in this world is ended." In the words of the late Dr. I. Epstein,[42]

> The World to Come, *Olam Haba*, has a twofold connotation, individual and universal. On the one hand, it denotes the heavenly world we each individually enter at death; on the other hand, it stands for the world in which the universality of mankind will enter upon its over-earthly destiny. The former is the sphere of Judgment and reward for our individual selves; the latter is the sphere of Resurrection and Judgment for all created beings. These two worlds are not distinct but represent two phases of the same process of fulfillment, the *Olam Haba* awaiting the individual at death having its consummation in the *Olam Haba* which follows the Resurrection.

"All Israel," states the *Mishnah*,[43] "have a portion in the world to come; as it is written 'And thy people shall be all righteous; they shall inherit the land forever, the branch of My planting, the work of My hands that I may be glorified' " (Isaiah 60:21).

RESURRECTION

The Prophets spoke eloquently of the resurrection. Isaiah declared, "Thy dead shall live, my dead bodies shall arise" (Isaiah 26:19). This belief in the resurrection of the dead is a fundamental principle of Judaism. "And he who does not believe in it, is not an adherent of Judaism," declared Maimonides,[44] the greatest rational Jewish philosopher of the Middle Ages.

The Sadducees (a Judean sect that flourished during the last two centuries of the Second Temple) denied resurrection of the dead and the immortality of the soul.[45] "At the close of every benediction in the Temple" the *Mishnah* records, "they used to say 'For everlasting,' but after the heretics had taught corruptly and said that there is but one world, it was ordained that they should say 'From everlasting to everlasting.' "[46]

Techiyat Hamesim min Hatorah (the belief in the resurrection of the dead) is of biblical origin, say the rabbis. Death is never regarded in the Bible as annihilation or the end of personal existence. "For Thou wilt not abandon my soul to the grave," sings the Psalmist, "neither wilt Thou suffer Thy godly one to see the pit" (Psalm 16:10–11).

Daniel states, "And many of them that sleep in the dust of the earth shall awake, some to everlasting life and some to reproaches and everlasting abhorrence" (Daniel 12:2).

The vision of Israel's resurrection from the dead is graphically described by the Prophet Ezekiel (Chapter 36–37). Josephus[47] explains that the Essenes believed in the immortality of the soul. He states that, while bodies are corruptible, souls are immortal. Good souls go to a refreshing place "beyond the ocean," whereas evil souls are assigned to "a gloomy and tempestuous recess, filled with incessant punishments." The Pharisees believed that "every soul is imperishable but the souls of the wicked suffer eternal punishment."

Several Qumran passages speak of the resurrection. In the *Manual of Discipline*[48] it states that those who walk according to the spirit of truth will receive "healing and abundance of peace, with length of days and fruitfulness and all blessings without end and eternal joy in everlasting light." In the Collection of Blessings, the priests are promised that they will be "in the company of God" and the angels "for everlasting time and for all ages forever."[49]

BODILY RESURRECTION

In the second benediction of the *Shemoneh Esreh* (the *Amidah*),[50] the resurrection is stressed and God is praised because "Thou keepest Thy faith to them that sleep in the dust."[51] The belief in the bodily resurrection was firmly held by Saadia Gaon (892–942),[52] Rashi[53] (1040–1105), and Rabbi Obadiah di Bertinoro (c. 1450–1510).[54] Even the Sibylline Oracle[55] (4:18) says: "The dead rise with the bodies in which they died in order that they may be recognized," while the Talmud[56] declares, "They would be appareled in their own clothes." The rabbis did not adopt a spiritual interpretation, as did Philo,[57] but believed in a real resurrection of the body.

The decomposition of the body did not present any difficulty to the sages of the Talmud and *Midrash*.[58]

THE PROPHET ELIJAH

Of the "seven prophetesses and the eight and forty prophets" who illumined the panorama of Jewish history, none has so fired the imagination of the Jewish people as Elijah.[59] No book of the Bible bears his name; he is not remembered for transcendent visions (like Isaiah), for lamentations and reproaches (like Jeremiah), for mystical profundities (like Ezekiel); yet his personality has become interwoven with the fabric of Jewish life. His activities were not confined to the period of his pilgrimage on earth, with the weak-willed King Ahab and the forceful Queen Jezebel or the idolatrous worshipers of Baal. His actions on Mount Carmel and on Mount Horeb were but the beginnings of an odyssey that has stretched over thousands of years.

According to legend, God gave Elijah a solemn charge: "Be thou now the protector and guardian of Me and the belief in Me throughout the whole world." Nobly, indeed, has the prophet carried out his mission. Like Enoch, Elijah made a miraculous ascension into Heaven. He has visited *tannaim, amoraim, geonim*, Kabbalists, and Chasidim. He has taken on many guises. He has appeared as beggar, Arab, architect, and slave. He has been peacemaker between husband and wife, helper in times of trouble, miraculous healer, painless dentist, erudite teacher, *minyan* man, and

Scarlet Pimpernel to the House of Israel. Many a medieval community, it is said, owed its survival to the timely intervention of Elijah the Tishbite, the wandering prophet of a wandering people.

Among the *dramatis personae* of eschatology, Elijah, the precursor of the Messiah, figures high. To him is allotted the task of restoring family purity, performing Seven Miracles, and introducing the Messiah. Elijah will appear three days before the advent of the Messiah and lament over the devastation of the Holy Land. The next day he will again appear and proclaim that "God will come upon the earth." And, finally, on the third day, Elijah will appear once more and promise that "salvation will come upon the earth." He will slay Satan, and the era of peace will begin. The resurrection would take place in the Holy Land. Some rabbis maintain that only those who are interred there would share in the future life. Other rabbis took the view that for those who have lived elsewhere, their bodies will have to be transferred there before they come back to life again.[60] The righteous whom God will resurrect will not return to the dust, and if they had blemishes while alive in this world, these would be healed in time for the resurrection.[61]

REINCARNATION

The belief that a soul, after death, passes into another body has been accepted as a matter of fact in the eastern part of the world. It was actually taught by ancient Greek philosophers. Reference to reincarnation is found in *Sefer Ha-Bahir* (The Book of Brilliance), which appeared in Provence in 1175, and was made by Nachmanides in his commentary to Job.[62] "All souls," says the *Zohar*,[63] "are subject to transmigrations." The *Zohar* goes on to say that "the Holy One . . . permits [the human being] . . . to start anew and to labor for himself, in order to make good his deficiencies." This is due to the mercy of the Almighty "from Whom no one is cast off forever." The *Zohar* mentions several causes that necessitate additional lives in the physical realm. It regards *gilgul* (transmigration) as the seventh ordeal, i.e., when the spirit is condemned to roam to and fro in the world and is not able to find a resting place until its appointed tasks have been completed. The term *gilgulim* (the wheels or the revolutions) originates from the biblical phrase in I Samuel 25:29 about lives being whirled round like a stone and then thrown out of a sling back into life.

Rabbi Isaac Luria (1534–1572), in his *Sefer ha-Gilgulim* (Book of Transmigrations), maintains that each person must carry out in his lifetime all of the commandments. If a single commandment is not fully observed, the soul reincarnates in order to fulfill all the unmet commandments and to make good the mistakes that were committed. Jewish sages transmigrated to compensate for neglected obligations in their former lives. This was regarded as both a blessing and a curse. It is hard to leave the bosom of the Divine Presence and to return to the physical world and suffer the tribulations of an earthly existence. On the other hand, it offers another chance to achieve salvation.

Rabbi Chayyim ben Joseph Vital (1542–1620) stressed that it was not enough merely to fulfill the commandments physically, but that they had to be carried out with the proper intention and concentration.

According to Jewish legends, Aaron the High Priest was reincarnated in Eli and Ezra; Cain in Jethro; Abel in Moses; Jacob in Mordecai; Phinehas in Elijah; and Tamar in Ruth. Rabbi Simon b. Yochai and, later, Rabbi Isaac Luria were reincarnations of Moses. David, Bathsheba, and Uriah were said to have the souls of Adam, Eve, and the serpent, and the soul of Terah, the father of Abraham, was given to Job.

In the course of time the theory of *gilgul* was modified. Each soul was allowed three rebirths only. If, by the end of the third rebirth, it had failed to achieve its purpose, it was condemned to roam the earth forever. "The soul that has fulfilled its task, that has done what it has to do in terms of creating or repairing its own part of the world and realizing its own essence, can wait after death for the perfection of the world as a whole. But not all the souls are so privileged: many stray for one reason or another. . . . In such cases the soul does not complete its task. . . . The sins of man are not eliminated so long as this soul does not complete that which it has to complete. From which it may be seen that most souls are not new; they are not in the world for the first time. Almost every person bears the legacy of previous existences. Generally one does not obtain the previous self again, for the soul manifests itself in different circumstances and in different situations."[64]

Rabbi Manasseh ben Israel (d. 1657), in his work *Nishmat Chayyim*,[65] devotes a large section to reincarnation. This doctrine of metempsychosis acquired great popularity among the chasidic masters, who all believed in *gilgul* and identified themselves and their colleagues with figures of a previous age. The Rabbi of Opatow, Rabbi Abraham Joshua Heschel (1748–1824), although not a *Kohen* himself, believed that he had been a High Priest in an earlier existence. He would change the prescribed text in the order of service of the High Priest, recited during the additional service (the *Avodah*) on the Day of Atonement in this way: Instead of saying, "Thus did he (the High Priest) say . . ." he would intone, "Thus did I say. . . ."

It was due to these mystical conceptions of the migration (*ibbur*) of souls that the idea of *dibbukim*[66] arose in medieval times.

The Kabbalistic school of Rabbi Isaac ben Solomon Ashkenazi Luria and his disciple Rabbi Chayyim Vital believed that a soul that had sinned returned to its earthly existence in order to make amends. Saadia Gaon,[67] Chasdai ben Abraham Crescas[68] (1340–1410), and Joseph Albo[69] (1380–1435) were skeptical of this belief.

SPIRITUALISM

It is forbidden for Jews to attempt to communicate with the dead. "There shall not be found among you . . . a sorcerer, or a charmer, or one that consulteth a ghost or a familiar spirit, or a necromancer. For whosoever doeth these things is an abomination unto the Lord."[70] Maimonides[71] says, "What is the meaning of necromancy?[72] It refers to one who starves himself and then stays overnight in the cemetery in order that a dead person should visit him in a dream to give him some information he requires."

The incident of Saul and the Witch of En Dor (I Samuel 28:7–19) and the esoteric experiences of a number of talmudic sages[73] are isolated instances. Judaism believes implicitly in the existence of the spirit, but rigorously opposes spiritualism, the attempt to contact these spirits. The dead should not be disturbed. Hence such practices are regarded as evil and undesirable and no better than idolatry and necromancy. Table-rapping, too, is strictly forbidden.[74]

THE CREATOR OF THE GOLEM

Rabbi Judah ben Bezalel Loew (1525–1609) of Prague was the creator of the *golem*. In biblical and mishnaic Hebrew the word *golem* has several connotations: an embryo, a mass of matter, the antithesis of "wise." It was widely believed among Jews that it was possible to create a *homunculus*, a superman, by means of the Ineffable Name, the Tetragrammaton, the *Shem Ha-Meforash*. According to rabbinic literature, Ben Sira (the author of Ecclesiasticus) strove to create a *golem* by means of the mystical *Sefer Yetzirah* (the Book of Creation—attributed to the Patriarch Abraham). As time went on, the Kabbalists became more proficient in this strange art. According to a legend in the Talmud, Rabah (third or fourth century) had created a *golem*; Rabbi Chaninah and Rabbi Oshayah formed a 3-year-old calf every Friday; Rashi (1040–1105) finds nothing surprising in this story. "They, Chaninah and Oshayah," says Rashi, "used to combine the letters of the code by which the Universe was created. This is not considered magic, for the creations of God were brought into being through His Holy Name." Among *golem* creators of the Middle Ages were Solomon Ibn Gabirol (1012–1058), the philosopher-poet, author of *Keter*

Malchut; and the German mystic Rabbi Samuel, father of the pietist Judah He-Chasid (d. 1217) of Regensburg, who wrote *Sefer Chasidim* (Book of the Saints). Ashkenazim and Sephardim were for once united by a common effort, and in the sixteenth century Rabbi Elijah of Chelm (d. 1583) joined the limited ranks of the robot makers.

With the aid of his son-in-law Isaac ben Shimshon Ha-Kohen and his disciple Jacob ben Chayyim Halevy, the *Maharal* created a *golem* on the twenty-fourth of *Adar*, 1580. The *golem* was named "Yossele" and he served as a *shammash* at the *Bet Din*. He served his purpose nobly. On *Lag B'Omer* in 1590, the *golem* was reduced to a heap of dust and his resting place, the attic of the *Altneu Schul* in Prague, became forbidden ground.

DIVINE GLORY

The late Professor Louis Ginzberg (1873–1953)[75] writes:

The Rabbis often speak of the reward awaiting the righteous after their death as consisting not in material pleasure but in enjoying divine glory. Nevertheless, the development of the religious thought of the Jew shows a marked tendency to fix the center of gravity of religion not in the thought of a world beyond but rather to fasten and establish it in the actual life of man on earth. In this respect the Scribes and the Rabbis were the true successors of the Prophets.

Chapter 12

Words of Comfort

❧ *PSALM 16* ❧

This Psalm gives us an insight into the quiet faith of an Israelite who has lived long in communion with God. He desires nothing else in life or death but the fellowship of God. In peril because impious enemies are closing in about him, the Psalmist appeals to God for help. His enemies are worldly men, seeking only this life's enjoyment. He, on the contrary, desires something far more satisfying—the beholding of God's majesty. Death cannot touch the heritage of the man whose heritage is the Lord.

Michtam of David.
Keep me, O God; for I have taken refuge in Thee.
I have said unto the Lord: "Thou art my Lord; I have no
   good but in Thee."
As for the holy that are in the earth,
They are the excellent in whom is all my delight.
Let the idols of them be multiplied that make suit unto
   another;
Their drink-offerings of blood will I not offer,
Nor take their names upon my lips.
O Lord, the portion of mine inheritance and of my cup,

Thou maintainest my lot.
The lines are fallen unto me in pleasant places;
Yea, I have a goodly heritage.
I will bless the Lord, who hath given me counsel;
Yea, in the night seasons my reins instruct me.
I have set the Lord always before me;
Surely, He is at my right hand, I shall not be moved.
Therefore my heart is glad, and my glory rejoiceth;
My flesh also dwelleth in safety;
For Thou wilt not abandon my soul to the nether-world;
Neither wilt Thou suffer Thy godly one to see the pit.
Thou makest me to know the path of life;
In Thy presence is fullness of joy,
At Thy right hand bliss for evermore.

❧ *PSALM 23* ❧

This Psalm is one of the most beautiful and best loved in
the entire Psalter. The Psalm breathes throughout a spirit of
the calmest and most assured trust in God's providence: It
speaks of a peace so deep, a serenity so profound, that even
the thought of the shadow of death cannot trouble it. The
Psalmist finds security not in a life of freedom from all
dangers but in a life spent under God's direction and care.
The picture is that of the shepherd leading his sheep through
the narrow and dark gorges where unknown terror may lie
in wait. But the shepherd is with them all the time and his
presence is their strength and support.

A Psalm of David.
The Lord is my shepherd; I shall not want.
He maketh me to lie down in green pastures;
He leadeth me beside the still waters.
He restoreth my soul;
He guideth me in straight paths for His name's sake.

Yea, though I walk through the valley of the shadow of
    death,
I will fear no evil,
For Thou art with me
Thy rod and Thy staff, they comfort me.
Thou preparest a table before me in the presence of
    mine enemies;
Thou hast anointed my head with oil; my cup runneth
    over.
Surely goodness and mercy shall follow me all the days
    of my life,
    And I shall dwell in the house of the Lord forever.

❧ . *PSALM 27* ☙

Under God's guardianship, the Psalmist knows no fear
in the midst of dangers. His highest desire is to enjoy God's
fellowship and protection as guest in His house. Earnestly
the Psalmist pleads that God will not forsake His servant and
appeals to His promises and past mercies.

The Lord is my light and my salvation; whom shall I
    fear?
The Lord is the stronghold of my life; of whom shall I be
    afraid?
When evil-doers came upon me to eat up my flesh,
Even mine adversaries and my foes, they stumbled and
    fell.
Though a host should encamp against me,
My heart shall not fear;
Though war should rise up against me,
Even then will I be confident.
One thing have I asked of the Lord, that will I seek after:
That I may dwell in the house of the Lord all the days of
    my life,

To behold the graciousness of the Lord, and to visit
    early in His Temple.
For He concealeth me in His pavilion in the day of evil;
He hideth me in the covert of His tent;
He lifteth me upon a rock.
And now shall my head be lifted up above mine
    enemies round about me;
And I will offer in His tabernacle sacrifices with a
    trumpet-sound;
I will sing, yea I will sing praises unto the Lord.
Hear, O Lord, when I call with my voice,
And be gracious unto me, and answer me.
In Thy behalf my heart hath said: 'Seek ye My face.'
Thy face, Lord, will I seek.
Hide not Thy face from me;
Put not Thy servant away in anger;
Thou hast been my help; cast me not off, neither forsake
    me,
O God of my salvation.
For though my father and my mother have forsaken me,
The Lord will take me up.
Teach me Thy way, O Lord,
And lead me in an even path,
Because of them that wait for me.
Deliver me not over unto the will of mine adversaries,
For false witnesses are risen up against me and such as
    breathe out violence.
If I had not believed to look upon the goodness of the
    Lord
in the land of the living!—
Wait for the Lord;
Be strong, and let thy heart take courage;
Yea, wait thou for the Lord.

❧ *PSALM 39* ❧

Though provoked by the presence of the wicked who
are unpunished and rich, the Psalmist keeps his silence.

With wicked men, the Psalmist will not discuss his physical
and mental sufferings. Prolonged sickness has brought him
to the very edge of the grave. He will, rather, address
himself to God, to learn something about the brevity and
emptiness of human existence. In the eternity of God, man is
but a very fleeting figure and the ungodly rich are but a
passing shadow. His hope is in God alone from whom he
asks forgiveness for all his sins.

Lord, make me to know mine end,
And the measure of my days, what it is:
Let me know how shortlived I am.
Behold, Thou hast made my days as hand-breadths;
And mine age is as nothing before Thee;
Surely every man at his best estate is altogether vanity.
  Selah.
Surely, man walketh as a mere semblance;
Surely for vanity they are in turmoil;
He heapeth up riches, and knoweth not who shall
  gather them.
And now, Lord, what wait I for?
My hope, it is in Thee.
Deliver me from all my transgressions;
Make me not the reproach of the base.
I am dumb, I open not my mouth;
Because Thou hast done it.
Remove Thy stroke from off me;
I am consumed by the blow of Thy hand.
With rebukes dost Thou chasten man for iniquity.
And like a moth Thou makest his beauty to consume
  away
Surely every man is vanity. Selah.
Hear my prayer, O Lord, and give ear unto my cry;
Keep not silence at my tears;
For I am a stranger with Thee
A sojourner, as all my fathers were.
Look away from me, that I may take comfort,
Before I go hence, and be no more.
                              (Verses 5–14)

❧ *PSALM 49* ❧

This Psalm deals with the problem: Why are the ungodly rich and powerful and the faithful poor and oppressed? In one way or another this problem constantly reappears in the Bible. Faced with the terrible ordeal of suffering, man is prone to doubt the goodness of the God whom he serves. The Psalmist resolves the problem by noting that all the wealth in the world cannot purchase exemption from death, and it must all be abandoned when its owner comes to die. The Psalmist expresses his own faith that righteousness will be finally triumphant.

For the Leader: A Psalm of the sons of Korah.
Hear this, all ye peoples;
Give ear, all ye inhabitants of the world.
Both low and high,
Rich and poor together.
My mouth shall speak wisdom,
And the meditation of my heart shall be understanding.
I will incline mine ear to a parable;
I will open my dark saying upon the harp.
Wherefore should I fear in the days of evil,
When the iniquity of my supplanters compasseth me
    about
Of them that trust in their wealth,
And boast themselves in the multitude of their riches?
No man can by any means redeem his brother,
Nor give to God a ransom for him—
For too costly is the redemption of his soul,
And must be left alone forever—
That he should still live alway,
That he should not see the pit.
For he seeth that wise men die,
The fool and the brutish together perish,
And leave their wealth to others.
Their inward thought is, that their houses shall continue forever,

And their dwelling-places to all generations;
They call their lands after their own names.
But man abideth not in honor;
He is like the beasts that perish.
This is the way of them that are foolish,
And of those who after them approve their sayings.
   Selah.
Like sheep they are appointed for the nether-world;
Death shall be their shepherd;
And the upright shall have dominion over them in the
   morning;
And their form shall be for the nether-world to wear
   away,
That there be no habitation for it.
But God will redeem my soul from the power of the
   nether-world;
For He shall receive me. Selah.
Be not thou afraid when one waxeth rich,
When the wealth of his house is increased;
For when he dieth he shall carry nothing away;
His wealth shall not descend after him.
Though while he lived he blessed his soul:
"Men will praise thee, when thou shalt do well to
   thyself:"
He shall go to the generation of his fathers;
They shall never see the light.
Man that is in honor understandeth not;
He is like the beasts that perish.

❧ *PSALM 103* ❧

   The Psalmist summons his soul and all his faculties to
praise God for pardon, redemption, and bountiful provision
for every need. Man may be frail and transitory, but those
who fear God can rest in the assurance of his eternal
faithfulness. Man is mortal and frail but God's mercy is
eternal.

As for man, his days are as grass;
As a flower of the field, so he flourisheth.
For the wind passeth over it, and it is gone;
And the place thereof knoweth it no more.
But the mercy of the Lord is from everlasting to ever-
　　lasting upon them that fear Him,
And His righteousness unto children's children.

(Verses 15–18)

❧ ISAIAH 55 ❧

God's thoughts transcend those of man as much as the heaven is higher than the earth. His purposes of redemption are too vast and sublime to be measured by the narrow conceptions of despairing minds. God is in truth near, although His thoughts and purposes are too exalted to be comprehended by the narrow and earthbound visions of selfish men.

Seek ye the Lord while He may be found,
Call ye upon Him while He is near;
Let the wicked forsake his way,
And the man of iniquity his thoughts;
And let him return unto the Lord,
and He will have compassion upon him,
And to our God, for He will abundantly pardon.
For my thoughts are not your thoughts
Neither are your ways My ways, saith the Lord
For as the heavens are higher than the earth,
So are My ways higher than your ways
and My thoughts than your thoughts.

(Verses 6–9)

❧ THE BOOK OF JOB ❧

The Book of Job wrestles with the problem of the meaning of sorrow. Job was a wealthy man living a seminomadic life, free from worldly cares, when suddenly catastrophe struck, and he was faced with the problem of human suffering. Satan is portrayed as asserting that Job serves God only because it is profitable. God accepts the challenge, and Satan is allowed to afflict Job in order to prove that the good man does not serve God merely because it pays him well to do so. Contrary to Satan's predictions, Job does not curse God in his misfortunes but blesses him. He believes that God effectively and at every moment controls the world and human life. The book was written for the purpose of seeking an answer to questions concerning the reason for human suffering and why a loving God allows it.

Then Job arose, and rent his mantle, and shaved his
    head, and fell down upon the ground, and wor-
    shiped; and he said:
Naked came I out of my mother's womb,
And naked shall I return thither;
The Lord gave, and the Lord hath taken away;
Blessed be the name of the Lord.
For all this Job sinned not, nor ascribed aught unseemly
    to God.

(Job 1:20–22)

We receive much good at the hand of God. Shall we not also, out of thanksgiving for the good, accept evil when He sends it? Job maintains that calamity is not a punishment or chastisement on account of sin but a trial of righteousness.

Shall we receive good at the hand of God,
and shall we not receive evil? . . .
Behold happy is the man whom God correcteth:
Therefore despise not thou the chastening of the Al-
    mighty. . . .
He delivereth the afflicted by his affliction.

(Job 2:10; 5:17; 36:15)

PROVERBS 31: THE WOMAN OF VIRTUE

This is a beautiful acrostic poem, the first verse beginning with the first letter of the Hebrew alphabet, and each of
the remaining twenty-one letters coming in turn. It is an ode
to the perfect wife, the ideal housewife. It shows the
elevated social position of woman among the Hebrews
compared with the woman's social position among other
ancient nations. The good wife is more precious than jewels.
Her kingdom is the home. The poem shows how happiness
in the domestic circle depends upon the foresight of this
queen of the hearth. This chapter is also interpreted by the
mystics as a reference to the *Shechinah,* the Queen Sabbath,
the Torah, wisdom, and the soul.

A woman of valor who can find?
For her price is far above rubies.
The heart of her husband doth safely trust in her,
And he hath no lack of gain.
She doeth him good and not evil
All the days of her life.
She seeketh wool and flax,
And worketh willingly with her hands.
She is like the merchant-ships;
She bringeth her food from afar.
She riseth also while it is yet night,
And giveth food to her household,
And a portion to her maidens.
She considereth a field, and buyeth it;
With the fruit of her hands she planteth a vineyard.
She girdeth her loins with strength,
And maketh strong her arms.
She perceiveth that her merchandise is good;
Her lamp goeth not out by night.
She layeth her hands to the distaff,
And her hands hold the spindle.
She stretcheth out her hand to the poor;
Yea, she reacheth forth her hands to the needy.

She is not afraid of the snow for her household;
For all her household are clothed with scarlet.
She maketh for herself coverlets;
Her clothing is fine linen and purple.
Her husband is known in the gates,
When he sitteth among the elders of the land.
She maketh linen garments and selleth them;
And delivereth girdles unto the merchant.
Strength and dignity are her clothing;
And she laugheth at the time to come.
She openeth her mouth with wisdom;
And the law of kindness is on her tongue.
She looketh well to the ways of her household,
And eateth not the bread of idleness.
Her children rise up, and call her blessed;
Her husband also, and he praiseth her:
"Many daughters have done valiantly,
But thou excellest them all."
Grace is deceitful, and beauty is vain;
But a woman that feareth the Lord, she shall be praised.
Give her of the fruit of her hands;
And let her works praise her in the gates.

(Verses 10–31)

❧ *NO RETURN* ❧

David will join his son in Sheol, the realm of the dead,
but none can return from there. This passage implies belief
in the continued existence of the soul in a state of conscious-
ness after death.

And the Lord struck the child that Uriah's wife bore
unto David, and it was very sick. David therefore
besought God for the child; and David fasted, and as
often as he went in, he lay all night upon the earth. And
the elders of the house arose and stood beside him, to
raise him up from the earth; but he would not, neither

did he eat bread with them. And it came to pass on the
seventh day, that the child died. And the servants of
David feared to tell him that the child was dead; for they
said: "Behold, while the child was yet alive, we
spoke unto him, and he hearkened not unto our voice;
how then shall we tell him that the child is dead, so that
he do himself some harm?" But when David saw that
his servants whispered together, David perceived that
the child was dead; and David said unto his servants:
"Is the child dead?" and they said: "He is dead." Then
David arose from the earth, and washed, and anointed
himself, and changed his apparel; and he came to the
house of the Lord, and worshiped; then he came to his
own house; and when he required, they set bread
before him and he did eat. Then said his servants unto
him: "What thing is this that thou hast done? Thou
didst fast and weep for the child while it was alive; but
when the child was dead, thou didst rise and eat
bread." And he said: "While the child was yet alive, I
fasted and wept; for I said: 'Who knoweth whether the
Lord will not be gracious to me, that the child may
live?' But now he is dead, wherefore should I fast? Can
I bring him back again? I shall go to him but he will not
return to me."

(II Samuel 12:16–23)

🦠 *ECCLESIASTES* 🦠

Ecclesiastes presents some practical considerations designed to alleviate misery and suggests that sorrow and even
death are blessings and that patience and wisdom will enable
man not only to bear but even to profit by inevitable
misfortunes. He who would live wisely must lay death to
heart and integrate it.

A good name is better than precious oil;
And the day of death than the day of one's birth.
It is better to go to the house of mourning,

Than to go to the house of feasting;
For that is the end of all men,
And the living will lay it to his heart.

(Ecclesiastes 7:1–2)

Man is a creature of time. Ecclesiastes recommends the frank recognition of our finite nature even in youth when life seems unquenchable. He is viewing the dissolution of the body and spirit, and he states that each returns to the source from which it sprang, the body to the dust and the spirit to God. The passages below describe the failings of an old man's physical powers. The Talmud (*Shabbat* 152a) explained the "sun" as forehead, "light" as nose, "moon" as soul, and "stars" as cheeks.

Remember then thy Creator in the days of thy youth,
Before the evil days come,
And the years draw nigh, when thou shalt say:
'I have no pleasure in them';
Before the sun, and light, and the moon,
And the stars, are darkened,
And the clouds return after the rain.

(Ecclesiastes 12:1–2)

And the dust returneth to the earth as it was,
And the spirit returneth unto God who gave it.

(Ecclesiastes 12:7)

The end of the matter, all having been heard: Fear God,
   and keep His commandments; for this is the whole
   man.

(Ecclesiastes 12:13)

THE RIGHTEOUS CANNOT DIE

Physical death is disregarded. The Wisdom of Solomon, one of the books of the Apocrypha, was probably written by an Alexandrian Jew who lived between 100 B.C.E. and 50 C.E. The author fixes his attention upon spiritual death. Suffering in the case of the righteous tests their goodness, while in the case of the unrighteous, it is purely retribution.

But the souls of the righteous are in the hand of God,
And no torment shall touch them.
In the eyes of the foolish they seemed to die;
And their departure was accounted to be their hurt,
And their going from us to be their ruin:
But they are in peace.
For though in the sight of men they be punished,
Their hope is full of immortality;
And having borne a little chastening, they shall receive
   great good;
Because God tested them, and found them worthy of
   Himself.
As gold in the furnace He proved them,
And as a whole burnt offering He accepted them.
               (The Wisdom of Solomon 3:1–6)

☙ DO AS MUCH AS IS IN THY POWER ☙

Rabbi Tarfon said, "The day is short, and the work is great, and the laborers are sluggish, and the reward is much, and the Master is urgent." He also said:

It is not thy duty to complete the work, but neither art thou free to desist from it; if thou hast studied much Torah, much reward will be given thee; and faithful is thy Employer to pay thee the reward of thy labor; and know that the grant of reward unto the righteous will be in the time to come.

                    (*Abot* 2:20–21)

Rabbi Jacob[2] said, "This world is like a vestibule before the world to come; prepare thyself in the vestibule, that thou mayest enter into the hall." He used to say:

Better is one hour of repentance and good deeds in this world than the whole life of the world to come; and better is one hour of blissfulness of spirit in the world to come than the whole life of this world.

(Abot 4:21)

❧ THE INCOMPARABLE WORTH ❧ OF THE TORAH

Rabbi Jose,[3] the son of Kisma, said:

I was once walking by the way, when a man met me and greeted me, and I returned his greeting. He said to me, "Rabbi, from what place art thou?" I said to him, "I come from a great city of sages and scribes." He said to me, "If thou art willing to dwell with us in our place, I will give thee a thousand thousand golden dinars and precious stones and pearls." I said to him, "Wert thou to give me all the silver and gold and precious stones and pearls in the world I would not dwell anywhere but in a home of the Torah; and thus it is written in the Book of Psalms by the hands of David King of Israel, The law of thy mouth is better unto me than thousands of gold and silver; and not only so, but in the hour of man's departure neither silver nor gold nor precious stones nor pearls accompany him, but only Torah and good works, as it is said, 'When thou walkest it shall lead thee; when thou liest down it shall watch over thee; and when thou awakest it shall talk with thee: — when thou walkest it shall lead thee — in this world; when thou liest down it shall watch over thee — in the grave; and when thou awakest it shall talk with thee — in the world to come.' And it says, 'The silver is mine, and the gold is mine, saith the Lord of hosts.' "

(Abot 6:9)

Rabbi Meir said:

> Whence do we learn that as you should say a blessing
> over the good, so you should say a blessing over the
> evil? Because it says, "Which the Lord thy God gives
> thee" (Deuteronomy 8:10). And "thy God" means "thy
> judge"; in every judgment with which He judges you,
> whether with the attribute of good or with the attribute
> of punishment, bless God.
>
> (*Berachot* 48b)

When Rabbi Jochanan[4] finished the Book of Job, he used to
say the following:

> The end of man is to die, and the end of a beast is to be
> slaughtered, and all are doomed to die. Happy is he
> who was brought up in the Torah and whose labor was
> in the Torah and who has given pleasure to his Creator
> and who grew up with a good name and departed the
> world with a good name; and of him Solomon said: "A
> good name is better than precious oil, and the day of
> death than the day of one's birth" (Ecclesiastes 8:1).
>
> (*Berachot* 17a)

When Rabban Jochanan ben Zakkai[5] fell ill, his disciples
went in to visit him. When he saw them he began to
weep. His disciples said to him: "Lamp of Israel, pillar
of the right hand, mighty hammer! Wherefore weepest
thou?" He replied, "If I were being taken today before a
human king who is here today and tomorrow in the
grave; whose anger, if he is angry with one, does not
last forever; who, if he imprisons me, does not imprison
me forever, and who, if he puts me to death, does not
put me to everlasting death; and whom I can persuade
with words and bribe with money; even so I would
weep. Now that I am being taken before the supreme
King of Kings; the Holy One, blessed be He, who lives
and endures forever and ever; whose anger, if He is

angry with me, is an everlasting anger; who if he imprisons me, imprisons me forever; who if He puts me to death puts me to death forever; and whom I cannot persuade with words or bribe with money—nay more, when there are two ways before me, one leading to Paradise and the other to *Gehinnom,* and I do not know by which I shall be taken, shall I not weep?"

(Berachot 28b)

It once came to pass that Hillel[6] the elder was coming from a journey, and he heard a great cry in the city, and he said: "I am confident that this does not come from my house." Of him Scripture says: "He shall not be afraid of the evil tidings; his heart is steadfast trusting in the Lord" (Psalm 112:7).

(Berachot 60a)

Raba[7] said, "When man is led in for judgment (in the next world) he is asked: 'Did you deal faithfully? Did you fix times for learning? Did you engage in procreation? Did you hope for salvation?' . . . Yet even so, if 'the fear of the Lord is his treasure' (Isaiah 33:6) it will go well with him: if not, it will not."

(Shabbat 31a)

Rabbi Simeon b. Pazzi said in the name of Rabbi Joshua b. Levi in Bar Kappara's name: "If one sheds tears for a worthy man, the Holy One, Blessed be He, counts them and lays them up in His treasure house, for it is said: 'Thou countest my grievings: Put thou my tears into thy bottle; Are they not in thy book?' " (Psalm 56:9).

(Shabbat 105b)

"Blessed shalt thou be when thou comest in, and blessed shalt thou be when thou goest out" (Deuteronomy 28:3)—that thine exit from the world shall be as

thine entry therein: Just as thou enterest it without sin,
so mayest thou leave it without sin.

(*Baba Metzia* 107a)

Rabbi Simlai said: "Six hundred and thirteen commandments were given to Moses, 365 negative commandments, answering to the number of the days of the year,
and 248 positive commandments, answering to the
number of the members of man's body. Then David
came and reduced them to eleven (eleven commandments are found in Psalm 15). Then came Isaiah, and
reduced them to six. Then came Micah, and reduced
them to three (as is seen in the great saying of Micah
6:8). Then Isaiah came again, and reduced them to two,
as it is said, 'Keep ye justice and do righteousness.'
Then came Amos, and reduced them to one, as it is
said, 'Seek ye Me and live.' Or one may say, then came
Habakkuk (2:4) and reduced them to one, as it is said,
'The righteous shall live by his faith.' "

(*Makkot* 23b–24a)

Rabbi Jochanan said: "If a man's first wife dies, it is as if
the Temple were destroyed in his day." Rabbi Alexandri
said: "If a man's wife dies the world becomes dark for
him." Rabbi Samuel ben Nachman said: "For everything there is a substitute except for the wife of one's
youth."

(*Sanhedrin* 22a)

A king had a vineyard in which he employed many
laborers, one of whom demonstrated special aptitude
and skill. What did the king do? He took this laborer
from his work and strolled through the garden con-
versing with him. When the laborers came for their
wages in the evening, the skillful laborer also appeared
among them and he received a full day's wages from the
king. The other laborers were angry at this and protested. "We have labored the whole day while this

manhas worked but two hours; why does the king give
him the full wage, even as to us?" The king said to
them: "Why are you angry? Through his skill he has
done in two hours more than you have done all day."
So it iswith Rabbi Abin ben Hiyya.[8] In the twenty-eight
years of his life he has attained more in Torah than
others in a hundred years.

> *(Yerushalmi, Berachot* 2:8; *Ecclesiastes Rabbah* 6)

"And God saw everything which He had made, and
behold it was very good" (Genesis 1:31). Why does
death befall the righteous and not only the wicked? It
had to befall the righteous, too, or else the wicked might
have said, "The righteous live because they practice the
Law and good works: We will do so too," and they
would have fulfilled the commandments deceitfully,
and not for their own sake. Again, death befalls the
wicked, because they cause vexation to God. But when
they die, they cease to vex Him. Death befalls the
righteous, because all their life they have a struggle with
their evil inclination; when they die, they are at peace.

> *(Genesis Rabbah* 9:5–9)

❧ THE TWO SHIPS ❧

Two ships were once seen to be sailing near land. One
of them was going forth from the harbor, and the other
was coming into the harbor. Everyone was cheering the
outgoing ship, everyone was giving it a hearty sendoff.
But the incoming ship was scarcely noticed.

A wise man was looking at the two ships, and he said:
"I see here a paradox; for surely, people should not
rejoice at the ship leaving the harbor, since they know
not what destiny awaits it, what storms it may encounter, what dangers it may have to undergo. Rejoice
rather over the ship that has reached port safely and
brought back all its passengers in peace."

It is the way of the world that when a human being is
born, all rejoice; but when he dies, all sorrow. Rather
ought the opposite to be the case. No one can tell what
troubles await the child on its journey into manhood.
But when a man has lived and dies in peace, all should
rejoice, seeing that he has completed his journey, and is
departing this world with the imperishable crown of a
good name.

(*Midrash Rabbah Va-Yachel* 48:1–2)

❧ *VANITY OF HUMAN PLEASURE* ❧

A hungry fox was eyeing some luscious fruit in a
garden, but to his dismay, he could find no way to
enter. At last he discovered an opening through which,
he thought, he might possibly get in, but he soon found
that the hole was too small to admit his body. "Well,"
he thought, "if I fast three days I will be able to squeeze
through." He did so; and he now feasted to his heart's
delight on the grapes and all the other good things in
the orchard. But when he wanted to escape, he discovered that the opening had again become too small for
him. Again he had to fast three days and as he escaped
he said: "O garden, what have I now for all my labor
and cunning?"

So it is with man. Naked he comes into the world,
naked must he leave it. After all his labor he carries
nothing away with him except the good deeds he leaves
behind.

(*Midrash, Ecclesiastes Rabbah* 5:1)

Not merely should we be ready to receive the evil as
well as the good from God, but a man should rejoice
over sufferings more than over good, for if a man is in
prosperity all his life, his sins will not be forgiven him.
But they are forgiven him through sufferings. Rabbi
Eliezer b. Jacob quoted the verse, Proverbs 3:12,

"Whom God loves He chastens, even as the father chastens the son of whom he is fond." What causes the son to be loved by his father? Sufferings. Rabbi Meir quoted the verse, Deuteronomy 8:5, "As a father chastens his son, so God has chastened thee." God says, "Thou, Israel, knowest the deeds that thou hast done, and that the sufferings that I have brought upon thee are not in proportion to thy deeds." Rabbi Jose b. Judah said: "Beloved are sufferings before God, for the glory of God rests upon sufferers."

(*Sifre, Deuteronomy Va-Etchanan* 32).

Rabbi Simeon ben Yochai[9] says: "Chastisements are precious; for the Holy One blessed be He, gave three gifts to Israel that the nations of the world desire, and he gave them to Israel only through chastisements. They are: the Torah, and the land of Israel, and the world to come. Whence do we know this of the Torah? For it is written: 'Happy is the man whom Thou chastenest, O Lord, and teachest him out of Thy Torah' (Psalm 94:12). Whence do we know this of the land of Israel? For it is written: 'So the Lord thy God chasteneth thee' (Deuteronomy 18:5) and afterwards: 'The Lord thy God bringeth thee into a good land, a land of brooks of water, of fountains and depths, springing forth in valleys and hills.' Whence do we know this of the world to come? For it is written: 'For the commandment is a lamp, and the teaching is light, and reproofs of instruction are the way of life' (Proverbs 6:23). Which is the way that brings a man to the world to come? It is chastisement."

(*Sifra* on Deuteronomy 36:5)[10]

When Aaron heard of the death of his two sons, he "held his peace" (Leviticus 10:3); he acknowledged the justice of the Divine decree. With the righteous it is habitual to act thus. So did Abraham, when he said, "I am but dust and ashes" (Genesis 18:27); so did Jacob and David.

(*Sifra*)[11]

Rabbi Meir[12] sat discoursing on a Sabbath afternoon in the house of study. While he was there, his two sons died. What did their mother[13] do? She laid them upon the bed and spread a linen cloth over them. At the outgoing of the Sabbath Rabbi Meir came home and said to her, "Where are my sons?" She replied, "They went to the house of study." He said, "I did not see them there." She gave him the *Havdalah* cup, and he said again, "Where are my sons?" She said, "They went to another place, and now they have returned." She gave him to eat and he ate and recited the blessing. Then she said, "I have a question to ask you." He replied, "Ask it." She said, "Early today a man came here, and gave me something to keep for him; now he has come back to ask for it again. Shall we return it to him or not?" He replied, "He who has received something on deposit must surely return it to its owner." She replied, "Without your knowledge I would not return it." Then she took him by the hand, and brought him up to the bed, and took away the cloth, and he saw his sons lying dead upon the bed. Then he began to weep, and said about each, "O my son, my son; O my rabbi, my rabbi! My sons, as all men would say; rabbi, rabbi because they gave light to their father's face through their knowledge of the Law." Then his wife said to him, "Did you not say to me that one must return a deposit to its owner? Does it not say, 'The Lord gave, the Lord hath taken away, Blessed be the name of the Lord' " (Job 1:21)? Thus she comforted him and quieted his mind.

(*Midrash* on Proverbs 31:10)

"Teach us to number our days" (Psalm 90:12). Rabbi Joshua[14] said: "If we knew for certain the exact number of days in our lives we would repent before we died." Rabbi Eleazar[15] taught: "Repent one day before thy death." When his disciples asked: "Is there a man who knows when he will die?" he replied: "All the more reason for a man to repent today, lest he die tomorrow. Thus all the days of his life will be spent in penitence."

(Midrash on Psalm 110:16)[16]

🍂 THE MAN AND HIS THREE FRIENDS 🍂

A certain man had three friends, two of whom he loved dearly, but the other he lightly esteemed. It happened one day that the king commanded his presence at court, at which he was greatly alarmed and wished to procure an advocate. Accordingly he went to the two friends whom he loved. One flatly refused to accompany him; the other offered to go with him as far as the king's gate, but no farther. In his extremity he called upon the third friend whom he least esteemed, and he not only went willingly with him, but so ably defended him before the king that he was acquitted.

In like manner, every man has three friends when Death summons him to appear before his Creator. His first friend, whom he loves most, namely, his money, cannot go with him a single step; his second, relations and neighbors, can only accompany him to the grave, but cannot defend him before the Judge; while his third friend, whom he does not highly esteem—his good works—goes with him before the King, and obtains his acquittal.

(Pirke de Rabbi Eliezer)[17]

It is related that an ass-driver came to Rabbi Akiva[18] and said to him, "Rabbi, teach me the whole Torah all at once." He replied, "My son, Moses our teacher stayed on the Mount forty days and forty nights before he learned it, and you want me to teach you the whole of it at once! Still, my son, this is the basic principle of the Torah: 'What is hateful to yourself, do not to your fellow-man. If you wish that nobody should harm you

in connection with what belongs to you, you must not
harm him in that way; if you wish that nobody should
take away from you what is yours, do not take away
from another what is his.' " The man rejoined his
companions, and they journeyed until they came to a
field full of seedpods. His companions each took two,
but he took none. They continued their journey, and
came to a field full of cabbages. They each took two, but
he took none. They asked him why he had not taken
any, and he replied, "Thus did Rabbi Akiva teach me:
'What is hateful to yourself, do not to your fellow-man.
If you wish that nobody should take from you what is
yours, do not take from another what is his.' "

(*Abot de Rabbi Nathan*)[19]

With regard to the great bliss which the soul is to attain
in the world to come—there is no possibility of compre-
hending or of knowing it whilst we are in this world;
seeing that here beneath we are sensible only of that
which is good for the body. But with respect to the
celestial bliss, it is so exceedingly great, that all earthly
good can bear no comparison with it, except metaphor-
ically. So that truly to estimate the happiness of the soul
in the world to come by the happiness of the body in
this world, as for instance in eating or drinking, is
utterly impossible. This is what David meant in exclaim-
ing, "Oh how abundant is Thy goodness, which Thou
hast laid up for them that fear Thee" (Psalm 31:20).

(*Mishneh Torah* 8:6)[20]

O my God, the soul which Thou gavest me is pure;
Thou didst create it, Thou didst form it, Thou didst
breathe it into me. Thou preservest it within me, and
Thou wilt take it from me, but wilt restore it unto me
hereafter. So long as the soul is within me, I will give
thanks unto Thee, O Lord my God and God of my
fathers, Sovereign of all works, Lord of all souls! Blessed
art Thou, O Lord, who restorest souls unto the dead.

(From the Morning Service)[21]

Since my brother is gone my world is no more wide; it is a prison, and the earth is like shackles. He that upheld the glory of all things, how is it that his back is now burdened with dust? Because he is gone the sun is the companion of jackals, the moon is the brother of mourning since his death. Now shall all understand that heaven's host will fade and shrivel as a withering bud (all this shall vanish as a clod of earth, and yet the memory of his glory never shall grow old). When my brother went to the grave, I knew that all creation is but vanity.

(Moses b. Jacob Ibn Ezra,
dirge on the death of his brother)[22]

The soul is likened to the moon, and the sun is God, who is blessed, as it is written: "The Lord God is a sun and a shield" (Psalm 84:12). Now just as the moon, when it approaches the sun, its light becomes stronger above; even so the Divine soul, when it draws nearer to God, who is blessed, and forsakes pleasures and worldly affairs, its light becomes fuller, and it attains bliss; for the way of life is upward to the wise. But when it removes itself from God, who is blessed, and clings to the affairs of the body, making God's service subordinate, it becomes dark on the upper part, and only sheds its light from its lower part upon bodily and worldly things. This is the cause of its perdition with regards to spiritual matters which occasion and bring about its welfare. It is on account of this circumstance that our teachers of blessed memory tell us that the preservation and light of the soul depend on its being turned toward God's countenance, and that its perdition and death are caused by its removing itself from Him; as it is written: "Lo, they that go far from Thee shall perish" (Psalm 78:27).

(Manasseh ben Israel, *Nishmat Chayyim*)[23]

An old Saxon chieftain on a wintry day was reveling with his warriors in the banqueting hall, when he noticed a sparrow fly in at one door, hover a moment over the light and warmth of the hearth-fire, fly across the hall to the other door, and vanish into the night whence it came. "So seems the life of man," he exclaimed. "Out of the darkness we come, we enjoy for a while the warmth and sunshine of the world, and then again into darkness we lapse." This is strikingly beautiful, but heathen, gloomy, false. Man's life is not a journey from darkness to darkness. There is within us a Divine spark. We come from God, we go back to God. "The dust returneth to the earth, as it was, but the spirit returneth unto God who gave it." If we have lived justly, loved mercy, and walked in humility with God and man, then the end of our toil is not a flight into darkness; but to that life which is wholly a Sabbath-rest with God, peace everlasting.

(Hertz, *The Authorized Daily Prayer Book,* p. 1102)[24]

❦ *WHO HAS LIVED?* ❦

"And Jacob lived" (Genesis 47:28). Of how few men, asks a famous modern Jewish preacher, can we repeat a phrase like "And Jacob *lived*"? When many a man dies, a death-notice appears in the press. In reality, it is a life-notice; because but for it, the world would never have known that that man had ever been alive. Only he who has been a force for human goodness, and abides in hearts and souls made better by his presence during his pilgrimage on earth, can be said to have *lived*, only such a one is heir to immortality.

(Hertz, *The Pentateuch and Haftorahs*, p. 180)

❦ *A PLEDGE FROM THE LIVING* ❦

The father's heart beat no more. The kindly eye was closed forever. The son had stepped into his parent's shoes. He had undertaken the responsibilities for the honor of his house. And there at the open grave he stood in the presence of the whole congregation of friends and strangers and those who were to lead in the age after him, and there at the saddest moment of his life he recalled neither sorrow nor his loss, but his duty. As a real Jew he knew the holiness of the moment, and he framed his resolution in the words holiest to Jewish hearts; then he opened his lips and made a pledge, a holy promise: "*Yisgadal Veyisskadash Shmay Rabboh*, Lord God, I do not murmur against Thy decree, I am a child of Jewry. Lord God, hear my voice at this moment. As my father lived for Thee, as his life was dedicated to Thy glory and Thy name, so do I declare *Yisgadal Veyisskadash* that Thy great name may be magnified and sanctified as the promise for my future. So do I undertake to remember his fidelity, and never to forget my own duty."

This was the meaning of *Kaddish* in the times when Jews were Jewish. This is the meaning of the words today when said for mother and father. Not a prayer for the dead, but a pledge from the living; not a superstitious phrase, but a man's motto of life.

(Jung, *The Jewish Library—Third Series*)[25]

❧ *EVERYTHING IS FOR THE BEST* ❧

One way of reasoning is, "Whatever Heaven does is for the best." This means that even suffering and hardship are only apparently evil; in reality they are good. The surgeon amputates a muscle or a limb that has been injured in order to preserve the health of the rest of the body, and to save the person from death. Though this seems cruel, it is in reality an act of mercy, and meant for the good of the person upon whom it is performed. That patient does not love the surgeon any less because of what he has done to him; on the contrary he loves him all the more. In like manner, if a man were to realize that whatever the Holy One, Blessed be He, does to him, whether it affects his body or his possessions, is intended for his benefit, neither suffering nor hardship would lessen his love for God in any way, though he may little understand in what manner he is benefited. On the contrary, his love would become even more intense and fervent.

(M. C. Luzzatto)[26]

THE LOSS OF A MITZVAH

When Rabbi Abraham Mordecai, the last remaining son of Rabbi Yitzchak Meir (1799–1866), the Rebbe of Ger, died in 1855, a Chasid sought to comfort the father with the traditional words from Job: "The Lord hath given and the Lord hath taken" (Job 1:12). The Rebbe of Ger replied: "My grief comes not because I have lost my son to everlasting life, since this was God's will. My sorrow arises from the knowledge that I shall now lack the opportunity to perform the *mitzvah:* 'Ye shall teach them diligently to your children' " (Deuteronomy 6:7).

(Rabbi Yitzchak Meir Alter)[27]

DEATH AS HOMECOMING

Is death nothing but an obliteration, an absolute negation? The view of death is affected by our understanding of life. If life is sensed as a surprise, as a gift, defying explanation, then death ceases to be a radical, absolute negation of what life stands for. For both life and death are aspects of a greater mystery, the mystery of being, the mystery of creation. Over and above the preciousness of particular existence stands the marvel of its being related to the infinite mystery of being creation.

Death, then, is not simply man's coming to an end. It is also entering a beginning.

(Abraham J. Heschel)[28]

Chapter 13

Memorial Prayers

ASHKENAZI PRAYERS FOR MOURNERS

Mourner's *Kaddish*

The following *Kaddish* is said by a mourner, during the first eleven months after the death of his parents or on the anniversary of their deaths.

Mourner יִתְגַּדַּל וְיִתְקַדַּשׁ שְׁמֵהּ רַבָּא. בְּעָלְמָא דִי בְרָא

כִרְעוּתֵהּ, וְיַמְלִיךְ מַלְכוּתֵהּ, בְּחַיֵּיכוֹן וּבְיוֹמֵיכוֹן, וּבְחַיֵּי דְכָל בֵּית

יִשְׂרָאֵל. בַּעֲגָלָא וּבִזְמַן קָרִיב, וְאִמְרוּ, אָמֵן. Cong. אמן

Cong. and Mourner יְהֵא שְׁמֵהּ רַבָּא, מְבָרַךְ לְעָלַם וּלְעָלְמֵי

עָלְמַיָּא. Cong. אמן

Mourner יִתְבָּרַךְ, וְיִשְׁתַּבַּח, וְיִתְפָּאַר, וְיִתְרוֹמַם, וְיִתְנַשֵּׂא,

Cong. and Mourner וְיִתְהַדָּר וְיִתְעַלֶּה וְיִתְהַלָּל, שְׁמֵהּ דְּקֻדְשָׁא,

בְּרִיךְ הוּא.

Mourner לְעֵלָּא (וּלְעֵלָּא (During the Ten Days of Penitence, add:

מִן־כָּל־בִּרְכָתָא וְשִׁירָתָא. תֻּשְׁבְּחָתָא וְנֶחֱמָתָא. דַּאֲמִירָן בְּעָלְמָא.

וְאִמְרוּ, אָמֵן. Cong. אמן

155

Mourner יְהֵא שְׁלָמָא רַבָּא מִן שְׁמַיָּא, וְחַיִּים עָלֵינוּ וְעַל כָּל

יִשְׂרָאֵל, וְאִמְרוּ, אָמֵן׃ Cong. אמן

Mourner עשֶׂה שָׁלוֹם בִּמְרוֹמָיו, הוּא יַעֲשֶׂה שָׁלוֹם, עָלֵינוּ

וְעַל כָּל יִשְׂרָאֵל, וְאִמְרוּ אָמֵן׃ Cong. אמן

ENGLISH TRANSLATION

Mourner—Magnified and sanctified be His great name in the world which He hath created according to His will. May He establish His kingdom during your life and during your days, and during the life of all the house of Israel, even speedily and at a near time, and say ye, Amen.

Congregation and mourner—Let His great name be blessed forever and to all eternity.

Mourner—Blessed, praised and glorified, exalted, extolled and honored, magnified and lauded be the name of the Holy One, blessed be He; though He be high above all the blessings and hymns, praises and consolations, which are uttered in the world, and say ye, Amen.

Mourner—May there be abundant peace from heaven, and life for us and for all Israel, and say ye, Amen.

Mourner—He who maketh peace in His high places, may He make peace for us and for all Israel, and say ye, Amen.

ASHKENAZI TRANSLITERATION OF THE MOURNER'S *KADDISH*

Yisgaddal v'yiskaddash sh'mey rabboh
B'olmoh dee-v'ro chir-usey,
V'yamlich malchusey
B'chay-yeychon uv'yo-meychon
Uv'chay-yey de-chol beys yisro-eyl
Ba-agoloh uvizman koreev
V'imru omeyn.
Y'hey sh'mey rabboh m'vorach
L'olam ul'olmey olmah-yoh

Yisborach, v'yishtabach,
V'yispo-ar v'yisromam
V'yisnassey, v'yis-haddar
V'yis-alleh v'yis-hallal
Sh'mey de-kudshoh, b'reech hu
L'eyloh[1] min kol birchosoh v'shirosoh
Tush-b'chosoh v'nechemosoh
Daa-amiron b'olmoh
V'imru omeyn.
Y'hey sh'lomoh rabboh min sh'mah-yoh,
V'chay-im oleynu v'al kol yisro-eyl
V'imru omeyn.
O-seh sholom bimromov
Hu ya-aseh sholom
Oleynu v'al kol yisro-eyl
V'imru omeyn.

SEPHARDI TRANSLITERATION OF THE MOURNER'S *KADDISH*

Yitgaddal v'yitkaddasy sh'mey rabbah.
B'olmah dee-v'ra chiru-teh,
V'yamlich malchuteh.
B'cha-yechon uv'yo-meychon,
Uv'cha-yey de-chol beit yisra-el.
Ba-agalah uvizman kareev,
V'imru Amen.
Y'hey sh'mey rabbah m'vorach,
L'alam ul'olmey almah-yah.
Yitbarach v'yishtabach, v'yitpa-ar v'yitromam
V'yitnasseh, v'yit-haddar v'yit-alleh v'yit-hallal,
Sh'mey de kudshah b'reech hu.
L'eylah[1] min kol birchatah v'shiratah,
Tush-b'chatah v'nechematah,
Da-amiran b'olmah v'imru Amen.
Y'heh sh'lamah rabbah min sh'mayah,
V'cha-yim alenu, v'al kol yisra-el,
V'imru Amen.

O-seh shalom bimromav,
Hu ya-aseh shalom,
Alenu v'al kol yisra-el,
V'imru Amen.

Scholar's *Kaddish*

Kaddish to be said after reading lessons from the works of the rabbis.

Reader יִתְגַּדַּל וְיִתְקַדַּשׁ שְׁמֵהּ רַבָּא, בְּעָלְמָא דִי־בְרָא
כִרְעוּתֵהּ, וְיַמְלִיךְ מַלְכוּתֵהּ, בְּחַיֵּיכוֹן וּבְיוֹמֵיכוֹן, וּבְחַיֵּי דְכָל־בֵּית
יִשְׂרָאֵל, בַּעֲגָלָא וּבִזְמַן קָרִיב, וְאִמְרוּ אָמֵן. :Cong. אמן

Cong. and Reader יְהֵא שְׁמֵהּ רַבָּא, מְבָרַךְ לְעָלַם, וּלְעָלְמֵי
עָלְמַיָּא:

Reader יִתְבָּרַךְ וְיִשְׁתַּבַּח, וְיִתְפָּאַר, וְיִתְרוֹמַם, וְיִתְנַשֵּׂא,
Cong. and Reader .שְׁמֵהּ דְּקֻדְשָׁא וְיִתְהַדָּר, וְיִתְעַלֶּה, וְיִתְהַלָּל
During the Ten Days of Penitence,) לְעֵלָּא Reader .בְּרִיךְ הוּא
(add: מִן־כָּל־בִּרְכָתָא וְשִׁירָתָא, תֻּשְׁבְּחָתָא וְנֶחֱמָתָא, וּלְעֵלָּא
דַּאֲמִירָן בְּעָלְמָא, וְאִמְרוּ אָמֵן. :Cong. אמן

Reader עַל יִשְׂרָאֵל וְעַל רַבָּנָן, וְעַל תַּלְמִידֵיהוֹן, וְעַל כָּל
תַּלְמִידֵי תַלְמִידֵיהוֹן, וְעַל כָּל מָאן דְּעָסְקִין בְּאוֹרַיְתָא, דִּי
בְאַתְרָא הָדֵין, וְדִי בְכָל אֲתַר וַאֲתַר, יְהֵא, לְהוֹן וּלְכוֹן, שְׁלָמָא
רַבָּא, חִנָּא וְחִסְדָּא, וְרַחֲמִין, וְחַיִּין אֲרִיכִין, וּמְזוֹנָא רְוִחֵי,
וּפוּרְקָנָא מִן־קֳדָם אֲבוּהוֹן דִּבִשְׁמַיָּא וְאַרְעָא, וְאִמְרוּ אָמֵן. :Cong.
אמן

Reader יְהֵא שְׁלָמָא רַבָּא מִן שְׁמַיָּא, וְחַיִּים טוֹבִים, עָלֵינוּ
וְעַל כָּל יִשְׂרָאֵל, וְאִמְרוּ אָמֵן. :Cong. אמן

Reader עֹשֶׂה שָׁלוֹם בִּמְרוֹמָיו, הוּא יַעֲשֶׂה בְרַחֲמָיו שָׁלוֹם,
עָלֵינוּ וְעַל כָּל יִשְׂרָאֵל, וְאִמְרוּ אָמֵן. :Cong. אמן

ENGLISH TRANSLATION OF THE SCHOLAR'S *KADDISH*

Reader—Magnified and sanctified be His great name in the world which He hath created according to His will. May He establish His kingdom during your life and during your days, and during the life of all the house of Israel, even speedily and at a near time, and say ye, Amen.

Congregation and Reader—Let His great name be blessed forever and to all eternity.

Reader—Blessed, praised and glorified, exalted, extolled and honored, magnified and lauded be the name of the Holy One, blessed be He; though He be high above all the blessings and hymns, praises and consolations, which are uttered in the world, and say ye, Amen.

Unto Israel, and unto the rabbis, and unto their disciples, and unto all the disciples of their disciples, and unto all who engage in the study of the Law, in this or in any other place, unto them and unto you be abundant peace, grace, loving-kindness, mercy, long life, ample sustenance, and salvation from the Father who is in heaven, and say ye, Amen.

Reader—May there be abundant peace from heaven, and a happy life for us and for all Israel, and say ye, Amen.

Reader—He who maketh peace in his high places, may He in his mercy make peace for us and for all Israel, and say ye, Amen.

ASHKENAZI TRANSLITERATION OF THE SCHOLAR'S *KADDISH*

Yisgaddal v'yiskaddash sh'mey rabboh
B'olmoh dee-v'ro chir-usey,
V'yamlich malchusey
B'chay-yeychon uv'yo-mechon
Uvchay-yey de-chol beys yisro-eyl,
Ba-agoloh uvizman koreev,
V'imru omeyn.

Y'hey sh'mey rabboh m'vorach
L'olam ul'olmey olmah-yoh.
Yisborach v'yishtabach,
V'yispo-ar v'yisromam
V'yisnassey, v'yis-haddar,
V'yis-alleh v'yis-hallal
Sh'mey de-kudshoh b'reech hu
L'eyloh[1] min kol birchosoh v'shirosoh
Tush-b'chosoh v'nechemosoh
Daa-amiron b'olmoh,
V'imru omeyn.

Al yisro-eyl v'al rabbonon, v'al talmeedeyhon v'al kol
talmeedey salmeedey-hon, v'al kol mon de-oskeen
b'oraysoh dee b'ass-roh hoh-deyn v'dee b'chol assar
va-assar. Y'hey l'hon ul'chon sh'lomoh rabboh,
chinoh v'chisdoh, v'rachamin v'chayin arichin
um'zono r'vicho ufurkonoh, min kodom avuhon dee
vishmah-yoh v'imru omeyn.

Y'hey sh'lomoh rabboh, min sh'mah-yoh,
V'chay-yim tovim, oleynu v'al kol yisro-eyl
V'imru omeyn.
O-seh sholom bimromov
Hu b'rachamov ya-aseh sholom
Oleynu v'al kol yisro-eyl
V'imru omeyn.

SEPHARDI TRANSLITERATION OF THE SCHOLAR'S KADDISH

Yitgaddal v'yitkaddash sh'meh rabbah.
B'olmah dee-v'ra chiru-teh,
V'yamlich malchuteh,
B'cha-yechon uv'yo-meychon,
Uv'cha-yey de-chol beit yisra-el,
Ba-agalah uvizman kareev,
V'imru Amen.

Y'hey sh'mey rabbah m'vorach
L'alam ul'olmey almah-yah.
Yitbarach v'yishtabach, v'yitpa-ar v'yitromam
V'yitnasseh, v'yit-haddar v'yit-alleh v'yit-hallal,
Sh'mey de kudshah b'reech hu.
L'eylah[1] min kol birchata v'shiratah,
Tush-b'chatah v'nechematah,
Da-amiran b'olmah, v'imru Amen.
Al yisra-el v'al rabbanan, v'al talmeedeh-hon, v'al kol
    talmeedeh talmeedeh-hon, v'al kol man de-askin
    b'oraytah, dee b'atrah ha-den, v'dee b'chol atar va-
    atar.
Y'heh l'hon ul'chon, sh'lamah rabbah, china v'chisdah,
    v'rachamin
V'chayin arichin,
Um'zona r'vicha ufurkanah, min kodam avuhon dee
    vishmayah, v'imru Amen.
Y'hey sh'lamah rabbah, min sh'mayah, v'cha-yim
    tovim, alenu v'al kol yisra-el,
V'imru Amen.
O'seh shalom bimromav, hu b'rachamav ya-aseh sha-
    lom, alenu v'al kol yisra-el,
V'imru Amen.

Burial *Kaddish*

The following *Kaddish* is said by children after the burial
of a parent.

Mourners. יִתְגַּדַּל וְיִתְקַדַּשׁ שְׁמֵהּ רַבָּא בְּעָלְמָא דִּי הוּא עָתִיד
לְאִתְחַדָּתָא וּלְאַחֲיָאָה מֵתַיָּא, וּלְאַסָּקָא יָתְהוֹן לְחַיֵּי עָלְמָא,
וּלְמִבְנֵא קַרְתָּא דִּי־יְרוּשְׁלֵם, וּלְשַׁכְלֵל הֵיכְלֵהּ בְּגַוַּהּ, וּלְמֶעְקַר
פֻּלְחָנָא נֻכְרָאָה מֵאַרְעָא, וּלְאָתָבָא פֻּלְחָנָא דִּי־שְׁמַיָּא לְאַתְרֵהּ,
וְיַמְלַךְ קֻדְשָׁא בְּרִיךְ הוּא בְּמַלְכוּתֵהּ וִיקָרֵהּ, בְּחַיֵּיכוֹן וּבְיוֹמֵיכוֹן
וּבְחַיֵּי דִּי־כָל־בֵּית יִשְׂרָאֵל בַּעֲגָלָא וּבִזְמַן קָרִיב, וְאִמְרוּ אָמֵן:

יְהֵא שְׁמֵהּ רַבָּא מְבָרַךְ לְעָלַם וּלְעָלְמֵי .Cong. and Mourners
עָלְמַיָּא.

יִתְבָּרַךְ וְיִשְׁתַּבַּח וְיִתְפָּאַר וְיִתְרוֹמַם וְיִתְנַשֵּׂא .Mourners
וְיִתְהַדָּר וְיִתְעַלֶּה וְיִתְהַלָּל שְׁמֵהּ דִּי־קֻדְשָׁא, בְּרִיךְ הוּא, לְעֵלָּא
מִן־כָּל־בִּרְכָתָא וְשִׁירָתָא תֻּשְׁבְּחָתָא וְנֶחֱמָתָא דִּי־אֲמִירָן בְּעָלְמָא,
וְאִמְרוּ אָמֵן:

יְהִי שֵׁם יְיָ מְבוֹרָךְ מֵעַתָּה וְעַד עוֹלָם: .Congregation

יְהֵא שְׁלָמָא רַבָּא מִן־שְׁמַיָּא וְחַיִּים עָלֵינוּ וְעַל־כָּל־ .Mourners
יִשְׂרָאֵל, וְאִמְרוּ אָמֵן:

עֶזְרִי מֵעִם יְיָ עֹשֵׂה שָׁמַיִם וָאָרֶץ: .Congregation

עֹשֶׂה שָׁלוֹם בִּמְרוֹמָיו הוּא יַעֲשֶׂה שָׁלוֹם עָלֵינוּ וְעַל־ .Mourners
כָּל־יִשְׂרָאֵל, וְאִמְרוּ אָמֵן:

ENGLISH TRANSLATION

Mourners—May His great name be magnified and sanctified in the world that is to be created anew, where He will
revive the dead and raise them up unto life eternal; will
rebuild the city of Jerusalem, and establish His Temple in the
midst thereof; and will uproot all alien worship from the
earth and restore the worship of the true God. O may the
Holy One, blessed be He, reign in His sovereignty and glory
during your life and during your days, and during the life of
all the house of Israel, even speedily and at a near time, and
say ye, Amen.

Congregation and mourners—Let His great name be
blessed forever and to all eternity.

Mourners—Blessed, praised and glorified, exalted, extolled and honored, magnified and lauded be the name of
the Holy One, blessed be He; though He be high above all

blessings and hymns, praises and consolations which are uttered in the world, and say ye, Amen.

Congregation—Let the name of the Lord be blessed from this time forth and forevermore.

Mourners—May there be abundant peace from heaven, and life for us and for all Israel, and say ye, Amen.

Congregation—My help is from the Lord, who made heaven and earth.

Mourners—He who maketh peace in His high places, may He make peace for us and for all Israel, and say ye, Amen.

ASHKENAZI TRANSLITERATION OF THE BURIAL *KADDISH*

Yisgaddal v'yiskaddash sh'mey rabboh
B'olmoh dee hu osid l'ischaddosoh ul'acha-yo-oh mey-sayoh
ul'assokoh yos-hon l'cha-yey olmoh. Ul'mivney kartoh dee
y'rushleym ul'shachleyl heych-ley b'gavah ul'meh-ekar
polchonoh nuchrohoh mey-ar-oh v'la-asovoh polchonoh
dee-sh'mayoh l'asrey v'yimlach kudshoh b'reech hu
b'malchoosey vee-korey

B'chay-yechon uv'yo-mechon
U'vcha-yey de-chol beys yisro-eyl
Ba-agoloh uvizman koreev
V'imru omeyn.
Y'hey sh'mey rabboh m'vorach
L'olam ul'olmey olmah-yoh
Yisborach v'yishtabbach
V'yispoar v'yisromam
V'yisnassey v'yis-haddar
V'yis-alleh v'yis-hallal
Sh'mey de-kudshoh b'reech hu
L'eyloh[1] min kol birchosoh v'shirosoh
Tush-b'chosoh v'nechemosoh
Daameeron b'olmoh

V'imru omeyn.
Y'hey sh'lomoh rabboh min sh'mayoh
V'chay-yeem oleynu v'al kol yisro-el
V'imru omeyn.
O-seh sholom bimromov
Hu ya-aseh sholom
Oleynu v'al kol yisro-eyl
V'imru omeyn.

SEPHARDI TRANSLITERATION OF THE BURIAL KADDISH

Yitgaddal v'yitkaddash sh'meh rabbah,
b'olmah diy hu atid le-it chadata,
ul'achaya'ah metaya, ulassaka
yat-hon lechayey olma, ulmivney
karta diy yerushleym, ulshachleyl
heychley begavah, ulme'kar polchana
nuchra'a mey'ara, vela'atava polchana
diy shmaya le'atrey, veyimlach kudsha
berich hu bemalchutey viykarey,
bechayeychon uveyomeychon, uvechayyey
diy chol bet yisrael, ba'agala uvizman
kareev ve'imru Amen. Y'hey sh'mey rabbah m'vorach,
L'alam ul'olmey almah-yah.
Yitbarach v'yishtabach, v'yitpa-ar v'yitromam
V'yitnasseh, v'yit-haddar v'yit-alleh v'yit-hallal,
Sh'mey de kudshah b'reech hu.
L'eylah[1] min kol birchatah v'shiratah,
Tush-b'chatah v'nechematah,
Da-amiran b'olmah, v'imru Amen.
Y'heh sh'lamah rabbah min sh'mayah,
V'cha-yim alenu v'al kol yisra-el,
V'imru Amen.
O'seh shalom bimromav,
Hu ya-aseh shalom,
Alenu v'al kol yisra-el,
Vimru Amen.

SEPHARDI PRAYERS FOR MOURNERS

Mourner's *Kaddish*

יִתְגַּדַּל וְיִתְקַדַּשׁ שְׁמֵיהּ רַבָּא (אמן): בְּעָלְמָא דִּי־בְרָא
כִרְעוּתֵיהּ, וְיַמְלִיךְ מַלְכוּתֵיהּ, וְיַצְמַח פּוּרְקָנֵיהּ, וִיקָרֵב מְשִׁיחֵיהּ
(אמן): בְּחַיֵּיכוֹן וּבְיוֹמֵיכוֹן וּבְחַיֵּי דְכָל־בֵּית יִשְׂרָאֵל בַּעֲגָלָא וּבִזְמַן
קָרִיב וְאִמְרוּ אָמֵן:

יְהֵא שְׁמֵיהּ רַבָּא מְבָרַךְ, לְעָלַם לְעָלְמֵי עָלְמַיָּא יִתְבָּרַךְ:
וְיִשְׁתַּבַּח, וְיִתְפָּאַר, וְיִתְרוֹמַם, וְיִתְנַשֵּׂא, וְיִתְהַדָּר, וְיִתְעַלֶּה,
וְיִתְהַלָּל, שְׁמֵיהּ דְּקוּדְשָׁא בְּרִיךְ הוּא: לְעֵילָא מִן כָּל־בִּרְכָתָא,
שִׁירָתָא, תֻּשְׁבְּחָתָא, וְנֶחֱמָתָא, דַּאֲמִירָן בְּעָלְמָא, וְאִמְרוּ אָמֵן:
יְהֵא שְׁלָמָא רַבָּא מִן שְׁמַיָּא (חיים), חַיִּים, וְשָׂבָע, וִישׁוּעָה,
וְנֶחָמָה, וְשֵׁיזָבָה, וּרְפוּאָה, וּגְאוּלָה, וּסְלִיחָה, וְכַפָּרָה, וְרֶוַח,
וְהַצָּלָה, לָנוּ, וּלְכָל־עַמּוֹ יִשְׂרָאֵל, וְאִמְרוּ אָמֵן: עֹשֶׂה שָׁלוֹם
בִּמְרוֹמָיו, הוּא בְרַחֲמָיו, יַעֲשֶׂה שָׁלוֹם עָלֵינוּ, וְעַל כָּל־יִשְׂרָאֵל
וְאִמְרוּ אָמֵן:

ENGLISH TRANSLATION

Magnified and sanctified be His great name (Amen) in the world which He hath created according to His will. May He establish His kingdom, cause His salvation to spring forth and hasten the coming of His anointed (Amen) in your lifetime and in your days, and in the lifetime of the whole house of Israel, speedily and at a near time, and say ye, Amen.

May His great name be blessed forever and ever. Lauded and glorified, exalted and extolled, honored, magnified and praised be the name of the Holy One, blessed be He; high though He be above all blessings, hymns, praises and consolations that are uttered in the world, and say ye, Amen.

May abundant peace from heaven with life, plenty, salvation, consolation, deliverance, health, redemption, pardon, expiation, enlargement, and freedom be granted to us and all His people Israel, and say ye, Amen.

May He who maketh peace in His high heavens through His infinite mercy grant peace unto us and unto all Israel, and say ye, Amen.

TRANSLITERATION OF THE SEPHARDI MOURNER'S *KADDISH*

Yitgaddal v'yitkaddash sh'meh rabbah (Amen).
B'olmah dee-v'ra chiru-teh,
V'yamlich malchuteh,
V'yatzmach Purkaneh.
Vekarev M'shicheh (Amen).
B'cha-yechon uv'yo-meychon,
Uv'cha-yey de-chol beit Yisra-el,
Ba-agalah uvizman kareev,
V'imru Amen.
Y'hey sh'mey rabbah m'varach
L'alam L'olmey almah-yah
Yitbarach.
V'yishtabach. V'yitpa-ar. V'yitromam.
V'yitnasseh, V'yit-hadar. V'yit-alleh. V'yit-hallal.
Sh'mey de-kudshah B'reech Hu.
L'eylah[1] min kol birchatah. Shiratah.
Tush-b'chatah v'nechematah.
Da-amiran b'olmah. V'imru Amen.
Y'hey sh'lamah rabbah min sh'mayah. Cha-yim.
    V'savah. Veeshuah.
V'nechamah. V'sheysavah. U'refuah. U'g'ulah.
    U's'lichah. V'chaparah.
V'revach. V'hatzalah. Lanu. Ul'chol amo Yisra-el.
    V'imru Amen.
O'seh Shalom bimromav. Hu B'rachamav. Ya-aseh
    shalom alenu.
V'al kol Yisra-el V'imru Amen.

Scholar's *Kaddish*

יִתְגַּדַּל וְיִתְקַדַּשׁ שְׁמֵיהּ רַבָּא (אמן)׃ בְּעָלְמָא דִי־בְרָא
כִרְעוּתֵיהּ, וְיַמְלִיךְ מַלְכוּתֵיהּ, וְיַצְמַח פּוּרְקָנֵיהּ, וִיקָרֵב מְשִׁיחֵיהּ
(אמן)׃ בְּחַיֵּיכוֹן וּבְיוֹמֵיכוֹן וּבְחַיֵּי דְכָל־בֵּית יִשְׂרָאֵל בַּעֲגָלָא וּבִזְמַן
קָרִיב וְאִמְרוּ אָמֵן׃

יְהֵא שְׁמֵיהּ רַבָּא מְבָרַךְ, לְעָלַם לְעָלְמֵי עָלְמַיָּא יִתְבָּרַךְ׃
וְיִשְׁתַּבַּח, וְיִתְפָּאַר, וְיִתְרוֹמַם, וְיִתְנַשֵּׂא, וְיִתְהַדָּר, וְיִתְעַלֶּה,
וְיִתְהַלָּל, שְׁמֵיהּ דְּקוּדְשָׁא בְּרִיךְ הוּא׃ לְעֵילָא מִן כָּל־בִּרְכָתָא,
שִׁירָתָא, תִּשְׁבְּחָתָא, וְנֶחֱמָתָא, דַּאֲמִירָן בְּעָלְמָא, וְאִמְרוּ אָמֵן׃

עַל יִשְׂרָאֵל, וְעַל רַבָּנָן, וְעַל תַּלְמִידֵהוֹן, וְעַל כָּל־תַּלְמִידֵי
תַלְמִידֵהוֹן דְּעָסְקִין בְּאוֹרַיְתָא קַדִּישְׁתָּא, דִּי בְּאַתְרָא הָדֵין, וְדִי
בְכָל־אֲתַר וַאֲתַר, יְהֵא לְנָא וּלְהוֹן, חִנָּא, וְחִסְדָּא, וְרַחֲמֵי, מִן
קֳדָם מָארֵיהּ שְׁמַיָּא וְאַרְעָא, וְאִמְרוּ אָמֵן׃

יְהֵא שְׁלָמָא רַבָּא מִן שְׁמַיָּא (חיים), חַיִּים, וְשָׂבָע, וִישׁוּעָה,
וְנֶחָמָה, וְשֵׁיזָבָה, וּרְפוּאָה, וּגְאוּלָה, וּסְלִיחָה, וְכַפָּרָה, וְרֶוַח,
וְהַצָּלָה, לָנוּ, וּלְכָל־עַמּוֹ יִשְׂרָאֵל, וְאִמְרוּ אָמֵן׃ עֹשֶׂה שָׁלוֹם
בִּמְרוֹמָיו, הוּא בְרַחֲמָיו, יַעֲשֶׂה שָׁלוֹם עָלֵינוּ, וְעַל כָּל־יִשְׂרָאֵל
וְאִמְרוּ אָמֵן׃

ENGLISH TRANSLATION

May His great name be exalted, and sanctified throughout the world which He created according to His will; may
He establish His kingdom, cause His redemption to spring
forth, and hasten the advent of His anointed, in your
lifetime, and in your days, and in the lifetime of the whole
house of Israel, speedily, and at a near time, and say ye,
Amen.

May His great name be blessed and glorified forever
and ever. May His hallowed name be praised, glorified,
exalted, magnified, honored, and most excellently adored;
blessed is He, far exceeding all blessings, hymns, praises,
and consolations that can be uttered in the world, and say
ye, Amen.

Unto Israel, their rabbis, their disciples and all their
successors, who diligently study the Law, in this, and in
every other place; may there be grace, favor and mercy, from
the Lord of heaven and earth, both to them and us, and say
ye, Amen.

May the fullness of peace from heaven, with life,
plenty, salvation, consolation, deliverance, health, redemption, pardon, expiation, enlargement, and freedom, be
granted unto us, and to all His people Israel, and say ye,
Amen. May He who establisheth peace in His high places,
bestow, through His infinite mercy, peace on us and on all
Israel, and say ye, Amen.

Burial *Kaddish*

יִתְגַּדַּל וְיִתְקַדַּשׁ שְׁמֵהּ רַבָּא (אמן), דְּהוּא עָתִיד לְחַדָּתָא
עָלְמָא, וּלְאַחָאָה מֵתַיָּא, וּלְשַׁכְלָלָא הֵיכְלָא, וּלְמִפְרַק חַיַּיָּא,
וּלְמִבְנֵי קַרְתָּא דִירוּשְׁלֵם, וּלְמֶעֱקַר פֻּלְחָנָא דֶאֱלִילַיָּא מֵאַרְעָא,
וּלְאָתָבָא פֻּלְחָנָא יַקִּירָא דִשְׁמַיָּא לְהַדְרֵהּ וְזִיוֵהּ וִיקָרֵהּ (אמן):
בְּחַיֵּיכוֹן וּבְיוֹמֵכוֹן וּבְחַיֵּי דְכָל־בֵּית יִשְׂרָאֵל, בַּעֲגָלָא וּבִזְמַן קָרִיב,
וְאִמְרוּ אָמֵן:

יְהֵא שְׁמֵהּ רַבָּא מְבָרַךְ, לְעָלַם לְעָלְמֵי עָלְמַיָּא יִתְבָּרַךְ:
וְיִשְׁתַּבַּח וְיִתְפָּאַר וְיִתְרוֹמַם וְיִתְנַשֵּׂא וְיִתְהַדָּר וְיִתְעַלֶּה וְיִתְהַלָּל
שְׁמֵהּ דְּקֻדְשָׁא, בְּרִיךְ הוּא (אמן), לְעֵלָּא מִן כָּל־בִּרְכָתָא,
שִׁירָתָא, תֻּשְׁבְּחָתָא, וְנֶחֱמָתָא, דַּאֲמִירָן בְּעָלְמָא וְאִמְרוּ אָמֵן:
תִּתְכְּלֵי חַרְבָּא, וְכַפְנָא, וּמוֹתָנָא, וּמַרְעִין בִּישִׁין, יַעֲדֵי מִנֶּנָּא

וּמִנְכוֹן וּמֵעַל עַמֵּהּ יִשְׂרָאֵל, וְאִמְרוּ אָמֵן:

יְהֵא שְׁלָמָא רַבָּא מִן שְׁמַיָּא (חיים), חַיִּים, וְשָׂבָע, וִישׁוּעָה,

וְנֶחָמָה, וְשֵׁיזָבָא, וּרְפוּאָה, וּגְאוּלָה, וּסְלִיחָה וְכַפָּרָה, וְרֶוַח

וְהַצָּלָה, לָנוּ וּלְכָל עַמּוֹ יִשְׂרָאֵל וְאִמְרוּ אָמֵן: עוֹשֶׂה שָׁלוֹם

בִּמְרוֹמָיו הוּא בְּרַחֲמָיו, יַעֲשֶׂה שָׁלוֹם עָלֵינוּ, וְעַל כָּל יִשְׂרָאֵל

וְאִמְרוּ אָמֵן:

ENGLISH TRANSLATION

May His great name be blessed forever and ever. Lauded and glorified, exalted and extolled, honored, magnified and praised be the name of the Holy One, blessed be He; high though He be above all blessings, hymns, praises, and consolations that are uttered in the world, and say ye, Amen. May the sword, famine, and pestilence be withheld and may He remove evil afflictions from us and from all His people Israel, and say ye, Amen.

May abundant peace from heaven with life, plenty, salvation, consolation, deliverance, health, redemption, pardon, expiation, enlargement, and freedom be granted to us and all His people Israel, and say ye, Amen.

May He who maketh peace in His high heavens through His infinite mercy grant peace unto us and unto all Israel, and say ye, Amen.

Magnified and sanctified be His great name (Amen), who will hereafter renew the world, quicken the dead, establish the temple, save the living, build up the city of Jerusalem, root out idolatry from the earth, and restore the worship of the glory of heaven to its beauty, splendor, and glory (Amen); in your lifetime and in your days and in the lifetime of the whole house of Israel, speedily and at a near time, and say ye, Amen.

ASHKENAZI PRAYERS IN MEMORY
OF LOVED ONES

A Memorial Prayer for an Adult

אֵל מָלֵא רַחֲמִים שׁוֹכֵן בַּמְּרוֹמִים אֱלוֹהַּ סְלִיחוֹת חַנּוּן
וְרַחוּם אֶרֶךְ אַפַּיִם וְרַב חֶסֶד, הַמּוֹצֵא כַפָּרַת פֶּשַׁע וְהַקָרְבַת יֶשַׁע
וּמְנוּחָה נְכוֹנָה תַּחַת כַּנְפֵי הַשְּׁכִינָה בְּמַעֲלוֹת קְדוֹשִׁים וּטְהוֹרִים
כְּזֹהַר הָרָקִיעַ מַזְהִירִים, אֶת נִשְׁמַת פּ״ב״פ שֶׁהָלַךְ (שֶׁהָלְכָה)
לְעוֹלָמוֹ (לְעוֹלָמָה), אָנָּא בַּעַל הָרַחֲמִים זָכְרָה-לוֹ (לָה) לְטוֹבָה
כָּל זְכִיּוֹתָיו (זְכִיּוֹתֶיהָ) וְצִדְקוֹתָיו (וְצִדְקוֹתֶיהָ) בְּאַרְצוֹת הַחַיִּים,
וּפְתַח לוֹ (לָה) שַׁעֲרֵי צֶדֶק וְאוֹרָה שַׁעֲרֵי חֶמְלָה וַחֲנִינָה, בְּסֵתֶר
כְּנָפֶיךָ תַּסְתִּירֵהוּ (תַּסְתִּירֶהָ) לְעוֹלָמִים, וּצְרוֹר בִּצְרוֹר הַחַיִּים אֶת
נִשְׁמָתוֹ (נִשְׁמָתָה), יְיָ הוּא נַחֲלָתוֹ (נַחֲלָתָה), וְיָנוּחַ (וְתָנוּחַ)
בְּשָׁלוֹם עַל מִשְׁכָּבוֹ (מִשְׁכָּבָהּ) וְנֹאמַר אָמֵן:

ENGLISH TRANSLATION

O Lord, who art full of compassion, who dwellest on
high; God of forgiveness, who art merciful, slow to anger
and abounding in loving-kindness, grant pardon of transgressions, speedy salvation, and perfect rest beneath the
shadow of Thy Divine Presence, in the exalted places among
the holy and pure, who shine as the brightness of the
firmament, to . . . who hath gone to his [her] eternal home.
We beseech Thee, O Lord of compassion, remember unto
him [her] for good all the meritorious and pious deeds which
he [she] wrought while on earth. Open unto him [her] the
gates of righteousness and light, the gates of pity and grace.
O shelter him [her] forevermore under the cover of Thy
wings; and let his [her] soul be bound up in the bond of
eternal life. The Lord be his [her] inheritance; may he [she]
rest in peace. And let us say, Amen. (End with Concluding
Prayer, p. 177.)

Prayer to be Recited on Visiting the Grave
of a Relative

יְיָ מָה־אָדָם וַתֵּדָעֵהוּ בֶּן־אֱנוֹשׁ וַתְּחַשְּׁבֵהוּ: אָדָם לַהֶבֶל דָּמָה
יָמָיו כְּצֵל עוֹבֵר: בַּבֹּקֶר יָצִיץ וְחָלָף לָעֶרֶב יְמוֹלֵל וְיָבֵשׁ: לִמְנוֹת
יָמֵינוּ כֵּן הוֹדַע וְנָבִיא לְבַב חָכְמָה: שְׁמָר־תָּם וּרְאֵה יָשָׁר כִּי
אַחֲרִית לְאִישׁ שָׁלוֹם: אַךְ־אֱלֹהִים יִפְדֶּה נַפְשִׁי מִיַּד שְׁאוֹל כִּי
יִקָּחֵנִי סֶלָה: כָּלָה שְׁאֵרִי וּלְבָבִי צוּר לְבָבִי וְחֶלְקִי אֱלֹהִים
לְעוֹלָם: וְיָשֹׁב הֶעָפָר עַל־הָאָרֶץ כְּשֶׁהָיָה וְהָרוּחַ תָּשׁוּב אֶל־
הָאֱלֹהִים אֲשֶׁר נְתָנָהּ: אֲנִי בְּצֶדֶק אֶחֱזֶה פָנֶיךָ אֶשְׂבְּעָה בְהָקִיץ
תְּמוּנָתֶךָ:

ENGLISH TRANSLATION

Lord, what is man, that Thou regardest him? Or the son of man, that Thou takest account of him? Man is like to vanity; his days are as a shadow that passeth away. In the morning he flourisheth, and sprouteth afresh; in the evening he is cut down and withereth. So teach us to number our days that we may get us a heart of wisdom. Mark the innocent man, and behold the upright: For the latter end of that man is peace. But God will redeem my soul from the grasp of the grave; for He will receive me. My flesh and my heart fail: but God is the strength of my heart and my portion for ever. And the dust returneth to the earth as it was, but the spirit returneth unto God who gave it. I shall behold Thy face in righteousness; I shall be satisfied, when I awake, with Thy likeness. Amen. (End with Concluding Prayer, p. 177.)

In Memory of a Father

יִזְכּוֹר אֱלֹהִים נִשְׁמַת אָבִי מוֹרִי . . . שֶׁהָלַךְ לְעוֹלָמוֹ. אָנָּא
תְּהִי נַפְשׁוֹ צְרוּרָה בִּצְרוֹר הַחַיִּים. וּתְהִי מְנוּחָתוֹ כָּבוֹד. שְׁבַע
שְׂמָחוֹת אֶת־פָּנֶיךָ. נְעִימוֹת בִּימִינְךָ נֶצַח. אָמֵן:

ENGLISH TRANSLATION

May God remember the soul of my respected fa-
ther . . . who has passed to his eternal rest. May his soul be
bound up in the bond of life, a living blessing in our midst,
Amen. (End with Concluding Prayer, p. 177.)

ASHKENAZI TRANSLITERATION

Yiz-kor e-lo-heem nish-mas avee mo-ree . . . sheh-
ho-lach l'o-lo-moh O-no t'hee naf-sho tz'ru-ro bi-tz'ror ha-
cha-yim, u-s'-hee m'nu-cho-so ko-vod, so-va s'mo-chos es
po-ne-cho, n'ee-mos bee-meen-cho ne-tzah. Omayn.

In Memory of a Mother

יִזְכּוֹר אֱלֹהִים נִשְׁמַת אִמִּי מוֹרָתִי . . שֶׁהָלְכָה לְעוֹלָמָהּ.
אָנָּא תְּהִי נַפְשָׁהּ צְרוּרָה בִּצְרוֹר הַחַיִּים. וּתְהִי מְנוּחָתָהּ כָּבוֹד.
שְׁבַע שְׂמָחוֹת אֶת־פָּנֶיךָ. נְעִימוֹת בִּימִינְךָ נֶצַח. אָמֵן:

ENGLISH TRANSLATION

May God remember the soul of my revered mother . . .
who hath gone to her repose. May her soul be bound up in
the bond of life. May her rest be glorious, with fullness of joy
in Thy presence, and bliss forevermore at Thy right hand.
Amen. (End with Concluding Prayer, p. 177.)

ASHKENAZI TRANSLITERATION

Yiz-kor e-lo-heem nish-mas imee mo-ro-see . . . sheh-ho-lacho l'o-lo-moh O-no t'hee naf-sho tz'ru-ro bi-tz'ror ha-cha-yim, u-s'-hee m'nu-cho-so ko-vod, so-va s'mo-chos es po-ne-cho, n'ee-mos bee-meen-cho ne-tzah. Omayn.

In Memory of a Husband

יִזְכּוֹר אֱלֹהִים נִשְׁמַת נַעֲלִי . . . שֶׁהָלַךְ לְעוֹלָמוֹ. אָנָּא תְּהִי
נַפְשׁוֹ צְרוּרָה בִּצְרוֹר הַחַיִּים. וּתְהִי מְנוּחָתוֹ כָּבוֹד. שֹׂבַע שְׂמָחוֹת
אֶת־פָּנֶיךָ. נְעִימוֹת בִּימִינְךָ נֶצַח. אָמֵן:

ENGLISH TRANSLATION

May God remember the soul of my beloved husband . . . who hath gone to his repose. May his soul be bound up in the bond of life. May his rest be glorious, with fullness of joy in Thy presence, and bliss forevermore at Thy right hand. Amen. (End with Concluding Prayer, p. 177.)

ASHKENAZI TRANSLITERATION

Yiz-kor e-lo-heem nish-mas bah-lee . . . sheh-ho-lach l'o-lo-moh O-no t'hee naf-sho tz'ru-ro bi-tz'ror ha-cha-yim, u-s'-hee m'nu-cho-so ko-vod, so-va s'mo-chos es po-ne-cho, n'ee-mos bee-meen-cho ne-tzah. Omayn.

In Memory of a Wife

יִזְכּוֹר אֱלֹהִים נִשְׁמַת אִשְׁתִּי . . . שֶׁהָלְכָה לְעוֹלָמָהּ. אָנָּא
תְּהִי נַפְשָׁהּ צְרוּרָה בִּצְרוֹר הַחַיִּים. וּתְהִי מְנוּחָתָהּ כָּבוֹד. שֹׂבַע
שְׂמָחוֹת אֶת־פָּנֶיךָ. נְעִימוֹת בִּימִינְךָ נֶצַח. אָמֵן:

May God remember the soul of my beloved wife . . .
who has gone to her repose. May her soul be bound up in
the bond of life. May her rest be glorious with fullness in Thy
presence and bliss forevermore at Thy right hand, Amen.
(End with Concluding Prayer, p. 177.)

ASHKENAZI TRANSLITERATION

Yiz-kor e-lo-heem nish-mas ish-tee . . . sheh-ho-lacho
l'o-lo-moh O-no t'hee naf-sho tz'ru-ro bi-tz'ror ha-cha-yim,
u-s'-hee m'nu-cho-so ko-vod, so-va s'mo-chos es po-ne-cho,
n'ee-mos bee-meen-cho ne-tzah. Omayn.

In Memory of a Son

יִזְכּוֹר אֱלֹהִים נִשְׁמַת בְּנִי ... שֶׁהָלַךְ לְעוֹלָמוֹ. אָנָּא תְּהִי
נַפְשׁוֹ צְרוּרָה בִּצְרוֹר הַחַיִּים. וּתְהִי מְנוּחָתוֹ כָּבוֹד. שָׂבַע שְׂמָחוֹת
אֶת־פָּנֶיךָ. נְעִימוֹת בִּימִינְךָ נֶצַח. אָמֵן:

ENGLISH TRANSLATION

May God remember the soul of my beloved son . . .
who hath gone to his repose. May his soul be bound up in
the bond of life. May his rest be glorious, with fullness of joy
in Thy presence, and bliss forevermore at Thy right hand.
Amen. (End with Concluding Prayer, p 177.)

ASHKENAZI TRANSLITERATION

Yiz-kor e-lo-heem nish-mas b'nee . . . sheh-ho-lach
l'o-lo-moh O-no t'hee naf-sho tz'ru-ro bi-tz'ror ha-cha-yim,
u-s'-hee m'nu-cho-so ko-vod, so-va s'mo-chos es po-ne-cho,
n'ee-mos bee-meen-cho ne-tzah. Omayn.

In Memory of a Daughter

יִזְכּוֹר אֱלֹהִים נִשְׁמַת בִּתִּי . . . שֶׁהָלְכָה לְעוֹלָמָהּ. אָנָּא תְּהִי
נַפְשָׁהּ צְרוּרָה בִּצְרוֹר הַחַיִּים. וּתְהִי מְנוּחָתָהּ כָּבוֹד. שְׂבַע
שְׂמָחוֹת אֶת־פָּנֶיךָ. נְעִימוֹת בִּימִינְךָ נֶצַח. אָמֵן:

ENGLISH TRANSLATION

May God remember the soul of my beloved daughter
. . . who hath gone to her repose. May her soul be bound up
in the bond of life. May her rest be glorious, with fullness of
joy in Thy presence, and bliss forevermore at Thy right
hand. Amen. (End with Concluding Prayer, p.177.)

ASHKENAZI TRANSLITERATION

Yiz-kor e-lo-heem nish-mas bi-ti . . . sheh-ho-lah a
l'o-lo-mo. O-no t'hee naf-sho tz'ru-ro bi-tz'ror ha'cha'ygim,
u-s'-hee m'nu-ho-so ko-vod, so-va s'mo-chos es po-ne-cho,
n'ee-mos bee-meen-ho ne-tzah. Omayn.

In Memory of a Brother

יִזְכּוֹר אֱלֹהִים נִשְׁמַת אָחִי . . . בֶּן . . . שֶׁהָלַךְ לְעוֹלָמוֹ. אָנָּא
תְּהִי נַפְשׁוֹ צְרוּרָה בִּצְרוֹר הַחַיִּים. וּתְהִי מְנוּחָתוֹ כָּבוֹד. שְׂבַע
שְׂמָחוֹת אֶת־פָּנֶיךָ. נְעִימוֹת בִּימִינְךָ נֶצַח. אָמֵן:

ENGLISH TRANSLATION

May God remember the soul of my beloved brother . . .
who hath gone to his repose. May his soul be bound up in
the bond of life. May his rest be glorious, with fullness of joy
in Thy presence, and bliss forevermore at Thy right hand.
Amen. (End with Concluding Prayer, p. 177.)

Yiz-kor e-lo-heem nish-mas ah-chee . . . sheh-ho-lach
l'o-lo-moh O-no t'hee naf-sho tz'ru-ro bi-tz'ror ha-cha-yim,
u-a'-hee m'nu-cho-so ko-vod, so-va s'mo-chos es po-ne-cho,
n'ee-mos bee-meen-cho ne-tzah. Omayn.

In Memory of a Sister

יִזְכּוֹר אֱלֹהִים נִשְׁמַת אֲחוֹתִי . . . בַּת . . . שֶׁהָלְכָה לְעוֹלָמָהּ.
אָנָּא תְּהִי נַפְשָׁהּ צְרוּרָה בִּצְרוֹר הַחַיִּים. וּתְהִי מְנוּחָתָהּ כָּבוֹד.
שֹׂבַע שְׂמָחוֹת אֶת פָּנֶיךָ. נְעִימוֹת בִּימִינְךָ נֶצַח. אָמֵן:

May God remember the soul of my beloved sister . . .
who hath gone to her repose. May her soul be bound up in
the bond of life. May her rest be glorious, with fullness of joy
in Thy presence, and bliss for evermore at Thy right hand.
Amen. (End with Concluding Prayer, p. 177.)

Yiz-kor e-lo-heem nish-mas ah-cho-tee . . . sheh-
hol-cho l'olo-moh O-no t'hee naf-sho tz'ru-ro bi-tz'ror ha-
cha-yim, u-s'hee m'nu-cho-so ko-vod, So-va s'mo-chos es
po-ne-cho, n'eemos bee-meen-cho ne-tzah. Omayn.

In Memory of a Child

אֵל מָלֵא רַחֲמִים שׁוֹכֵן בַּמְּרוֹמִים. הַמְצֵא מְנוּחָה נְכוֹנָה
תַּחַת כַּנְפֵי הַשְּׁכִינָה. בְּמַעֲלוֹת קְדוֹשִׁים וּטְהוֹרִים. כְּזֹהַר הָרָקִיעַ
מַזְהִירִים. אֶת־נִשְׁמַת הַיֶּלֶד (הַיַּלְדָה) . . . שֶׁהָלַךְ (שֶׁהָלְכָה)
לְעוֹלָמוֹ (לְעוֹלָמָהּ). אָנָּא בַּעַל הָרַחֲמִים הַסְתִּירֵהוּ (הַסְתִּירֶהָ)
בְּסֵתֶר כְּנָפֶיךָ לְעוֹלָמִים. וּצְרוֹר בִּצְרוֹר הַחַיִּים אֶת נִשְׁמָתוֹ
(נִשְׁמָתָהּ). יְיָ הוּא נַחֲלָתוֹ (נַחֲלָתָהּ) וְיָנוּחַ (וְתָנוּחַ) בְּשָׁלוֹם עַל
מִשְׁכָּבוֹ (מִשְׁכָּבָהּ) וְנֹאמַר אָמֵן:

ENGLISH TRANSLATION

O God who art full of compassion, who dwellest on high, grant perfect rest beneath the shadow of Thy Divine Presence, in the exalted places among the holy and pure, who shine as the brightness of the firmament, to the child . . . who hath gone to his [her] eternal rest. We beseech thee, O Lord of compassion, shelter his [her] soul forevermore under the cover of Thy wings. The Lord is his [her] portion. May he [she] rest in peace. And let us say, Amen.

Concluding Prayer

אַב הָרַחֲמִים אֲשֶׁר בְּיָדְךָ נַפְשׁוֹת הַחַיִּים וְהַמֵּתִים. תַּנְחוּמֶיךָ
יְשַׁעַשְׁעוּ נַפְשֵׁנוּ בְּזָכְרֵנוּ אֶת קְרוֹבֵינוּ הָאֲהוּבִים וְהַנִּכְבָּדִים אֲשֶׁר
הָלְכוּ לִמְנוּחָתָם: אָנָּא יְיָ אַמְּצֵנוּ לִשְׁמוֹר אֶת פְּקוּדָתָם כָּל עוֹד
נִשְׁמָתֵנוּ בְּקִרְבֵּנוּ. וְנַפְשָׁם תָּנוּחַ בְּאֶרֶץ הַחַיִּים לַחֲזוֹת בְּנוֹעַמְךָ
וּלְהִתְעַנֵּג מִטּוּבֶךָ:

אָנָּא פְּנֵה הַיּוֹם בְּחֶסֶד וּבְרַחֲמִים אֶל תְּפִלַּת עֲבָדֶיךָ
הַשּׁוֹפְכִים אֶת נַפְשָׁם לְפָנֶיךָ: אָנָּא חַסְדְּךָ מֵאִתָּנוּ אַל-יָמוּשׁ:
הַטְרִיפֵנוּ לֶחֶם חֻקֵּנוּ וְאַל תַּצְרִיכֵנוּ לִידֵי מַתְּנַת בָּשָׂר וָדָם: הָסֵר
מֵעָלֵינוּ כָּל-דְּאָגָה וְתוּגָה כָּל-צָרָה וָפַחַד כָּל-חֶרְפָּה וָבוּז:
בְּיִרְאָתְךָ הַטְּהוֹרָה תְּחַזְּקֵנוּ וּבְתוֹרָתְךָ הַתְּמִימָה תְּאַמְּצֵנוּ: אֵל נָא
אַל תַּעַזְבֵנוּ בַּחֲצִי יָמֵינוּ וּנְמַלֵּא בְשָׁלוֹם אֶת מִסְפַּר יָמֵינוּ: יָדַעְנוּ
אַךְ יָדַעְנוּ כִּי חָדֵל כֹּהֵנוּ וּטְפָחוֹת נָתַתָּ יָמֵינוּ: עָזְרֵנוּ אֱלֹהֵי
יִשְׁעֵנוּ לְהִתְנַהֵג בֶּאֱמֶת וּבְתָמִים יְמֵי שְׁנֵי חַיֵּי מְגוּרֵינוּ: וְכַאֲשֶׁר
יַגִּיעַ קִצֵּנוּ לְהִפָּרֵד מִן הָעוֹלָם הֱיֵה אַתָּה עִמָּנוּ וְנִשְׁמָתֵינוּ
תִּהְיֶינָה צְרוּרוֹת בִּצְרוֹר הַחַיִּים עִם נִשְׁמוֹת אֲבוֹתֵינוּ וּקְרוֹבֵינוּ
וְנִשְׁמוֹת הַצַּדִּיקִים הָעוֹמְדִים לְפָנֶיךָ. אָמֵן וְאָמֵן:

ENGLISH TRANSLATION

Father of mercy, in whose hand are the souls of the living and the dead, may Thy consolation cheer us as we remember our beloved and honored kinsfolk who have gone to their rest. We beseech Thee, O Lord, grant us strength to be faithful to their charge while the breath of life is within us. And may their souls repose in the land of the living, beholding Thy glory and delighting in Thy goodness.

O turn this day in loving-kindness and tender mercy to the prayers of Thy servants who pour out their souls before Thee. May Thy loving-kindness not depart from us. Give us our needful sustenance, and let us not be in want of the gifts of flesh and blood. Remove from us care and sorrow, distress and fear, shame and contempt. Strengthen us in our reverence for Thee and fortify us to keep Thy perfect law. O God, take us not hence in the midst of our days. Let us complete in peace the number of our years. Verily we know that our strength is frail, and that Thou hast made our days as handbreadths. Help us, O God of our salvation, to bear ourselves faithfully and blamelessly during the years of our pilgrimage. And when our end draws nigh and we depart this world, be Thou with us, and may our souls be bound up in the bond of life with the souls of our parents and kinsfolk, and with the souls of the righteous who are ever with Thee. Amen, and Amen.

Prayer in Memory of the Jewish Martyrs

יִזְכֹּר אֱלֹהִים נִשְׁמוֹת כָּל־אַחֵינוּ בְּנֵי יִשְׂרָאֵל שֶׁמָּסְרוּ נַפְשָׁם עַל־קִדּוּשׁ הַשֵּׁם. אָנָּא יִשָּׁמַע בְּחַיֵּינוּ הֵד גְּבוּרָתָם וּמְסִירוּתָם וְיֵרָאֶה בְּמַעֲשֵׂינוּ טֹהַר לִבָּם וְתִהְיֶינָה נַפְשׁוֹתֵיהֶם צְרוּרוֹת בִּצְרוֹר הַחַיִּים וּתְהִי מְנוּחָתָם כָּבוֹד. שֹׂבַע שְׂמָחוֹת אֶת־פָּנֶיךָ נְעִימוֹת בִּימִינְךָ נֶצַח. אָמֵן:

ENGLISH TRANSLATION

May God be mindful of the souls of all our brothers, departed members of the house of Israel who sacrificed their lives for the sanctification of the holy name and the honor of Israel. Grant that their heroism and self-sacrificing devotion find response in our hearts and the purity of their souls be reflected in our lives. May their souls be bound up in the bonds of eternal life, an everlasting blessing among us. Amen.

Prayer for the Victims of Nazi Persecution

אֵל מָלֵא רַחֲמִים שׁוֹכֵן בַּמְּרוֹמִים, הַמְצֵא מְנוּחָה נְכוֹנָה תַּחַת כַּנְפֵי הַשְּׁכִינָה. בְּמַעֲלוֹת קְדוֹשִׁים וּטְהוֹרִים, כְּזֹהַר הָרָקִיעַ מַזְהִירִים, אֶת נִשְׁמוֹת אַחֵינוּ אֲשֶׁר נִשְׂרְפוּ וְנֶהֶרְגוּ בִּידֵי הַגֶּרְמָנִים הָאַכְזָרִים וְהָרוֹצְחִים, בָּאֲרָצוֹת תַּחַת מֶמְשֶׁלֶת גֶּרְמַנְיָא. אָנָּא בַּעַל הָרַחֲמִים, הַסְתִּירֵם בְּסֵתֶר כְּנָפֶיךָ לְעוֹלָמִים. וּצְרוֹר בִּצְרוֹר הַחַיִּים אֶת נִשְׁמָתָם. יְיָ הוּא נַחֲלָתָם, וְיָנוּחוּ בְשָׁלוֹם עַל מִשְׁכָּבָם. וְנֹאמַר אָמֵן:

ENGLISH TRANSLATION

O God, Who art full of compassion. Who dwellest on high, grant perfect rest beneath the shelter of Thy Divine Presence, in the exalted places among the holy and pure who shine as the brightness of the firmament, to our brethren whose blood was spilt and who perished at the hands of the Nazi oppressors in the countries of their domination. We beseech Thee, Lord of Compassion, shelter them forevermore under the cover of Thy wings, and let their souls be bound up in the bond of eternal life. The Lord is their inheritance; may they rest in peace. And let us say, Amen.

Prayer for Members of the Israel Defense Force

אֵל מָלֵא רַחֲמִים, שׁוֹכֵן בַּמְּרוֹמִים, הַמְצֵא מְנוּחָה נְכוֹנָה*
עַל כַּנְפֵי הַשְּׁכִינָה,* בְּמַעֲלוֹת קְדוֹשִׁים וּטְהוֹרִים* כְּזֹהַר הָרָקִיעַ
מַזְהִירִים, לְנִשְׁמוֹת חַיָּלֵי צְבָא הֲגַנָּה לְיִשְׂרָאֵל אֲשֶׁר מָסְרוּ נַפְשָׁם
עַל קְדֻשַּׁת הַשֵּׁם וְעַל כִּבּוּשׁ הָאָרֶץ. בְּעַל הָרַחֲמִים יַסְתִּירֵם
בְּסֵתֶר כְּנָפָיו לְעוֹלָמִים, וְיִצְרוֹר בִּצְרוֹר הַחַיִּים אֶת נִשְׁמוֹתֵיהֶם,
יְיָ הוּא נַחֲלָתָם, בְּגַן עֵדֶן תְּהֵא מְנוּחָתָם, וְיָנוּחוּ בְּשָׁלוֹם עַל
מִשְׁכְּבוֹתָם. וְנֹאמַר: אָמֵן.

ENGLISH TRANSLATION

    O God, full of mercy, Who dwells on high, grant proper rest on the wings of the Divine Presence—in the lofty levels of the holy and the pure ones, who shine like theglow of the firmament—for the souls of the members of the Israel Defense Force, who gave up their lives for the sanctification of Your name and for the defense of the land. May the Master of Mercy shelter them in the shelter of His wings for eternity and may He bind their souls in the Bond of Life. Hashem is their heritage. May their resting place be in the Garden of Eden. May they repose in peace in their resting places. Now let us respond: Amen.

SEPHARDI PRAYERS IN MEMORY OF LOVED ONES

A Memorial Prayer for Adult Men

וְהַחָכְמָה מֵאַיִן תִּמָּצֵא. וְאֵיזֶה מְקוֹם בִּינָה: אַשְׁרֵי אָדָם מָצָא
חָכְמָה. וְאָדָם יָפִיק תְּבוּנָה:

לפרנס חברת הרוחצים ולש״ץ ולאדם רשום מתחילין מכאן

מָה רַב טוּבְךָ אֲשֶׁר צָפַנְתָּ לִירֵאֶיךָ, פָּעַלְתָּ לַחוֹסִים בָּךְ נֶגֶד בְּנֵי אָדָם: מַה־יָּקָר חַסְדְּךָ אֱלֹהִים, וּבְנֵי אָדָם בְּצֵל כְּנָפֶיךָ יֶחֱסָיוּן: יִרְוְיֻן מִדֶּשֶׁן בֵּיתֶךָ, וְנַחַל עֲדָנֶיךָ תַשְׁקֵם:]

טוֹב שֵׁם מִשֶּׁמֶן טוֹב, וְיוֹם הַמָּוֶת מִיּוֹם הִוָּלְדוֹ: סוֹף דָּבָר הַכֹּל נִשְׁמָע, אֶת הָאֱלֹהִים יְרָא, וְאֶת מִצְוֹתָיו שְׁמוֹר, כִּי זֶה כָּל־הָאָדָם: יַעְלְזוּ חֲסִידִים בְּכָבוֹד, יְרַנְּנוּ עַל מִשְׁכְּבוֹתָם:

מְנוּחָה נְכוֹנָה, בִּישִׁיבָה עֶלְיוֹנָה, תַּחַת כַּנְפֵי הַשְּׁכִינָה, בְּמַעֲלַת קְדוֹשִׁים וּטְהוֹרִים, כְּזֹהַר הָרָקִיעַ מְאִירִים וּמַזְהִירִים, וְחִלּוּץ עֲצָמִים, וְכַפָּרַת אֲשָׁמִים, וְהַרְחָקַת פֶּשַׁע, וְהַקְרָבַת יֶשַׁע, וְחֶמְלָה וַחֲנִינָה, מִלִּפְנֵי שׁוֹכֵן מְעוֹנָה, וְחֻלָקָא טָבָא, לְחַיֵּי הָעוֹלָם הַבָּא, שָׁם תְּהֵא מְנָת וּמְחִיצַת וִישִׁיבַת נֶפֶשׁ הַשֵּׁם הַטּוֹב (פלוני) רוּחַ יְיָ תְּנִיחֶנּוּ בְּגַן עֵדֶן, דְּאִתְפְּטַר מִן עָלְמָא הָדֵין, כִּרְעוּת אֱלָהָא מָרֵה שְׁמַיָּא וְאַרְעָא, הַמֶּלֶךְ בְּרַחֲמָיו, יָחוֹס וְיַחְמוֹל עָלָיו: וִילַוֶּה אֵלָיו הַשָּׁלוֹם, וְעַל מִשְׁכָּבוֹ יִהְיֶה שָׁלוֹם, כְּדִכְתִיב, יָבוֹא שָׁלוֹם יָנוּחוּ עַל מִשְׁכְּבוֹתָם, הוֹלֵךְ נְכוֹחוֹ: הוּא וְכָל־בְּנֵי יִשְׂרָאֵל הַשּׁוֹכְבִים עִמּוֹ בִּכְלַל הָרַחֲמִים וְהַסְּלִיחוֹת, וְכֵן יְהִי רָצוֹן וְנֹאמַר אָמֵן:

בִּלַּע הַמָּוֶת לָנֶצַח, וּמָחָה יְיָ אֱלֹהִים דִּמְעָה מֵעַל כָּל־פָּנִים, וְחֶרְפַּת עַמּוֹ יָסִיר מֵעַל כָּל־הָאָרֶץ, כִּי יְיָ דִּבֵּר: יִחְיוּ מֵתֶיךָ נְבֵלָתִי יְקוּמוּן, הָקִיצוּ וְרַנְּנוּ שֹׁכְנֵי עָפָר, כִּי טַל אוֹרֹת טַלֶּךָ, וָאָרֶץ רְפָאִים תַּפִּיל: וְהוּא רַחוּם יְכַפֵּר עָוֹן, וְלֹא יַשְׁחִית, וְהִרְבָּה לְהָשִׁיב אַפּוֹ, וְלֹא יָעִיר כָּל־חֲמָתוֹ:

ENGLISH TRANSLATION

[For a distinguished rabbi begin here]
Where shall wisdom be found? and where is the place of understanding? Happy is the man that findeth wisdom, and the man that getteth understanding.

[For a warden of the Lavadores, or a Hazan, or a Member of the Midrash, begin here]
How great is Thy goodness, which Thou hast treasured up for those that fear Thee; which Thou hast wrought for those that trust in Thee, before the sons of men. How excellent is Thy loving-kindness, O God! Thou shelterest the children of men under the shadow of Thy wings. Thou satisfiest them abundantly with the richness of Thy house: and causest them to drink of the stream of Thy delights. Amen.

[In general cases begin here]
A good name is more fragrant than rich perfume, and the day of death better than the day of one's birth. The sum of the matter, after all hath been heard, is, to fear God, and keep His commandments, for this is the whole of man. Let the pious rejoice in glory; let them sing aloud upon their couches.

May the Lord who sitteth on high in His infinite mercy grant in the celestial abode under the wings of the divine glory in the high station of the holy and pure—that shine luminously as the brightness of the firmament—repose, renewal of strength, forgiveness of trespass, removal of transgression, speeding of salvation, compassion and mercy, and a goodly portion in the life to come. May this be the allotted portion and resting-place of the soul of the deceased . . . . May God vouchsafe peace and rest in Paradise to him who departed from this world according to the will of God, the Lord of heaven and earth. May the supreme King of Kings, through His infinite mercy, have pity and compassion on him and grant him peace. And may his rest be in peace as it is written. He shall come in peace; they shall rest on their couches; everyone who walketh in uprightness. May he, and all the children of Israel who slumber in the dust with him be included in mercy and forgiveness. May this be His Divine will! and let us say, Amen.

He will destroy death forever; and the Lord God will wipe away the tear from off all faces; and the reproach of His people will He remove from off the whole earth; for the Lord hath spoken it. Thy dead shall live again; the deceased of My people shall rise up.

Awake and sing, ye that dwell in the dust; for thy dew is as the dew of the morn; and the earth shall cast forth the dead. And He, being merciful, forgiveth iniquity, and destroyeth not; yea, He frequently turneth away his anger, and doth not stir up all His wrath. Save us, O Lord! answer us, O King! on the day when we call.

A Memorial Prayer for Adult Women

השכבה לאשה

אֵשֶׁת חַיִל מִי יִמְצָא, וְרָחוֹק מִפְּנִינִים מִכְרָהּ:

לבתולה מתחילין מכאן

רַבּוֹת בָּנוֹת עָשׂוּ חָיִל, וְאַתְּ עָלִית עַל כֻּלָּנָה:
שֶׁקֶר הַחֵן וְהֶבֶל הַיּוֹפִי, אִשָּׁה יִרְאַת יְיָ הִיא תִתְהַלָּל: תְּנוּ לָהּ
מִפְּרִי יָדֶיהָ: וִיהַלְלוּהָ בַשְּׁעָרִים מַעֲשֶׂיהָ:
רַחֲמָנָא דְרַחֲמָנוּתָא דִלֵהּ הִיא, וּבְמֵימְרֵהּ אִתְבְּרִיאוּ עָלְמַיָּא,
עָלְמָא הָדֵין וְעָלְמָא דְאָתֵי, וּגְנַז בֵּיהּ צַדְקָנִיּוֹת וְחַסְדָּנִיּוֹת דְּעָבְדָן
רְעוּתֵהּ, וּבְמֵימְרֵהּ וּבִיקָרֵהּ וּבִתְקְפֵּהּ יֵאמַר לְמֵיעַל קֳדָמוֹהִי דִּכְרַן
הָאִשָּׁה הַכְּבוּדָה וְהַצְּנוּעָה וְהַנִּכְבֶּדֶת מָרַת (פלונית) רוּחַ יְיָ
תְּנִיחֶנָּה בְּגַן עֵדֶן, דְּאִתְפְּטָרַת מִן עָלְמָא הָדֵין, כִּרְעוּת אֱלָהָא

מָרֵא שְׁמַיָּא וְאַרְעָא: הַמֶּלֶךְ בְּרַחֲמָיו יָחוֹס וְיַחְמוֹל עָלֶיהָ, וְיִלְוֶה
אֵלֶיהָ הַשָּׁלוֹם, וְעַל מִשְׁכָּבָהּ יִהְיֶה שָׁלוֹם, כְּדִכְתִיב, יָבֹא שָׁלוֹם,
יָנוּחוּ עַל מִשְׁכְּבוֹתָם, הוֹלֵךְ נְכֹחוֹ: הִיא וְכָל־בְּנוֹת יִשְׂרָאֵל
הַשּׁוֹכְבוֹת עִמָּהּ, בִּכְלַל הָרַחֲמִים וְהַסְּלִיחוֹת, וְכֵן יְהִי רָצוֹן
וְנֹאמַר אָמֵן:

וּבִפְנֵי הָאָבֵל אוֹמְרִים אֵלּוּ הַפְּסוּקִים אַחַר הַהַשְׁכָּבָה:

בִּלַּע הַמָּוֶת לָנֶצַח, וּמָחָה יְיָ אֱלֹהִים דִּמְעָה מֵעַל כָּל־פָּנִים,
וְחֶרְפַּת עַמּוֹ יָסִיר מֵעַל כָּל־הָאָרֶץ, כִּי יְיָ דִּבֵּר: יִחְיוּ מֵתֶיךָ
נְבֵלָתִי יְקוּמוּן, הָקִיצוּ וְרַנְּנוּ שֹׁכְנֵי עָפָר, כִּי טַל אוֹרֹת טַלֶּךָ,
וָאָרֶץ רְפָאִים תַּפִּיל: וְהוּא רַחוּם יְכַפֵּר עָוֹן, וְלֹא יַשְׁחִית,
וְהִרְבָּה לְהָשִׁיב אַפּוֹ, וְלֹא יָעִיר כָּל־חֲמָתוֹ: יְיָ הוֹשִׁיעָה, הַמֶּלֶךְ
יַעֲנֵנוּ בְיוֹם קָרְאֵנוּ:

ENGLISH TRANSLATION

[For married women begin here]
Who can find a valiant woman? for her value is far
above gems.

[For unmarried women begin here]
Many daughters have done valiantly, but thou hast
surpassed them all. Grace is deceitful and beauty is vain; but
the woman that feareth the Lord, she shall be praised. Give
her of the fruit of her hands, and her works will praise her in
the gates.

May the Most Merciful, to whom mercy appertaineth,
and by whose word the worlds were created, both this, and
the world to come, in which are treasured up the souls of the
righteous and pious women who performed His will, command by His word, glory, and power that the remembrance
of the worthy, modest, and virtuous woman, . . . shall
appear before him. May God grant peace in Paradise to her

who hath departed this world, according to the will of God,
the Lord of heaven and earth. May the supreme King of
Kings, through His infinite mercy, have pity and compassion
on her, and grant her peace; and may her rest be in peace; as
it is written, "He shall come in peace; they shall rest on their
couches; every one walketh in uprightness." May she, and
all the daughters of Israel, who slumber in the dust with her,
be included in mercy and forgiveness. May this be His
Divine will, and let us say, Amen.

He will destroy death forever; and the Lord God will
wipe away the tear from off all faces; and the reproach of His
people will he remove from off the whole earth; for the Lord
hath spoken it. Thy dead shall live again; the deceased of my
people shall rise up. Awake and sing, ye that dwell in the
dust; for thy dew is as the dew of the morn; and the
earthshall cast forth the dead. And He, being merciful,
forgiveth iniquity, and destroyeth not; yea, He frequently
turneth away His anger, and doth not stir up all His wrath.
Save us, O Lord! Answer us, O King, on the day when we
call.

A Memorial Prayer for a Child

השכבה לילד

הָאֵל אָב הָרַחֲמָן, אֲשֶׁר רִחַם עַל אֲבוֹתֵינוּ הַקְּדוֹשִׁים עוֹשֵׂי
רְצוֹנוֹ, הוּא יְרַחֵם עַל נֶפֶשׁ הַיֶּלֶד הַנָּעִים (הַיַּלְדָּה הַנְּעִימָה) ...
רוּחַ יְיָ תְּנִיחֶנּוּ בְּגַן עֵדֶן, וִינַהֲלֵהוּ לְהִתְעַנֵּג בֵּין הַצַּדִּיקִים: וְיִהְיֶה
כַפָּרָה עַל אָבִיו וְאִמּוֹ כְּקָרְבַּן אִשֶּׁה: וְיִסְלַח לְכָל־עֲוֹנָם, וְיִרְפָּא
לְכָל־מַכּוֹתָם, וְיִתֵּן לָהֶם בָּנִים זְכָרִים אֲשֶׁר יִחְיוּ וְיַעַסְקוּ בַתּוֹרָה:
וְיָסִיר מֵהֶם יָגוֹן וַאֲנָחָה, וְכֵן יְהִי רָצוֹן וְנֹאמַר אָמֵן:

ובפני האבל אומרים אלו הפסוקים אחר ההשכבה:

בִּלַּע הַמָּוֶת לָנֶצַח, וּמָחָה אֲדֹנָי אֱלֹהִים דִּמְעָה מֵעַל כָּל־

פָּנִים, וְחֶרְפַּת עַמּוֹ יָסִיר מֵעַל כָּל־הָאָרֶץ, כִּי יְיָ דִּבֵּר: יִחְיוּ מֵתֶיךָ
נְבֵלָתִי יְקוּמוּן, הָקִיצוּ וְרַנְּנוּ שֹׁכְנֵי עָפָר, כִּי טַל אוֹרוֹת טַלֶּךָ,
וָאָרֶץ רְפָאִים תַּפִּיל: וְהוּא רַחוּם יְכַפֵּר עָוֹן, וְלֹא יַשְׁחִית,
וְהִרְבָּה לְהָשִׁיב אַפּוֹ, וְלֹא יָעִיר כָּל־חֲמָתוֹ: וּכְתִיב, כְּאִישׁ אֲשֶׁר
אִמּוֹ תְּנַחֲמֶנּוּ, כֵּן אָנֹכִי אֲנַחֶמְכֶם, וּבִירוּשָׁלַם תְּנֻחָמוּ:

ENGLISH TRANSLATION

May God the Father of mercy, who had compassion upon our fathers, that did His will, have mercy upon the soul of this child . . .; to him may the spirit of the Lord give repose in Paradise. May he rejoice with the spirits of the pious and may he bring atonement to his father and mother. May God pardon them their sins, heal their wounds, and keep them from further sorrow. May He grant them other children and may these live to follow the paths of His law. May this be the Divine will, and let us say, Amen.

He will destroy death forever; and the Lord God will wipe away the tear from off all faces; and the reproach of His people will He remove from off the whole earth; for the Lord hath spoken it. Thy dead shall live again; the deceased of my people shall rise up. Awake and sing, ye that dwell in the dust; for thy dew is as the dew of the morn; and the earth shall cast forth the dead. And He, being merciful, forgiveth iniquity, and destroyeth not; yea, He frequently turneth away His anger, and doth not stir up all His wrath. And it is written, "As one whom his mother comforteth, so will I comfort you; and ye shall be comforted in Jerusalem."

Family Record

YAHRZEIT DATES

Name of Deceased		Date of Death	
English	Hebrew	Civil	Hebrew

Notes

NOTES TO CHAPTER 1

1. The Holy One, Blessed be He, visited the sick, for it is written: "And the Lord appeared unto him by the oaks of Mamre" (Genesis 18:1), so do thou also visit the sick (*Sotah* 14a). Tradition has it that God visited Abraham on the third day of his circumcision (*Baba Metzia* 86b).
2. Mishnah *Peah*, Chapter 1; *Shabbat* 127a.
3. *Gittin* 61a; *Yoreh Deah* 335.9, "One must visit the sick of the gentiles so as to promote good will."
4. *Nedarim* 40a; *Yoreh Deah* 335.4.
5. Israel Abrahams, ed., *Hebrew Ethical Wills* (Philadelphia: The Jewish Publication Society of America, 1926), vol. 1, p. 40.
6. Proverbs 10:2, 11:4.
7. Abrahams, op. cit., p. 44.
8. *Yoreh Deah* 335.5.
9. Genesis 20:17; Numbers 12:13; Isaiah 38:2-5; *Nedarim* 40a; *Shabbat* 12b; *Berachot* 34b.
10. Proverbs 10:2, 11:4.
11. J. H. Hertz, *The Authorised Daily Prayer Book* (London: Shapiro Vallentine, 1962), p. 492. Future references to this title will be notated A.P.B.
12. *Yoreh Deah* 335.6.
13. *Rosh Hashanah* 16b.

14. Judah He-Chasid, *Sefer Chasidim*, ed. J. Wistinetzki (Berlin: Mekitzay Nirdamim, 1891), par. 365.

15. Israel Isserlein, *Terumat Hadeshen* (Venice: 1519), no. 234. Jacob b. Judah Weil, *Responsa* (Hanau: 1610), no. 182. Cf. H. J. Zimmels, *Magicians, Theologians and Doctors* (London: Edward Goldstone, 1952), p. 143.

16. J. D. Eisenstein, *Ozar Dinim U' Minhagim* (New York: J. D. Eisenstein, 1917), p. 220.

17. *Shnei Luchot Haberit* (Fuerth, 1764), fol. 214b. See also *Sefer Chasidim* 478 and Herman Pollack, *Jewish Folkways in German Lands 1648–1806* (Cambridge MA: The M.I.T. Press, 1971), p. 48.

18. *Yoma* 85a; *Orach Chayyim* 32.

19. *Shabbat* 151b.

20. *Yoreh Deah* 337.1; *Moed Katan* 26b.

21. *Orach Chayyim* 287.1.

22. A.P.B., p. 49.

23. *Baba Metziah* 85b; *Chullin* 7b; *Sanhedrin* 17b; *Bet Yosef Yoreh Deah* 336.

24. *Makkot* 22b.

25. *Baba Kamma* 85a. The school of R. Ishmael taught: "And the words 'And He shall cause him to be thoroughly healed' (Exodus 21:19) are the source whence it can be derived that authority was granted by God to the medical man to heal" (*Berachot* 60a).

26. Cecil Roth, *The Jewish Contribution to Civilization* (Oxford: The East and West Library, 1938), p. 192.

27. Ecclesiastes *Rabbah* 5:6.

28. *Avodah Zarah* 18a.

29. *Sanhedrin* 37a.

30. *Yoreh Deah* 338.1.

31. A.P.B., pp. 419–420; *Yoreh Deah* 338.

32. *Yoreh Deah* 338, 338.1.

33. *Zohar, Terumah* 174b; cf. Louis Ginzberg, *The Legends of the Jews* (Philadelphia: Jewish Publication Society of America, 1913), vol. 2, p. 131.

34. Genesis 49:2–27.

35. Genesis 50:24–25.

36. Deuteronomy 33:2–29.

37. I Kings 2:1–9.

38. I Maccabees 3:49–69.

39. Abrahams, op. cit., p. 23.
40. Also II Kings 20:1.
41. *Gittin* 13a.
42. Cf. Targum on Isaiah 60:4 and *Rema* (*Even Ha-Ezer* 121.7 and *Choshen Mishpat* 211.2): "Brings up a secretion in his throat on account of the narrowing of his chest."
43. *Gittin* 28a.
44. *Yoreh Deah* 399.1.
45. Ibid., p. 4.
46. A.P.B., p. 420.
47. Cf. Commentaries of Ibn Ezra and Rabbi Jacob ben Asher, *Baal Haturim* on Genesis 46:4.
48. *Zohar, Vayyechi* 218b: "At a time of a man's death he is vouchsafed to see his dead relatives and companions from the other world." Also p. 226: ". . . the eyes which have just beheld a holy vision should now dwell on a sight of different character."
49. Moses Sofer (Schreiber), *Teshuvat Chatam Sofer* (Vienna–Budapest: 1855–1858); *Yoreh Deah* 338.
50. *Orach Chayyim* 311.1.
51. Ibid., 526.3; Israel Meir Kagan, *Mishnah Berurah* (Warsaw: 1910).
52. A circular entitled "Guidance for Hospital Authorities" issued by the office of the Sexton, Burial Society of the United Synagogue (January 1960), reads as follows: "Where it is not possible to obtain the services of a Jewish chaplain, it is permissible for the hospital staff to carry out the following: Close the eyes. Tie up the jaw. Keep arms and hands straight, by sides of the body. Any tubes or instruments in the body should be removed and the incision plugged. The corpse should then be wrapped in a plain sheet without religious emblems, and placed in the mortuary or other special room for Jewish bodies."

NOTES TO CHAPTER 2

1. *Shabbat* 105b.
2. *Berachot* 19a.
3. *Kiddushin* 31b. It is said only by children.
4. *Yoreh Deah* 341.6.

5. *Shabbat* 151b.
6. R. E. Prothero, *The Psalms in Human Life* (New York: E. P. Dutton, 1908), pp. 1–5.
7. Cf. Deuteronomy 23, "His body shall not remain all night upon the tree but thou shalt surely bury him the same day." The *Mishnah Sanhedrin* 46b states: "Whoever leaves his dead lie overnight, transgresses both a positive command ('but thou shalt surely bury him the same day') and the negative command 'his body shall not remain all night upon the tree.' "
8. *Sanhedrin* 47a; *Yoreh Deah* 357.1.
9. Norman Linzer, *Understanding Bereavement and Grief* (New York: Ktav, 1977), p. 11.
10. *Noda Beyehudah*, part 2, *Yoreh Deah* 210 (Vilna: 1904).
11. *Chatam Sofer Yoreh Deah* (Vienna: 1855).
12. M.D. Silberstein, "Baayat Nituah Hametim Upitrona" in *Yavneh* (Jerusalem: 1949), p. 214, quoted by Immanuel Jakobovitz in *Jewish Medical Ethics* (New York: Bloch, 1959), p. 150.
13. I. Jakobovitz, op. cit., p. 150. Cf. Norman Lamm and Walter S. Wurtzburger, "The Dissection of the Dead in Jewish Law" in *A Treasury of Tradition* (New York: Hebrew Publishing Company, 1967), pp. 285–317.
14. Iser Judah Unterman, *Shevet Miyehudah* (1955), p. 313; Dayan Myer Steinberg, *Responsum* (London: 1957), p. 12; *Noam*, vol. 3, p. 313.
15. *Yoreh Deah* 349.2. Cf. *Keseph Mishnah* to *Yad Evel*; Greenwald, op. cit., p. 57.
16. Josephus, Flavius (38–100 C.E.) *Antiquities* 16:7.
17. "Why did Joseph die before his brethren?" Rabbi said: "Because he embalmed his father" (Genesis *Rabbah* 100.2).
18. Moses Hyamson, *Rules and Regulations of the Chevrah Kaddisha Orach Chaim* (New York: Chevrah Kaddisha Orach Chaim, 1942), p. 7.
19. Gerald Friedlander, ed., *Pirke de Rabbi Eliezer* (London: Kegan Paul, 1916), p. 156; *Tanchumah* (Vilna: 1833) and Genesis *Rabbah* 22:8 read "Two clean birds."
20. *Historiae* 5.5.
21. Leviticus 21:19, 18:10, 20:14; *Sanhedrin* 9.1; *Sifra, Kedoshim* 9.16; *Yevamot* 21a.
22. Molten lead or a mixture of lead and tin was poured down the

throat of the criminal. *Sanhedrin* 7:2; *Yerushalmi, Sanhedrin* 7.24b.

23. *Avodah Zarah* 1.3. Both Rashi and Bertinoro explain the Mishnah "Death at which burning of articles of the dead takes place is attended by idolatry."

24. II Kings 23:10; II Chronicles 23:3, 28:3.

25. *Gittin* 56b.

26. *Hilchot Avel* 12.1; *Sefer Ha-Mitzvot* (Lvov: 1860), no. 231; *Yoreh Deah* 362.1.

27. Josephus, the Jewish historian, also states, "And they buried the bodies in their fairest country called Arura." *The Antiquities of the Jews*, ed. H. St. J. Thackeray (London: New English Library, 1965), vol. 6, p. 375.

28. He is often confused with the other proselyte, Aquila, who flourished in the second century C.E. and who translated the Bible into Greek.

29. The *maneh* was a weight in gold or silver equal to fifty or a hundred common *shekels*. One *maneh* of Tyrian weight equals twenty-five *selas*.

30. Essay on resurrection.

31. Saadia, *Emunot Vedeot* 8.

32. *Sanhedrin* 90b.

33. Leviticus *Rabbah* 18:1; Genesis *Rabbah* 28:5; *Tosafot, Baba Kamma* 16b; *Zohar* 1:69b; Rashi on Ecclesiastes 12:5.

34. *The Jewish Chronicle*, London, December 9, 1887, and September 3, 1926.

35. *The Jewish Chronicle*, London, October 2, 1891, p. 10.

36. *Laws and Byelaws of the Burial Society of the United Synagogue* (London: United Synagogue, 1955), p. 61, section F.14.

NOTES TO CHAPTER 3

1. "One who is troubled" or "sorrowful" (Genesis 35:18). *Ben Oni* and Hosea 9:4, "bread of mourning." The root *onen* is found in Numbers 11:1 (*Mithonenim*, murmurers or complaining): "He will lament" (Lamentations 3:39).

2. *Moed Katan* 23b; *Yoreh Deah* 341.1.

3. *Sukkah* 25a.

4. *Semachot* 10.

5. *Tosafot, Berachot* 17b.
6. Joseph Soloveitchik, *Jewish Reflections on Death,* ed. Jack Riemer (New York: Schocken Books, 1975), pp. 77–78.
7. Some authorities maintain that in a place where there is a *Chevrah Kaddisha,* the relatives are not legally subject to the laws of *aninut* and are obliged to read the *Shema* and recite the *Amidah* (*Kitzur Shulchan Aruch* 196.5).
8. *Mishnah Berachot* 3:1
9. *Berachot* 17b.
10. *Yerushalmi Berachot* 3.1.
11. *Moed Katan* 23b; *Yoreh Deah* 341.1.
12. Ibid.; *Berachot* 18a.
13. Greenwald, *Kol Bo Al Avelut,* p. 130.
14. If, however, he is not preoccupied with the burial arrangements, he is obliged to build a *sukkah.*
15. He may do so if there is no one else.
16. He may recite it on the following day without a benediction, *Mishnah Berurah, Biur Halachah* 489.
17. Chayyim Joseph David Azulai, *Pirke Yoseph on Yoreh Deah* (Vienna: 1859), p. 4341.
18. *Mishnah Berurah* 693.13.
19. But not at night because at night he is not obliged to feast (*Kitzur Shulchan Aruch* 142.21).
20. Greenwald, op. cit., pp. 137, 157b.
21. Greenwald, op. cit., p. 151.
22. If there is no other person he may officiate (*Kitzur Shulchan Aruch* 196.9).
23. Some authorities forbid it.
24. This is the view of Rabbi Solomon b. Yehudah Luria. Moses Isserles, however, maintains that the *brit* should take place after the interment.
25. Greenwald, op. cit., pp. 155–156.
26. *Yerushalmi, Yebamot* 11.7.
27. *Bet Yoseph, Yoreh Deah* 263.
28. *Yoreh Deah* 339.5.
29. That is, water contained in vessels.
30. That is, the three houses including the one in which the dead lies.
31. Abudraham, *Sefer Abudraham,* ed. Solomon Wertheimer (Jerusalem: Usha Press, 1963), p. 371; *Beer Hetev* on *Orach Chayyim* 90.23.

32. Op. cit., p. 371, *Beer Hetev* on *Orach Chayyim* 90.23.
33. *Yoreh Deah* 340.1.
34. *Moed Katan* 25a; *Yoreh Deah* 340.5.
35. *Yoreh Deah* 340.1.
36. J. H. Hertz, *Book of Jewish Thoughts* (London: Oxford University Press, 1935), p. 297.
37. *Moed Katan* 22b; *Sukkah* 32b; *Niddah* 26a.
38. *Yoreh Deah* 340.30.
39. *Yoreh Deah* 340.14.
40. Solomon Ganzfried, ed. *Kitzur Shulchan Aruch* (Leipzig: Feldman, 1933), 195.11.
41. *Ibid.*, Section 13; *Yoreh Deah* 340.27.
42. Mishnah *Makkot* 3:5.
43. *Moed Katan* 27b.
44. A book containing dissertations, prayers to be offered for the sick and the dead.
45. Other associations held the *seudah* on the thirty-third of the *omer* days (eighteenth of *Iyyar*) or on the eve of the new moon of *Shevat* or fifteenth of *Kislev*.
46. *Sefer Chasidim* 650.
47. *Yerushalmi Shabbat* 23.5.
48. H. J. Zimmels, *Ashkenazim and Sephardim* (London: Oxford University Press, 1958), p. 183.
49. *Laws and Byelaws of the Burial Society* (London: United Synagogue, 1955), p. 91.
50. *The Handbook of Life* (London: The Chevrah Kaddisha, 1909), pp. 32–33.
51. *Yoreh Deah* 364.4.
52. *Mishnah Sanhedrin* 6.5.
53. *The Handbook of Life*, p. 34.
54. The white garment traditionally worn in some Ashkenazi rites by members of the congregation during prayer on the High Holy Days, by the celebrant at the *seder* table, and in some communities by the groom during the marriage ceremony. It is also worn by the officiant at the Additional Service on the first day of Passover and the eighth day of Tabernacles.
55. Gamaliel II, also called Gamaliel of Javneh, flourished late first and early second century.
56. *Moed Katan* 27b.
57. *Shabbat* 114a. Cf. *Midrash* Genesis *Rabba* 100.2, "Rabbi Jochanan gave instructions before his death: 'Do not bury me in white or

in black but colored shrouds, so that if I am summoned with the righteous, the wicked may not be aware of me; while if I am summoned with the wicked, the righteous may not be aware of me.' "

58. Genesis *Rabbah* 100.2.
59. *Mishnah Eduyot* 5.6.
60. *Yerushalmi, Kilayim* 9.4. Rabbi Judah Hanasi instructed: "Lower my coffin deep in the earth," i.e., the board beneath shall be removed so that the coffin shall be in close touch with the earth (*Tur Yoreh Deah* 362).
61. Genesis *Rabbah* 19.8.
62. *Yerushalmi, Kilayim* 9.3.
63. *Yoreh Deah* 349.
64. Cf. Code *Orach Chayyim* 526: "If a body has to be buried on the first day of *Yom Tov*, non-Jews shall perform the labor even if the death occurred on the same day and it would be possible without danger of decomposition to keep the body until the next day. This, however, refers only to the work of making shrouds while the dressing of the body, heating of water for washing it, carrying out the body, and placing it in the grave may be carried out by Jews. If one died on the first day of *Yom Tov*, it is permitted to keep the body overnight until the second holy day in order that Jews may perform the services of the funeral."
65. That is, the grave diggers. Cf. *Mishnah Berurah*, vol. 5, p. 194.
66. *Betzah* 6a.

NOTES TO CHAPTER 4

1. Ecclesiastes 12:5.
2. Cf. Job 30:23, "House appointed for all living."
3. *Moed Katan* 9b.
4. *Sanhedrin* 96b.
5. Cecil Roth, *A History of the Jews in England* (Oxford: Clarendon Press, 1941), p. 13.
6. Albert M. Hyamson, *The Sephardim of England* (London: Methuen, 1951), p. 14.
7. *Yoreh Deah* 368.2.
8. Israel Abrahams, *Jewish Life in the Middle Ages* (London: Edward Goldstone, 1932), p. 93.

9. S. W. Baron, *The Jewish Community* (Philadelphia: Jewish Publication Society, 1942), vol. 1, p. 218.
10. Cecil Roth, *History of the Great Synagogue* (London: Edward Goldstone, 1950), p. 103, note 3.
11. *Megillah* 29a.
12. *Yoreh Deah* 368.1.
13. *Contra Apion* 2.
14. *Berachot* 19b–20a; *Yoreh Deah* 374.1.
15. *Nazir* 47–48; *Megillah* 3b.
16. *Baba Kamma* 71a.
17. *Yoreh Deah* 354.1.
18. *Peah* 1.
19. *Ketubot* 17a and *Yoreh Deah* 361.1, "Schoolchildren are not suspended from their studies."
20. *Berachot* 18a; *Derech Eretz Zuta* 9.
21. *Yoreh Deah* 361.3.
22. *Yerushalmi, Bikkurim* 3.3; *Yoreh Deah* 361.4.
23. *Contra Apion* 11.27.
24. *The Art Scroll Siddur* (New York: Mesorah, 1987), p. 796. Future reference to this title will be A.S.S.; *Berachot* 58b.
25. *Ketubot* 46b.
26. *Ketubot* 2.10; *Baba Batra* 6.7; *Oholot* 18.4; *Baba Batra* 100b.
27. *Yoreh Deah* 358.3 *(Rema)*.
28. A.P.B., p. 24; A.S.S., p. 810.
29. Ecclesiastes 1:2; *Baba Batra* 100b.
30. Ibid.
31. A quotation from Exodus 18:23, "All this people shall go to their place in peace" (A.P.B., p. 427).
32. *Maavar Yabok* (Amsterdam: 1732) mentions five spadesful.
33. A.S.S., p. 798; A.P.B., pp. 424–425. In Anglo Jewry, *Tzidduk Ha-Din* is recited prior to the funeral and Psalm 91 after the burial.
34. *Avodah Zarah* 18a; *Sifre* on Deuteronomy 32.
35. *Yoreh Deah* 401.6 *(Rema)*.
36. *Kitzur Shulchan Aruch* 198:14; Greenwald, op. cit. p. 211.
37. Ibid.
38. *Yerushalmi, Berachot* 3:2; *Megillah*, Rashi, 23b; *Baba Batra* 100b.
39. *Sanhedrin* 19a.
40. *Moed Katan*, chapter 1.
41. *Yoreh Deah* 376.4.
42. A.S.S., p. 802; A.P.B., p. 427.

43. Deuteronomy 21:7. Some people do not dry their hands with a towel so as not to seem to wish to wipe off the memory of the deceased.

44. S. Hurwitz, ed., *Machsor Vitry,* (Nurnberg: I. Bulka, 1923), p. 247; *Yoreh Deah* 376.4.

45. *Berachot* 53a; *Baba Kamma* 16b.

46. *Betzah* 6a and *Orach Chayyim* 526.4.

47. *Mishnah Moed Katan* 3.8.

48. Rav urged Rabbi Samuel ben Shilath: "Be fervent in my funeral eulogy, for I will be standing there." *Shabbat* 153a; *Moed Katan* 8a, 25b; *Yerushalmi, Ketubot* 12.3.

49. *Moed Katan* 25b; Emanuel Feldman, *Biblical and Post Biblical Defilement and Mourning Law as Theology* (New York: Yeshivah University Press, Ktav, 1977), pp. 110–118.

50. To strike, to beat, cf. Isaiah 32:12, "Smiting upon the breasts."

51. A.E. Cowley, *Aramaic Papyri of the 5th Century* B.C. (Oxford: Clarendon Press, 1923), p. 112. See also "Fasts and Fasting" by Rev. A. W. Greenup in *Essays in Honor of the Rev. Dr. J. H. Hertz,* ed. I. Epstein et al. (London: Edward Goldstone, 1942), pp. 203–215.

52. *Mishnah Baba Batra* 2.9; *Semachot* 14; *Tosefta Baba Batra* 1:1.

53. *Ketubot* 111a.

54. Deuteronomy 32:43: "The earth shall atone for his people."

55. *Ketubot* 3a.

56. *Tanchumah* Genesis, *Vayyechi,* ed. Buber (Vilna: 1885), p. 214.

NOTES TO CHAPTER 5

1. *Moed Katan* 20a; *Yerushalmi, Moed Katan* 3.5.

2. *Vayyechi* 26a.

3. *Sanhedrin* 108b.

4. *Yerushalmi, Moed Katan* 3.5.

5. *Yerushalmi, Ketubot* 1.1.

6. *Yoreh Deah* 399.1.

7. *Mishnah Moed Katan* 19a; *Yoreh Deah* 399.6.

8. *Moed Katan* 27b; *Yoreh Deah* 378.1.

9. *Moed Katan* 27a.

10. *Ketubot* 8b: Following the scriptural precept, "Give strong drink unto him that is ready to perish, and wine unto the bitter in soul" (Proverbs 31:6–7), the rabbis ordered ten cups of wine

to be served with the "meal of consolation." "Wine was created," declared Rabbi Chanan, "for the sole purpose of consoling the bereaved" (*Sanhedrin* 70a).

11. *Hosea* 9:4; *Ezekiel* 24:17.
12. *Baba Batra* 16b; *Yoreh Deah* 378.9.
13. *Midrash* Genesis *Rabbah* 63.14.
14. *Yoreh Deah* 378.5.
15. Only if the burial took place on *Chol Ha-Moed*. The mourner must eat it while sitting at the table, for there is no mourning on *Chol Ha-Moed* (*Kitzur Shulchan Aruch* 205.8). Cf. *Talmudic Encyclopaedia* (Jerusalem: Talmudic Encyclopaedia Institute, 1957), vol. 8, p. 146, note 111.
16. *Tosafot Moed Katan* 24b; *Tur Shulchan Aruch, Yoreh Deah* 278; *Yerushalmi, Moed Katan* 3.5; *Yoreh Deah* 378.12.
17. Samuel Halevy, *Nachalat Shivah* (Warsaw: 1884), 73. It was also customary to keep a glass of water and a towel during the *shivah*. Rabbi Abraham Danzig, in *Chochmat Adam* (Warsaw: 1908), p. 461, disapproves of this *minhag*.
18. *Ketubot* 103a.
19. *Moed Katan* 15a–b; *Yoreh Deah* 378.1.
20. *Yoreh Deah* 380.1, 382.1; *Moed Katan* 15b.
21. *Yoreh Deah* 382.2.
22. *Orach Chayyim* 614.3.
23. *Moed Katan* 15b; *Yoreh Deah* 381.1.
24. *Yoreh Deah* 381.1.
25. "Rabban Gamaliel washed himself the first night of his wife's death. His disciples said to him: 'Master, didst thou not teach us that a mourner is forbidden to wash himself?' He replied, 'I am not in this respect like other men. I am of delicate health' " (*Berachot* 2.6; *Yoreh Deah* 381.3).
26. *Yoreh Deah* 381.6.
27. *Shabbat* 152a.
28. Cecil Roth, *The History of the Great Synagogue* (London: Edward Goldstein, 1950), p. 61, note 11.
29. V. D. Lipman, *Social History of the Jews in England 1850–1950* (London: Watts, 1954), p. 72.
30. A.P.B., pp. 429–430.
31. *Keritot* 6a; A.R.P, pp. 219–220.
32. A.P.B., pp. 60–68.
33. Ibid., p. 426.
34. Ibid., pp. 75–76.

35. Ibid., pp. 5, 55.
36. Ibid., p. 147.
37. Greenwald, op. cit., p. 281.
38. Ibid., pp. 282, 370. Some authorities permit the use of spices.
39. A.P.B., pp. 380–381.
40. Some authorities maintain that on *Chanukah, Hallel* should be recited with the congregation, even in the house of a mourner.
41. A.P.B., p. 79; A.S.S., p. 56.
42. *Yoreh Deah* 380.1, 388.1; *Moed Katan* 15a.
43. Phylacteries: small cases containing passages from the Scriptures and affixed to the forehead and arm during the recital of prayers (Deuteronomy 6:8). *Tefillin* are identified with a joyous heart. See Rabbi Solomon Ibn Adret, *Sheelot Uteshuvot* (New York: 1958–1959), p. 106.
44. If there be a mourner at the synagogue, the congregation does not in this respect do as he does, and they have to say *Tachanun* while the mourner himself need not say it (*Kitzur Shulchan Aruch* 22.5).
45. *Kitzur Shulchan Aruch* 128.10.
46. *Yoreh Deah* 374.11 (*Rema*).
47. *Yoreh Deah* 374.11.

NOTES TO CHAPTER 6

1. *Yerushalmi, Moed Katan* 111.5.
2. That is, such writing as is permitted on *Chol Ha-Moed*.
3. *Yoreh Deah* 380.21.
4. *Yoreh Deah* 22.
5. *Semachot* 11.9; *Moed Katan* 27a.
6. *Halachot*—the Law; the legal literature of the Jew. *Aggadot*—ethical or homiletical portions of rabbinic literature. *Moed Katan* 21a; *Yoreh Deah* 384.1; *Semachot* 6.1.
7. *Yerushalmi, Moed Katan* 3.5. In the name of Rabbi Jochanan.
8. *Yoreh Deah* 384.4.
9. *Moed Katan*, Chapter 3.
10. Joyful occasions. A minor tractate of the Talmud that deals with death and mourning customs.
11. *Moed Katan* 15a; *Yoreh Deah* 385.1.
12. *Yoreh Deah* 385.1.

13. *Midrash Rabbah* Esther 8:2.
14. *Maimonides, Yad Evel* 10:1; cf.*Yoreh Deah* 385.3.
15. *Yerushalmi, Moed Katan* 3.5.
16. Solomon Schechter, *Avot De Rabbi Nathan* (New York: Philipp Feldheim, 1945), p. 45: English translation by Judah Goldin (*The Fathers According to Rabbi Nathan* [New Haven: Yale University Press, 1955]).
17. *Sotah* 14a; *Moed Katan* 22a.
18. Ecclesiastes *Rabbah* 7.4 in the name of Rabbi Phineas.
19. *Sanhedrin* 113a.
20. Teachers quoted in the *Mishnah* or *Beraita.*
21. The name given to the rabbinic authorities responsible for the *Gemara.*
22. *Moed Katan* 21b.
23. *Berachot* 6a.
24. Jack D. Spiro, *A Time to Mourn* (New York: Bloch, 1967), p. 32.
25. I. Grunfeld, *Horeb* (London: The Soncino Press, 1962), vol. 2, pp. 433–434.
26. *Yoreh Deah* 389.1.
27. *Yoreh Deah* 389.1.
28. *Moed Katan* 14a; *Yoreh Deah* 390.1.
29. *Yoreh Deah* 6.
30. *Yoreh Deah* 391.3.
31. *Yoreh Deah* 393.4. *Rema:* "In every matter connected with a religious duty that cannot be performed without the mourner, he is permitted to go out in order to perform the *mitzvah.*"
32. *Yoreh Deah* 393.2.
33. *Moed Katan* 15b, 21a; *Yoreh Deah* 383.1; also during *aninut* period, *Yoreh Deah* 341.5 (*Rema*).
34. *Yoreh Deah* 383.1 (*Rema*).
35. *Mishnah Moed Katan* 19a; *Yoreh Deah* 400.1; *Semachot* 7.1.
36. *Moed Katan* 3.5.
37. *Yoreh Deah* 400.1.
38. *Kitzur Shulchan Aruch* 195.6: "Changing one's apparel for the Sabbath means putting on other weekly garments and not the usual Sabbath apparel."
39. *Moed Katan* 22b.
40. Cf. *Yoreh Deah* 393.4. "Those who adopt the practice when they are mourners not to change their places in the synagogue on the Sabbath are correct in doing so." The *Rema*, however, says:

"Some say that on the Sabbath he should also change his place, and this is the common practice, and one should not alter this custom."

41. Rabbenu Tam (1100–1171), a French *tosafist* and a grandson of Rashi.
42. *Yoreh Deah* 400.1.
43. "The Third Meal commences after *Minchah* and lasts until the end of the Sabbath." "They shall recite the Afternoon Prayer," says Maimonides, "and commence the Third Meal and eat and drink until the expiry of the Sabbath."
44. *Orach Chayyim* 284.7 (*Rema*). On the other hand, a number of rabbinic authorities do not permit it on Sabbath *Rosh Chodesh,* v. *Mishnah Berurah* ad. loc.
45. J. H. Hertz, *Daily Prayer Book* (London: Shapiro Vallentine, 1947), p. 359.
46. Maimonides, *Hilchot Avel* 10.13.
47. *Orach Chayyim* 128.43.
48. Lit., "termination." The completion of the study of a tractate of the Talmud. A special meal (*seudah*) is held where the *hadran* (concluding lecture) is delivered. See Greenwald, op. cit., p. 397.
49. Bridegrooms of the Law, honorary titles bestowed on those who are called up to the reading of certain sections of the law during the morning service of *Simchat Torah.* See Abraham Zevi Hirsch Eisenstadt, *Pitchei Teshuvah* on *Yoreh Deah* 399:1.
50. Zimmels, *Ashkenazim and Sephardim,* p. 185.
51. Around the reading desk while *Hoshanot* are chanted at the conclusion of the repetition of the *Musaf Amidah.*
52. *Orach Chayyim* 661.2 (*Rema*).
53. *Orach Chayyim* 559.6.
54. Greenwald, op. cit., p. 344.
55. *Orach Chayyim* 696.4.
56. *Orach Chayyim* 696.4 (*Rema*). The fifteenth of *Adar* is known as *Shushan Purim* since in the capital, Shushan, the Jews had to defend themselves against their enemies on the fourteenth and celebrated the Festival a day later.
57. *Kitzur Shulchan Aruch* 141.20.
58. *Orach Chayyim* 696.4 (*Rema*).
59. *Kitzur Shulchan Aruch* 142.7.
60. Ibid.; *The Magen Avraham,* by Abraham Gombiner on *Orach Chayyim* (696.12) permits it. Rabbi David ben Samuel Ha-Levi

in his commentary, *Turei Zahav*, on the *Shulchan Aruch* (Lublin: 1646), forbids it.

61. A benediction pronounced on occasions of importance. Greenwald, op. cit. p. 288, note 20. Some authorities do not permit an *avel* to recite *Shehecheyanu* in public.

62. "One upon whom the people of the household depend and who are guided by him whether he is a brother or a young man" (*Yoreh Deah* 375.2).

63. Josephus, *The Jewish War*, trans. H. St. J. Thackeray and Ralph Marcus (New York and London: Washington Square Press and New English Library, 1965), p. 242.

64. *Baba Kamma* 91b.

65. *Semachot* 4.

66. Wanton destruction of property.

67. *Kiddushin* 32.

68. *Sanhedrin* 74a; *Yerushalmi, Sanhedrin* 3.5; *Yoreh Deah* 157.

69. *Taanit* 29a.

70. A stronghold west of the Dead Sea.

71. Josephus, op. cit. 7.1–7, 9.2.

72. *Berachot* 61b.

73. *Semachot* 2; *Yoreh Deah* 345.1.

74. *Yoreh Deah* 345.4.

75. *Semachot* 2.4.

76. *Pitche Teshuvah* on *Yoreh Deah* 345.

77. *Yoreh Deah* 345.3.

78. *Yoreh Deah* 345.5 and *Kitzur Shulchan Aruch* 201.4; *Semachot* 2.10.

79. *Kitzur Shulchan Aruch* 201.5.

NOTES TO CHAPTER 7

1. A.P.B., p. 80; A.S.S., p. 56.

2. Joseph B. Soloveitchik, *Jewish Reflections on Death*, ed. Jack Riemer (New York: Schocken Books, 1970).

3. *Targum Yerushalmi* on Genesis 49:2 and Deuteronomy 6:4.

4. *Soferim* 19:12 and *Siddur* of R. Amram, son of Sheshna, Gaon of Sura (d. 875). His *Siddur* was first published in Warsaw in 1865.

5. *Shabbat* 119b.

6. *Berachot* 3a.

7. *Shabbat* 119b.

8. Isaac b. Moses, *Or Zarua* (Zhitomir: 1862), II, p. 11b: "It is our custom in the land of Canaan and it is the custom in the land of *Benei Rinus* that after the community recites *Ein Keloheinu*, the orphan recites *Kaddish*."

9. David De Sola Pool, *The Old Jewish Aramaic Prayer, the Kaddish* (Leipzig: Rudolf Haupt, 1909), p. 82.

10. *Yesh Nochalin*, p. 35; David De Sola Pool, op. cit. p. 34. Elyakim b. Joseph the *Ravya* (d. 1150) writes: "It is not generally accepted that through the recitation of the *Kaddish* the son brings his father and mother to Paradise, and that he who frequently repeats the *Kaddish* atones by that action for the sins of his parents and helps them to enter into the future world. For there is no foundation for the view that the *Kaddish* is for the mourners. There is no basis for it in either the Jerusalem or the Babylonian Talmud or in the Tosefta. The only source is the legend of Rabbi Akiva, and we do not base laws upon legends." See A. Z. Idelsohn, *Jewish Liturgy and Its Development* (New York: Schocken Books, 1967), p. 87. Popular Judaism, however, adopts a more sentimental view.

11. Exodus *Rabbah* 15.5.

12. A. Marmorstein, *The Doctrine of Merits in Old Rabbinical Literature* (London: Oxford University Press, 1920), pp. 115–116.

13. *Sanhedrin* 104a.

14. Marmorstein, op. cit., p. 156; *Kallah*, ed. N. N. Coronel (Vienna: 1864), pp. 4b, 19b. In a work of the tenth century, *Seder Eliyahu Rabba VeSeder Eliyahu Zuta*, ed. M. Friedmann, (Jerusalem: 1959), p. 22. The story is told in the name of Rabban Jochanan ben Zakkai.

15. *Sotah* 10b.

16. I. Abrahams, quoted in *A Book of Jewish Thoughts* (1921 ed.), p. 198.

17. *Berachot* 60b.

18. Leopold Kompert (1822–1886), quoted in *A Book of Jewish Thoughts*, pp. 199–200.

19. *Veyatzmach Purkonay Vikoraiv Meshichai*, "May He bring forth His salvation and hasten the coming of His anointed one." In the *Siddur Ari* (Rabbi Isaac Luria) the text reads *Keitz Meshichai*, "the end of the appointed time."

20. Genesis 31:47; Ezra 5:23–5:25, 6:13–18; Daniel 2:4, 7:8.

21. A.S.S., pp. 154–156; A.P.B., pp. 76–78; *Yekum Purkan* in the Sabbath Morning Service, A.S.S., pp. 448–449; A.P.B., pp.

201–203; the introductory sentences of the Passover *Haggadah* (*HaLachma Anya*), the emotive *Kol Nidre,* opening words of the Evening Service commencing the Day of Atonement, and *piyyutim* for penitential days.

22. The *Zohar* (*Terumah* 129b) gives an additional reason: "The *Kaddish* breaks down iron walls and weighty seals and all the shells and defences of Evil. By its merits the glory of the Holy One, Blessed be He, is more greatly exalted than through any other prayer, because it causes the power of the 'other side' to wane and its empire to decline. Therefore, it must be said in Aramaic, which is the language of the 'other side.' " Cf. Marvin Luban, *The Kaddish* in *Studies in Torah Judaism* (New York: Yeshiva University Press, 1962), p. 20.

23. *Kol Bo,* an anonymous halachic work printed by Marco Giustiniani (Venice: 1547).

24. *Berachot* 58b.

25. *Rosh Hashanah* 17a; *Shabbat* 33b.

26. *Yoreh Deah* 376.4 (*Rema*).

27. Greenwald, op. cit., p. 375.

28. *Yoreh Deah* 376.4 (*Rema*).

29. Greenwald, op. cit., p. 376, in the name of Rabbi Ezekiel Landau, *Noda BeYehudah* on *Orach Chayyim* (Zolkiew: 1823), 8.

30. Zecharia Mendel of Cracow, *Beer Hetev, Orach Chayyim,* 132.5: See also Rabbi Yair Chayyim Bacharach, *Chavot Yair;* Immanuel Jakobovitz, *Journal of a Rabbi* (London: W. H. Allen, 1967), pp. 256–257.

31. *Zohar* 129b. "The *Shechinah* unites herself with the Holy tongue and all sanctifications with which the *Shechinah* is connected can be uttered only in the presence of at least ten persons." Cf. *Soferim* 10:7.

32. *Berachot* 21b. It is derived from the verse: "I shall be sanctified in the midst of the children of Israel" (Leviticus 22:32).

33. A.S.S., p. 160, 254, 280.

34. Ibid., p. 162.

35. Ibid., p. 486.

36. Ibid., p. 56.

37. *Yoreh Deah* 376.

38. A.S.S., p. 52.

39. A teaching of the *tannaim* that has been excluded from the *Mishnah*.

40. A.S.S., p. 52.

41. A.P.B., *Mishnah Shabbat* 2, pp. 390–393. This chapter contains the regulations concerning the material proper for the Sabbath lights.
42. *Keritot* 6a; A.P.B., pp. 547–548; A.S.S., pp. 476–478. The passage deals with the incense that was burned in the Temple morning and evening.
43. A.S.S., p. 328.
44. Ibid., p. 480.
45. Ibid., p. 125.
46. L. Kompert (1822–1886) quoted in J. H. Hertz, *Book of Jewish Thoughts* (London: 1920), pp. 199–200.

NOTES TO CHAPTER 8

1. *Moed Katan* 27b.
2. *Ketubot* 103b.
3. It is interesting to note that the Hebrew word *avel* has been used as a mnemonic to remind people where their duty lay. For *alef*, the first letter, can stand for *ish* (man), *ishah* (woman), *av* (father), *em* (mother), *ach* (brother), or *achot* (sister); while *bet*, the second letter, stands for *ben* (son) or *bat* (daughter). In addition, *lamed*, the third letter, is the sign for thirty (*sheloshim*). See also Abraham Lewysohn, *Sefer Mekore Minhagim Hanehugim Bivnei Yisroel* (Berlin: 1846), p. 136.
4. *Kitzur Shulchan Aruch* 216.2.
5. *Yoreh Deah* 402.
6. *Yoreh Deah* 340.18.
7. *Yoreh Deah* 402.7.
8. *Yoreh Deah* 391.2.
9. *Yoreh Deah* 391.2.
10. *Kitzur Shulchan Aruch* 212.1.
11. *Yoreh Deah* 391.3.
12. *Yoreh Deah* 391.3.
13. *Unterfuhrer* (Yiddish): a close relative who conducts the bride or groom under the wedding canopy.
14. *Yoreh Deah* 391.3.
15. Ibid.
16. *Yoreh Deah* 391.3 (*Rema*).
17. Provided there is no musical entertainment there. The *Minchat Eleazer*, however, forbids it.

18. Chaim N. Denburg, *Shulchan Aruch Yoreh Deah* (Montreal: The Jurisprudence Press, 1954), p. 330, note 38.
19. *Yoreh Deah* 399.1.
20. *Yoreh Deah* 399.1.
21. *Yoreh Deah* 339.9.
22. *Moed Katan* 24b; *Yoreh Deah* 399.7.
23. Ibid., section 1.1.
24. Ibid., section 2.
25. Ibid.
26. *Yoreh Deah* 390.4 (*Rema*).
27. Responsa on *Orach Chayyim* (Pressburg: 1855), no. 158, p. 61.
28. *Yoreh Deah* 390.7.
29. *Yoreh Deah* 390.5.
30. *Yoma* 39b.
31. I. Abrahams, op. cit., p. 315.
32. *Baba Kamma* 59b. When Eliezer Zeera was asked: What grounds have you for wearing black shoes? He said to them, "I am mourning for Jerusalem."
33. A. Asher, *The Itinerary of Rabbi Benjamin of Tudelo* (London and Berlin: A. Asher, 1840), p. 113; Abrahams, op. cit., p. 315, note 4.
34. Cecil Roth, *History of the Great Synagogue* (London: Edward Goldstone, 1954), p. 104.
35. *Yoreh Deah* 392.1.
36. Ibid.
37. *Moed Katan* 23a.
38. *Yoreh Deah* 392.2.
39. *Kitzur Shulchan Aruch* 213.3.
40. *Vayeychi* 225a.
41. *Shabbat* 152b.
42. Zimmels, *Ashkenazim and Sephardim* (London: Oxford University Press, 1958), p. 185.
43. *Taanit* 16a; *Sotah* 34b.
44. Numbers 13:7.
45. *Sotah* 34b.
46. *Abba Areka* (160–247), founder of the Sura Academy.
47. *Sanhedrin* 47b.
48. *Taanit* 16a.
49. *Hagigah* 3b.
50. *Niddah* 17a; *Sanhedrin* 65b.
51. *Orach Chayyim* 559.10 (*Rema*).

52. *Orach Chayyim* 581.4 (*Rema*).
53. *Orach Chayyim* 605 (*Rema*).
54. See below.
55. From the sentence in Proverbs 16:1, "The preparations of the heart are man's but the answer of the tongue is from the Lord."
56. *Sefer Chasidim,* ed. J. Wistinetzki (Berlin: Mekize Nirdamim, 1891), p. 271.
57. *Kitzur Shulchan Aruch* 26.14, 210.5.
58. Ibid.
59. Six feet.
60. *Yoreh Deah* 371.5.
61. Leviticus 21:1, "He shall not defile himself for the dead among his people." See also *Sifra* and *Yoreh Deah* 374.4.

NOTES TO CHAPTER 9

1. *Nedarim* 12a; *Yevamot* 122a and Rashi *ad. loc; Shevuot* 20a.
2. Zimmels, op.cit., p. 186, note 5. See also *Responsa* No. 80 and R. Isaac of Tyrnau in *Jewish Encyclopedia* (New York: Funk and Wagnalls, 1925), vol. 7, p. 65.
3. This is based on the story of the Creation. "It was evening, it was morning the first day" (Genesis 1:5); the evening came first.
4. That is, if a person died on *Rosh Chodesh Kislev* in a year when there was only one day of *Rosh Chodesh,* then, in a year when there are two days of *Rosh Chodesh, yahrzeit* should be observed on the second day of *Rosh Chodesh* (which is actually the first day of *Kislev*), since this is the real anniversary of the death. If, however, a person died on the first day of *Rosh Chodesh Kislev* in a year where there is only one day of *Rosh Chodesh,* the *yahrzeit* should be observed on the twenty-ninth day of *Cheshvan,* which is the true anniversary. In a case when the first *yahrzeit* fell in a year where there are two days of *Rosh Chodesh,* he should keep the *yahrzeit* on the first day of *Rosh Chodesh.* He is then considered as having set a precedent for observing the *yahrzeit* on the first day of *Rosh Chodesh* and should continue to do so in subsequent years, whether there are one or two days of *Rosh Chodesh* in them. One who has *yahrzeit* on any of the days of *Chanukah,* falling on or subsequent to *Rosh Chodesh Tevet,* should be careful not to count the

yahrzeit according to the particular days of *Chanukah*. The dates of the days of *Chanukah* in *Tevet* vary as to whether there are one or two days of *Rosh Chodesh*.

5. Isaac Luria, see Abraham Lewysohn, op. cit.
6. Conclusion. The portion selected from the books of the Prophets and read after the Reading of the Law.
7. A.P.B., p. 199.
8. Rashi, *Yevamot* 122a.
9. Joseph ben Moses, *Leket Yosher* (Breslau: 1903–1904), part 1, p. 49. See also Zimmels, op. cit., p. 187.
10. *Maavar Yabok* 15.94b.
11. I Samuel 31:13; II Samuel 1:12; Joel 1:17; Zechariah 7:4–7, 9.
12. *Nedarim* 12a.
13. Compendium. Name of a medieval Jewish legal codification often ascribed to either Rabbi Joseph b. Tobias or Rabbi Shemaryah b. Simchah.
14. See *Rema* on *Yoreh Deah* 402:12.
15. *Kitzur Shulchan Aruch* 221.6.
16. Ibid.
17. *Yoreh Deah* 376.4; Danzig, *Chochmat Adam* p. 171.
18. *Baba Batra* 10a.
19. Vessels. This chapter has seventeen *mishnayot* numerically equal to the Hebrew word *tov* (good).
20. Purity. The name is a euphemism for ritual uncleanliness, and all the treatises of the Order deal with the laws concerning impurity.
21. *Tohorot* is the sixth and last order of the *Mishnah*. It consists of twelve tractates. A.S.S., pp. 802–806.
22. *Kitzur Shulchan Aruch* 221.7, Abraham Zevi Hirsch Eisenstadt, *Pitche Teshuvah*.
23. The thirty-third day of the *Omer*, corresponding to the eighteenth day of *Iyyar*.
24. *Etz Chayyim* (Sudylkov: 1818), 22; *Sefirat Ha-Omer* 7.
25. A.P.B., p. 436; A.S.S., p. 870.
26. *Orach Chayyim* 621.5.
27. Jacob ben Judah Weil, first half of the fifteenth century, *Responsa* (Hanau: 1610) (quoted by J. D. Eisenstein, p. 97; Hurwitz, pp. 173, 392; *Sefer Chasidim* 1171–1172; *Siddur Rashi*, ed. S. Buber (Berlin: Mekitsei Nirdamim, 1910–1911), p. 214.
28. *Jewish Encyclopedia*, vol. 8, p. 456.
29. A.S.S., pp. 454–455.

30. *Die Synagogale Poesie des Mittelalters* (Berlin: Verlag von Julius Springer, 1855), chapter 2, quoted in A.P.B., p. 513.
31. A.S.S., p. 454; A.P.B., p. 423.
32. *Tanchumah Yelamdenu, Haazinu* and *Kol Bo.*
33. *Orach Chayyim* 284.7 *(Rema).*
34. I. Abrahams, *Hebrew Ethical Wills,* vol. 2 (Philadelphia: The Jewish Publication Society of America, 1962), p. 276.
35. Moses Gaster, *The Book of Prayer and Order of Service According to the Custom of the Spanish and Portuguese Jews* (London: University Press, 1936), vol. 1, pp. 200–201.
36. A.P.B., p. 423; A.S.S., p. 814.
37. A.P.B., pp. 1004–1005.
38. David De Sola Pool, *The Traditional Prayer Book* (New York: Behrman House, 1960), p. 474.

NOTES TO CHAPTER 10

1. Ezekiel 39:15; II Kings 23:17; II Samuel 18:17.
2. *Shekalim* 1:1; *Moed Katan* 6a.
3. *Shekalim* 2:5.
4. *Antiquities of the Jews* 13:6; *The Jewish War* 52.2.
5. *Yoreh Deah* 403.1–10.
6. Symbol of the soul of man, which is a spark of the heavenly fire.
7. Herald of the Messianic era.
8. H. J. Leon, "New Material about the Jews of Ancient Rome," in *Jewish Quarterly Review,* New Series (Philadelphia, 1929–1930), vol. 20, pp. 301–312.
9. S. W. Baron, in op. cit., p. 151.
10. *The Jewish Encyclopedia,* vol. 12, p. 193.
11. Israel Abrahams, *Jewish Life in the Middle Ages,* op.cit. p. 40.
12. *Laws and Byelaws of the Burial Society,* p. 16. See also Cecil Roth, *History of the Great Synagogue,* p. 103.
13. *The Laws and Byelaws of the Burial Society of the United Synagogue* states: "The propriety and orthography of inscriptions and of designs and emblems on a tombstone shall be subject to the approval of the Treasurers, whose decision shall be final. The name in Hebrew of the deceased and the Hebrew שלום or ת״נ״צ״ב״ה

must form part of every inscription. The dates according to the Jewish and Civil eras shall be permitted in the inscription" (p. 70).

14. A.P.B., pp. 434–435.
15. A.P.B., pp. 434–435.
16. Greenwald, op.cit., p. 384.
17. *The Jewish Encyclopedia*, vol. 12, p. 192.

NOTES TO CHAPTER 11

1. *Hagigah* 14b.
2. *Ecclesiasticus* 3:2.
3. Numbers 6:1–21.
4. *Yerushalmi* at end of *Kiddushin*.
5. I. Epstein, *The Faith of Judaism* (London: Soncino Press, 1954), p. 261.
6. *Avot* 6:9.
7. Maimonides, *Commentary on the Mishnah*, Introduction to *Sanhedrin* 10.
8. Also known as *Yechidah* (the only one) and *Chayyah* (living being), *Midrash* Genesis *Rabbah* 14.9.
9. Moses Nachmanides.
10. *Hagigah* 12b.
11. A.S.S., p. 18; A.P.B., p. 6; *Berachot* 60b.
12. *Berachot* 10a.
13. *Midrash Tehillim* (*Shocher Tov*), ed. S. Buber (Vilna: 1891). Psalm 103, p. 433.
14. *Tanchuma*, ed. S. Buber (Vilna: 1913), *Vaetchanan* 6.
15. *Shabbat* 55b.
16. *Shabbat* 55b.
17. Louis I. Newman, *The Hasidic Anthology* (New York: Bloch 1944), p. 71.
18. *Sotah* 1:7.
19. *Avot* 2:1.
20. *Shabbat* 31b.
21. *Avot* 1:3.
22. A.S.S., p. 178; A.P.B., p. 94.
23. *Avot* 4.19.
24. *Eruvin* 19a.

25. II *Kings* 16:3, 21:6.
26. *Menachot* 89b; *Eruvin* 19a; *Taanit* 10a.
27. *Berachot* 28b.
28. *Eduyot* 2:10.
29. Louis Newman, op. cit., p. 3.
30. Samuel Krauss, *Antoninus und Rabbi* (Frankfurt am Main: Sanger and Friedberg, 1910) identifies him with Avidius Cassius, general of Marcus Aurelius and a procurator of Judea.
31. *Sanhedrin* 91a–b.
32. Newman, op. cit., p. 4.
33. A.P.B., p. 255.
34. Genesis 2:8.
35. *Sifre*, Deuteronomy 10.67; *Midrash* to Psalm 11.7.51a; *Yalkut Shimoni, Genesis* (Polonnoye: 1806), 6.
36. *Shabbat* 152a. Cf. Dr. A. Cohen, *Everyman's Talmud* (London: J. M. Dent, 1937), p. 408.
37. *The Wisdom of Solomon* 3:1–4.
38. *Baba Batra* 75a.
39. *Berachot* 17a.
40. *Yad Ha-Chazakah Hilchot Melachim* 12:5.
41. A. Cohen, op. cit., p. 386.
42. Isidore Epstein, *The Faith of Judaism* (London: The Soncino Press, 1960), p. 323.
43. *Sanhedrin* 10:1.
44. *Commentary to Mishnah Sanhedrin* 10.1.
45. Abraham Wasserstein, *Flavius Josephus, Selections from His Works*, B'nai B'rith Jewish Heritage Classics (New York: The Viking Press, 1974), p. 189.
46. *Berachot* 9.5.
47. Norman Bentwich, *Josephus* (Philadelphia: The Jewish Publication Society of America, 1940), pp. 116–117.
48. B. Beall Todd, *Josephus' Description of the Essenes Illustrated by the Dead Sea Scrolls* (Cambridge, MA: Harvard University Press, 1988), p. 106.
49. Ibid.
50. A.S.S., p. 98; A.P.B., p. 95.
51. A.S.S., p. 100; A.P.B, p. 47.
52. *Emunot Ve-Deot, The Book of Beliefs and Opinion*, trans. by S. Rosenblatt (New Haven: Yale University Press, 1955), 7:7–19.
53. Commentary on *Sanhedrin* 92a.
54. Commentary on *Mishnah Sanhedrin* 10:1.
55. Series of verse prophecies in Greek hexameters from the

second century B.C.E. to the fourth century C.E. Didactic in nature and national in spirit, they unfold in mystical form the principles of Judaism.

56. Leviticus *Rabbah* 18.1, "Hadrian asked Rabbi Joshua ben Channaniah: 'From which part of the body will the Holy One, blessed be He, in time to come, cause man to sprout forth?' He answered: 'From the nut of the spinal column.' "

57. *De Cherubim* 1:159; Josephus, *Wars* 3:8.

58. Leviticus *Rabbah* 18.1.

59. *Pesikta Rabbata,* ed. M. Friedmann (Vienna: 1880), p. 161. "The resurrection of the dead will come through Elijah" (*Sotah* 9.15).

60. *Ketubot* 11a.

61. *Sanhedrin* 72a, 91a.

62. Charles B. Chavel, *Kitvei Ha-Rambam* (Jerusalem: Shilo Publishing House, 1963), vol. 1, p. 101.

63. *Zohar* 11:94a and 99b (*Mishpatim*).

64. Adin Steinsaltz, *The Thirteen Petalled Rose* (New York: Basic Books, 1980), pp. 63–64.

65. (Amsterdam: 1651), chapter 6, p. 28. Printed by Manasseh ben Israel.

66. *Dibbuk*—the soul of a sinner that attaches itself to a living body.

67. *Emunot Vedeot* (Belief and Opinions), trans. Samuel Rosenblatt (New Haven: Yale University Press, 1948), pp. 259–263.

68. *Or Adonai,* ed. S. G. Stern (Vienna: 1859), 4:7.

69. *Sefer Ha-Ikkarim* (Philadelphia: Jewish Publication Society of America, 1930), 4:29.

70. Deuteronomy 18:10–12; Leviticus 19:31, 20:8.

71. *Hilchot Avodah Zarah* 11:13; cf. A. E. Silverstone, *The Great Beyond and Other Essays* (London: A. H. Stockwell, 1932), p. 23.

72. A necromancer or a wizard. From Isaiah 8:19, it would appear that an *Ov* was a kind of ventriloquist who impersonated the dead.

73. *Berachot* 18b; *Gittin* 56b, 57a; *Shabbat* 152b; Genesis *Rabbah* 100.7.

74. *Berachot* 18b; *Gittin* 56b, 57a; *Shabbat* 152b; Genesis *Rabbah* 100.7.

75. Rabbi Zevi Hirsch Spira of Munkacz (d. 1913) in *Darchei Teshuvah Yoreh Deah* (Munkacz: 1903–1904), note 6, p. 179.

76. Louis Ginzberg, *Students, Scholars and Saints* (Philadelphia: The Jewish Publication Society of America, 1943), pp. 97–98.

NOTES TO CHAPTER 12

1. Rabbi Tarfon flourished toward the end of the first and the beginning of the second centuries.
2. Rabbi Jacob ben Korshai flourished toward the end of the second century. He was a disciple of Rabbi Meir and a teacher of Rabbi Judah Hanasi.
3. Rabbi Jose flourished at the beginning of the second century. He was a colleague of Rabbi Chananya ben Teradyon.
4. Rabbi Jochanan ben Nappacha (190–279) was head of the Academy at Tiberias.
5. Rabban Jochanan ben Zakkai flourished during the first century and belonged to the first generation of *tannaim*. He was one of the younger disciples of Hillel who spoke of him as "Master of Wisdom" and "Master of all time to come" (*Yerushalmi, Nedarim* 5.6).
6. Hillel, called "The Elder," flourished in the first century C.E. He was the founder of the school known as the "House of Hillel" and ancestor of a dynasty of patriarchs who held office until the fifth century.
7. Raba, a leading Babylonian Amora, who flourished in the middle of the fourth century. He established an academy in his native Mahoza.
8. Rabbi Zera, in a funeral oration at the untimely death of Rabbi Abin at the age of 28.
9. Rabbi Simeon ben Yochai (ca. 130–160 C.E.) was a disciple of Rabbi Akiva.
10. Friedmann edition, 73b.
11. I. H. Weiss and J. Schlossberg, eds. *Sifra* (Vienna: 1862), 45a.
12. Rabbi Meir flourished during the second century and was a disciple of Rabbi Akiva.
13. Beruryah, wife of Rabbi Meir.
14. Rabbi Joshua ben Chananyah was a disciple of Rabbi Jochanan ben Zaccai.
15. Rabbi Eleazar ben Arach flourished in the late first century.
16. William G. Braude, *The Midrash on Psalms*, Yale University Series, vol. 13 (New Haven: Yale University Press, 1959), vol. 2, p. 97.
17. Gerald Friedlander, *Pirke de Rabbi Eliezer* (London: Kegan Paul, 1916), Chapter. 34, pp. 256–257.
18. Rabbi Akiva ben Joseph was put to death by the Romans between 132 and 135 C.E.

18. Solomon Schechter, *Avot De Rabbi Nathan* (New York: Philipp Feldheim, 1945), second ed., p. 26.
19. Moses Maimonides, *Mishneh Torah, Book of Knowledge,* section on repentance, chapter 8.
20. A.S.S, p. 18; A.P.B., p. 5; *Berachot* 60b.
21. Moses ben Jacob Ibn Ezra (1055–1135), a Spanish Hebrew poet quoted by Chayyim Brody in *Festschrift zum achzigsten Geburstage Moritz Steinschneider* (Leipzig: Otto Harrassowitz, 1896), p. 430.
22. Manasseh ben Israel (1604–1657) was a rabbi, apologist, and theologian. This quotation is from his work *Nishmat Chayyim* (The Soul of Life) (Amsterdam: printed by the author on his own printing press, 1652), part II, Chapter 30.
23. Dr. Joseph Herman Hertz (1872–1946) was Chief Rabbi of the British Empire from 1913 to 1946. His publications include English commentaries on the Pentateuch and prayer book.
24. Rabbi Dr. Leo Jung, late spiritual leader of the New York Jewish Center, was the author and editor of many standard works of Judaica, including *The Jewish Library*, third series (New York: Jewish Publishing Co., 1934).
25. Moses Chayyim Luzzatto (1700–1747) was a Kabbalist, poet, and author of *Mesillat Yesharim* (Paths of the Upright), a major work on Jewish ethics. It was translated by Mordecai M. Kaplan (Philadelphia: Jewish Publication Society of America, 1936).
26. Rabbi Yitzchak Meir Alter, the *Chiddushei Harim,* was the founder of the Chasidic dynasty of Ger.
27. From "Death as Homecoming" in *Jewish Reflections on Death,* ed. J. Riemer (New York: Schocken Books, 1975), p. 59.
28. Abraham Joshua Heschel (1907–1972) was one of the great creative Jewish thinkers of modern times.

NOTES TO CHAPTER 13

1. During the Ten Days of Penitence from New Year to Day of Atonement, repeat the word *L'eyloh.* The two words *Min Kol* are contracted into one word *Mikol.*

Glossary

Adar—The twelfth month of the Jewish calendar.

Adar Sheni—In a leap year an extra month is added. This extra month is called *Adar Sheni* (the Second Adar).

Aggadah—Ethical or homiletical portions of rabbinic literature.

Alav Hashalom—May peace be to him. A phrase used when the name of a departed is mentioned.

Alehah Hashalom—May peace be to her.

Alenu—It is our duty. A prayer that is read at the end of all services.

Aliyah—Going up. A term used when one is called up to the Reading of the Law.

Altneuschul—Oldest synagogue in Prague, possibly founded in the eleventh century.

Amidah—The name by which the Prayer of the Eighteen Blessings (*Shemoneh Esray*) is known. The term *Amidah* (prayer said standing) is also known as *Tefillah*. It originally contained eighteen benedictions and now contains nineteen, while on the Sabbath and on festivals it has only seven benedictions.

Amora—Speaker or interpreter. The name given to the rabbinic authorities responsible for the *Gemara*.

Anim Zemirot—Hymn of Glory.

Aninut—The interval between death and burial.

Annos—a *sephardi* term for anniversary of a death.

Arba Turim—Code of Jewish law by Jacob ben Asher (1269-1342). It is divided into four parts: *Orach Chayyim, Yoreh Deah, Even Ha-Ezer,* and *Choshen Mishpat.*

Aron—A coffin.

Ashkenazim—Jews of Germany and their descendants.

Av—The fifth month of the Jewish calendar.

Av Bet Din—Vice-President of the court.

Avel (Avelim)—Mourner, one who has suffered the loss of a father or mother, a husband or wife, a son or daughter, or a brother or sister including a half-brother or half-sister.

Avelut—Mourning; the periods of formal mourning.

Av Ha-Rachamim—Requiem for the martyrs.

Bal Tashchit—Warning not to destroy something of value. Wanton destruction of property.

Bar—A son. Frequently appearing in personal names.

Bar Yochai—Son of Yochai. A reference to Rabbi Simeon ben Yochai, who flourished mid-second century. He was noted as a miracle worker.

Bar Mitzvah—Son of Commandment. A boy attaining thirteen years of age.

Barechu—"Bless ye the Lord Who is to be blessed." The invocation to prayer with which the Public Service now opens.

Bat-Kol—(Lit. "daughter of a voice," i.e., an echo.) In rabbinic literature the term denotes a heavenly voice.

Bedikat Chametz—Searching for leavened bread. The ceremony generally performed by the head of the house on the eve of the fourteenth of *Nisan.*

Bensch—Ashkenazi term meaning to "bless."

Beraita—Outside. A teaching of the *Tannaim* that has been excluded from the Mishnah.

Bet Din—House of law or judgment. A gathering of three or more learned men acting as a Jewish Court of Law.

Bet Hamidrash—House of Study.

Bet Olam—Eternal House, i.e., a cemetery.

Bet Taharah—A building in the cemetery used for ritual washing.

Bikkur Cholim—Visiting the sick.

Bimah—The platform in a synagogue on which the law is read and from which the Reader leads the congregation in prayer.

Brit Milah—Covenant. Circumcision ceremony.

Kabbalah—Jewish mysticism.

Chacham—Sage.

Chanukah—Dedication. The festival is celebrated for eight days from the twenty-fifth of *Kislev*. It commemorates the rededication of the Second Temple by Judah the Maccabee in 165 B.C.E.

Chasidim—Pietists, followers of Rabbi Israel Baal Shem **Tov** (1700–1760).

Chatam Sopher—Rabbi Moses Schreiber (1762–1839), known after his most distinguished work *Chatam, Sopher.*

Cheshvan—Popularly called *Marcheshvan*. Second month of the Jewish religious year, approximating October–November.

Chevrah Kaddisha—Holy Brotherhood. Title applied to charitable confraternity now generally limited to associations for burial of the dead.

Chodesh—Month.

Chol Ha-Moed—The half festive days or the secular days of Passover and *Sukkot*.

Chukkat Ha-goy—Pagan custom.

Dibbuk—A soul of a sinner that attaches itself to a living body.

Din—Law.

Duchaning—The priestly benediction prescribed in Numbers 6:23–27 and introduced into the repetition of the *Amidah* in the Morning Service and Additional Service. It is recited in the Diaspora only during the Additional Service on Festivals (except on a Sabbath) and the Day of Atonement.

Eichah—The opening word of the Book of Lamentations. The third of the Five Scrolls ascribed to the Prophet

Jeremiah. The book is read in the synagogue during the evening and morning services on the ninth of *Av*.

El Malay Rachamim—God full of compassion. A memorial prayer.

Elul—Sixth month of the Jewish calendar.

Eretz Yisrael—The land of Israel.

Etrog—A citron. One of the "four kinds of plants" used during the festival of *Sukkot*.

Gan Eden—Heaven, Garden of Eden, Paradise.

Gaon, pl. Geonim—The title of the head of the rabbinical academies in Babylon.

Gedol Ha-bayit—Head of the family.

Gehinnom—Hell, the Valley of Hinnom.

Gemara—See Talmud

Gevater—One who carries the infant during circumcision ceremony.

Gilgul—Transmigration of a soul.

Gosess—A dying person (Yiddish).

Guter Ort—The good place (a cemetery).

Hadlakah—Bonfire.

Haftarah—Conclusion. Concluding the Reading of the Torah with a passage from the Prophets.

Haggadah—Telling. The *Haggadah* is the book that tells the story of the Exodus from Egypt. It is part of the ritual of the Passover *Seder* (order) on the first two nights of Passover.

Hakkafot—Circuits. Processions with the Torah around the *Bimah* on *Simchat Torah*.

Halachah, pl. Halachot—Guidance. The law or the legal literature of the Jews.

Halbashah—Dressing of the dead.

Hallel—Hymns of praise consisting of six Psalms and recited on certain festive days of the year.

Halvayat Hamet—Attending a funeral.

Hashkavah—Memorial prayer among the Sephardim corresponding to the Ashkenazi prayer of *El Malay Rachamim*.

Havdalah—Division. The benedictions recited at the termination of the Sabbath and Festivals.

Hazkarat Neshamot—Memorial services.

Hesped—Eulogy.

Hevel—Vanity.

Hitlahavut—Religious ecstasy.

Hortus Judaeorum—Jewish graveyard.

Iyyar—The second month of the Jewish calendar.

Kaddish, pl. Kaddishim—Holy or sacred. Refers to the doxology recited in the synagogue by mourners during the period of mourning and on the anniversary of a death.

Kaddish De-Rabbanan—Scholar's Kaddish.

Kevod Hamet—Respect for the dead.

Keriah—Rending. The custom of rending the garment. Performed by near relatives before burial as a sign of deep grief.

Kiddush Hashem—Sanctification of God's Name, hence martyrdom.

Kinot—Lamentations recited on the ninth day of *Av.*

Kislev—The ninth month of the Jewish calendar.

Kittel—White garment worn as a shroud and by officials and many individuals in the synagogue during service on New Year and the Day of Atonement.

Kohen—A priest, a descendant of Aaron.

Kol Bo—Name of a medieval Jewish legal codification.

Kol Chamira—All manner of leaven.

Kol Nidrei—The Evening Service of the Day of Atonement is preceded by the chanting of *Kol Nidrei* (All Vows).

Lag B'Omer—The thirty-third day of the *Omer* corresponding to the eighteenth of *Iyyar,* the Scholar's Feast.

Lechah Dodi—Come my beloved. A hymn sung during the Friday evening service.

Leshon Ha-Kodesh—The holy tongue, Hebrew.

Maariv—Evening Service.

Maftir—Concluding. The last portion of the *Sidrah* is known as *Maftir.*

Maneh—Weight in gold or silver equal to fifty or one hundred common shekels.

Masorah—The body of tradition that concerns itself with the

correct spelling, writing, and reading of the Hebrew Bible.

Matzah — Unleavened bread.

Matzevah — Tombstone.

Me'abed Atzmo Ladaat — A suicide.

Megillah — "Scroll." A term commonly applied to the Book of Esther.

Memorbucher — Memorial books.

Menachem Avel — Comforting the mourner.

Menorah — Candelabrum.

Met Mitzvah — The corpse lying unattended with nobody to arrange for its burial. The duty of burying it is the responsibility of whoever discovers it, even if he is a high priest.

Midrash, pl. Midrashim — Expositions. The books devoted to the homiletic exposition of the Scriptures and the five *Megillot*.

Minchah — Afternoon Service.

Minhag — Custom, rite.

Minyan — Number or quorum. Ten men above the age of thirteen.

Mi-Sheberach — It is usual for a blessing to be invoked upon the one who is called up to the Reading of the Law. As a rule such a blessing is accompanied by an offering to the congregation or toward some charitable cause.

Mishloach Manot — Gifts to friends and neighbors during *Purim*.

Mishnah — Repetition. The collection of the statements of the *Tannaim* edited by Rabbi Judah the Patriarch (135–220). English translation by H. Danby, Oxford, 1933.

Mitnagged — (Lit. opponent.) Those who opposed Chasidism.

Mittah — Bed or bier.

Mitzvah — The obligation or duty ordained either by God or the rabbis.

Mohel — Circumciser.

Musaf — Additional prayers on Sabbath, holidays ,and *Rosh Chodesh*.

Nasi — Prince.

Nefesh—The soul.

Nefilat Appayim—"Falling on the face." Part of the *Tachanun* prayer. See also *Tachanun*.

Neshamah—Soul.

Nichum Avelim—The practice of visiting the *Avelim* to extend condolences.

Nisan—The first month of the Jewish calendar.

Ohel—Sepulcher.

Olam Haba—The world to come.

Omer—Sheaf. The seven weeks counted between Passover and Pentecost.

Onen—A mourner while his dead relatives are awaiting burial.

Or Zarua—Ritual code of Rabbi Isaac b. Moses (c. 1250).

Pardes—The realm of mysteries.

Passover—The festival commemorating the liberation of the Jews from their bondage in Egypt. The festival is kept for eight days, from the fifteenth of *Nisan* to the twenty-second (to the twenty-first in Israel).

Pidyon Ha-ben—Redemption of the firstborn son in a ceremony held on the thirty-first day of birth.

Piyyutim—Liturgical poetry for Sabbaths and the holidays.

Purim—"Lots." The festival is celebrated on the fourteenth of *Adar* in commemoration of the deliverance of the Jews in Persia from the hands of Haman.

Rashi—Abbreviation of Rabbi Solomon b. Isaac (1040–1105), the great commentator of the Bible and Talmud.

Rema—Glosses to *Shulchan Aruch* by Rabbi Moses Isserlis.

Responsa—Written replies (*Teshuvot*) given to questions on all aspects of Jewish law by qualified authorities from the time of the late *Geonim* to the present day.

Rosh Chodesh—New Moon.

Rosh Hashanah—New Year, the first and second days of *Tishri*.

Ruach—Breath (the soul).

Sandek—The one who holds the baby on his knees during the circumcision.

Seder—Order. The order of the home service on Passover.

Sefer Torah—The Book of the Law. The handwritten scroll of the Torah from which readings are made.

Sefer Zikaron—Book of Remembrance.

Selichot—Penitential prayers.

Semachot—(Heb.—joys) Euphemistic title of the small tractate *Evel Rabbati* that deals with the laws of mourning.

Sephardim—Jews who trace their descent to the Jews of Spain (*Sepharad*) and of its sister country, Portugal.

Seudah—Festive meal.

Seudah Shelishit—(Heb.—Third Meal) The third meal eaten on Sabbath afternoon.

Seudat Havraah—Meal provided for mourners by neighbors on return from the funeral.

Seudat Mitzvah—Meal of the Commandment, i.e., a meal that is a religious occasion.

Shabbat Ha-Gadol—Name given to the Sabbath before Passover.

Shacharit—Morning prayer recited daily.

Shalach Manot/Mishloach Manot—The sending of gifts to friends, usually two kinds of sweetmeats on *Purim*.

Shalom Aleichem—Peace be upon you. Opening words of hymn welcoming the Sabbath angels to the home.

Shalosh Seudot—See *Seudah Shelishit*

Shammash—(Heb.—servant) A sexton or usher of the Bet Din.

Shavuot—Pentecost or the Feast of Weeks celebrated on the sixth and seventh of *Sivan*.

Shechinah—The Divine Presence.

Shehecheyanu—Who has kept us alive. A benediction pronounced as a blessing of thanksgiving for certain things when they are enjoyed for the first time. The occasion may be general (e.g., the acquisition of new things) or seasonal (like the advent of a Festival).

Sheloshim—Thirty. The thirty days of full mourning after which the bereaved observed a period of semi-mourning till the expiration of twelve months.

Shema—Hear. Refers to those sections of Scripture recited

every morning and evening (Deuteronomy 6:4–9, 11:13–21; Numbers 15:37–41).

Shemini Atzeret—The Feast of the Eighth Day or the Eight Days of Solemn Assembly (Numbers 30:35). Last day of the Festival of *Sukkot* (Tabernacles).

Shene Luchot Haberit—*Two Tablets of the Covenant* by Rabbi Isaiah Horowitz (1565–1630). The work deals with Kabbalistic tendencies in Jewish laws and customs.

Sheol—The nether world of the grave.

Shevat—The eleventh month of the Jewish calendar.

Shinnui Hashem—Change of name.

Shivah—Seven, refers to the seven days of mourning.

Shochet—A ritual slaughterer.

Shofar—A ram's horn used in the services of *Rosh Hashanah* and at the conclusion of *Yom Kippur*.

Shulchan Aruch—Table Prepared. A Code of Jewish Law by Rabbi Joseph Caro (1488–1575), and first published in 1565.

Shushan Purim—The day succeeding *Purim*. Referred to in Esther 9:18 as that on which the Jews of Shushan (Susa) celebrated their triumph; celebrated as a minor festival.

Siddur—The prayer book of the Jews.

Sidra—Weekly Torah portion.

Simchah—A joyous occasion.

Simchat Torah—Rejoicing of the Law. The festival immediately after *Shemini Atzeret*.

Sivan—Ninth month of the Jewish calendar.

Siyyum—Completion. When a course of study is completed the occasion is marked by a celebratory meal.

Sukkah—The festive booth for Tabernacles (Leviticus 23:34).

Sukkot—This Festival commemorates the wandering of the children of Israel in the wilderness and is observed from the fifteenth to the twenty-third of *Tishri*.

Tabernacles—See *Sukkot*

Tachanun—Supplicatory prayers. Recited at morning and afternoon services.

Tachrichim—Shrouds of the dead.

Taharah—The ritual of cleansing a corpse.

Tahorot—Cleanliness and purification. One of the six orders of the Mishnah.

Tallit—The prayer shawl.

Talmud—The general sense of the word is study of the law. It is more common in the narrow sense of the comments and the discussions (*Gemara*) on the text of the *Mishnah* by the Palestinian and Babylonian scholars from the third to the fifth centuries C.E. that constitute the Palestinian Talmud and the Babylonian Talmud. The Babylonian Talmud (*Bavli*) contains nearly 3,000 pages and was edited by Rav Ashi (352–427), whereas the Palestinian Talmud (*Yerushalmi*) was finished in the fifth century and is only one-seventh as long as the Babylonian Talmud.

Tammuz—The fourth month of the Jewish calendar.

Tanna—A teacher quoted in the *Mishnah* or *Beraita*.

Targum—Aramaic translation of the Bible.

Techinah—Supplication. A supplementary devotional prayer in Yiddish.

Tefillin—Phylacteries. Small cases containing passages from the Scriptures and affixed to the forehead and arm during the recital of morning prayers (Deuteronomy 6:8).

Tevet—Tenth month of the Jewish calendar.

Tisha B'Av—The fast of the ninth of *Av* commemorates the destruction of both the First and the Second Temples (586 B.C.E. and 70 C.E.).

Tishri—The seventh month of the Jewish calendar.

Torah—Hebrew word meaning teaching, instruction, or guidance. Torah represents the whole body of Jewish teaching from the commencement of the Bible right down to our own day.

Tosafot—Critical glosses on the Talmud by French rabbis of the twelfth and thirteenth centuries. Printed together with Rashi in all standard editions of the Talmud.

Tur—Code by Rabbi Jacob ben Asher. The full title is *Arba Turim*.

Tzaddik—A righteous man. A person outstanding for his faith and piety, especially a chasidic rabbi or leader.

Tzedakah—Righteousness, charity.

Tzidduk Ha-Din—Acknowledgment of Divine judgment. Part of burial service.

Tzitzit—The biblical name of the fringes that are attached to each of the four corners of the garment (Numbers 14:38).

Unterfuhrer—The person who leads the bride or bridegroom under the wedding canopy. The *Unterfuhrers* are usually the parents of the bride and groom, or in their absence, a married couple, if possible, closely related to them.

Viddui—Confession.

Yahrzeit—Anniversary of death.

Yetziat Neshamah—Departure of the soul.

Yizkor—Popular name for Memorial Service; the full title is Hazkarat Neshamot. This is recited on Passover, *Shavuot, Sukkot,* and *Yom Kippur.*

Yom Ha-Shoah—Holocaust Remembrance Day.

Yom Kippur—The Day of Atonement.

Yom Tov—A good day. Generally applied to holidays and festivals.

Yoreh Deah—Second part of the *Shulchan Aruch.* Deals mainly with dietary and ritual laws including mourning.

Zecher Tzaddik Livrachah—May the memory of the righteous be for a blessing.

Zechut Avot—The merit of the Fathers.

Zechur Retov—May he be remembered for good.

Zohar—Title of the mystical work introduced into Spain by Moses de Leon at the end of the thirteenth century and attributed to Rabbi Simeon bar Yochai of the second century. It was first published in Mantua, 1558–1560. English translation edited by M. Simon, five volumes (London: Soncino Press, 1932).

Zuz—Silver coin, one-fourth of a shekel.

BIBLIOGRAPHY

Abrahams, I., ed. *Hebrew Ethical Wills*. Philadelphia: The Jewish Publication Society of America, 1926.

_____. *Jewish Life in the Middle Ages*. London: Edward Goldstone, 1932.

The Art Scroll Siddur. New York: Mesorah, 1987.

Baron, S. W. *The Jewish Community*. Philadelphia: Jewish Publication Society of America, 1942.

Bender, A. P. "Belief, Rites and Customs of the Jews Connected with Death, Burial and Mourning." *The Jewish Quarterly Review* 1895;7:101–118, 259–270.

Buber, S., ed. *Siddur Rashi*. Berlin: Mekitsei Nirdamin, 1910–1911.

Chavel, C. B. *Rambam: His Life and Teachings*. New York: Philipp Feldheim, 1960.

Cowley, A. E. *Aramaic Papyri of the Fifth Century B.C.* Oxford: Clarendon Press, 1923.

Denburg, C. N., trans. *Code of Hebrew Law (Shulchan Aruch, Yoreh Deah, 3350–3403)*. Montreal: The Jurisprudence Press, 1954.

De Sola Pool, D. *The Old Jewish Aramaic Prayer, the Kaddish*. Leipzig: Rudolf Haupt, 1909.

_____. *The Traditional Prayer Book*. New York: Behrman House, 1960.

Eisenstein, J. D. *Ozar Dinim U Minhagim*. New York: J. D. Eisenstein, 1917.

Feldman, E. *Biblical and Post-Biblical Defilement and Mourning Law as Theology*. New York: Ktav, 1977.

Friedlander, G., ed. *Pirke De Rabbi Eliezer*. London: Kegan Paul, 1916.

Friedmann, M., ed. *Seder Eliyahu Rabba VeSeder Eliyahu Zuta*, 2nd ed. Jerusalem: Bamberger Wahrman, 1960.

Ganzfried, S.,ed. *Kitzur Shulchan Aruch*. Leipzig: Feldman, 1933.

Ginzberg, L. *The Legends of the Jews*. Philadelphia: Jewish Publication Society of America, 1913.

Greenberg, S., ed. *A Treasury of Comfort*. Hartford, CT: Hartmore House, 1954.

Greenwald, L. *Kol Bo Al Avelut*. New York: Moriah Printing Company, 1947.

————. *Kol Bo Al Avelut, Chelek Sheni*. Brooklyn: Hadar Linotyping & Publishing Co., 1949–1950.

The Handbook of Life. London: The Chevra Kadisha, 1909.

Hertz, J. H. *Authorised Daily Prayer Book*. London: Shapiro Vallentine, 1962.

————. *Book of Jewish Thoughts*. London: Oxford University Press, 1935.

Higger, M. *Samachot and Samachot of Rabbi Chiyya*. New York: Bloch, 1931.

Hurwitz, S., ed. *Machsor Vitry*. Nuremberg: I. Bulka, 1923.

Hyamson, A. M. *The Sephardim of England*. London: Methuen, 1951.

Hyamson, M. *Rules and Regulations of the Chevrah Kaddisha Orach Chaim*. New York: Orach Chaim, 1942.

Idelson, A. Z. *Jewish Liturgy and Its Development*. New York: Schocken Books, 1967.

Jakobovitz, I. *Jewish Medical Ethics*. New York: Bloch, 1975.

————. *Journal of a Rabbi*. London: W. H. Allen, 1967.

Jewish Encyclopedia. New York: Funk & Wagnalls, 1925.

Joseph, M. *A Jewish Book of Comfort for Mourners*. London: Eyre & Spottiswoode, 1917.

Jung, L. *The Jewish Library–Third Series*. New York: Jewish Library Publishing Co., 1934.

Kagan, I. M. *Mishnah Berurah*. Warsaw: 1910.

Lamm, M. *The Jewish Way in Death and Mourning*. New York: Jonathan David Publishers, 1975.

Lamm, N., and Wurtzburger, W. S. *A Treasury of Tradition*. New York: Hebrew Publishing, 1967.

Laws and Byelaws of the Burial Society. London: United Synagogue, 1955.

Lewysohn, A. *Sefer Mekore Minhagim Hanehugim Bivnei Yisroel*. Berlin: 1946.

Linzer, N., ed. *Understanding Bereavement and Grief*. New York: Ktav, 1977.

Lipman, V. D. *Social History of the Jews in England 1850–1950*. London: Watts, 1954.

Luban, M. *The Kaddish*. New York: Yeshiva University Press, 1962.

Maimonides, M. *Mishneh Torah Hilchot Avel*. New York: 1947.

Marmorstein, A. *The Doctrine of Merits in Old Rabbinic Literature*. London: Oxford University Press, 1920.

Nachmanides, M. *Torat ha-Adam*. Warsaw: 1841.

Newman, L. I. *The Hasidic Anthology*. New York: Bloch, 1944.

Pachino, M. B. *Towards an Understanding of Jewish Funeral and Mourning Practices*. New York: Union of Orthodox Jewish Congregations of America, 1966.

Pollack, H. *Jewish Folkways in Germanic Lands, 1648–1806*. Cambridge, MA.: The M.I.T. Press, 1971.

Prothero, R. E. *The Psalms in Human Life*. New York: E. P. Dutton, 1908.

Riemer, J. *Jewish Reflections on Death*. New York: Schocken Books, 1975.

Roth, C. *History of the Great Synagogue*. London: Edward Goldstone, 1950.

———. *A History of the Jews in England*. Oxford: Clarendon Press, 1941.

———. *The Jewish Contribution to Civilization*. Oxford: The East and West Library, 1938.

Schechter, S,. ed. *Abot de Rabbi Nathan*. New York: Philipp Feldheim, 1945.

Silverstone, A. E. *The Great Beyond and Other Essays*. London: A. H. Stockwell, 1932.

Soloveitchik, J. B. *Jewish Reflections on Death*. New York: Schocken Books, 1975.

Sperka, S. J. *Eternal Life: A Digest of All Laws of Mourning*. New York: Bloch, 1939.

Spiro, J. D. *A Time to Mourn*. New York: Bloch, 1967.

Stavsky, D. *For Thou Art with Me, a Manual of Mourning*. New York: Philipp Feldheim, 1965.

Steinberg, D. M. *Responsum*. London: Beth Din, 1957.

Steinsaltz, A. *The Thirteen Petalled Rose*. New York: Basic Books, 1980.

Students, Scholars and Saints. Philadelphia: The Jewish Publication Society of America, 1943.

Todd, B. B. *Josephus' Description of the Essenes Illustrated by the Dead Sea Scrolls*. New York: Cambridge University Press, 1988.

Toperoff, S.P. *Eternal Life, a Handbook for the Mourner*. Newcastle-upon-Tyne: Old Hebrew Congregation, 1972.

Tuchachinsky, Y. M. *Gesher ha-Chayyim*. 2 vols. Jerusalem: 1944.

Unterman, I. J. *Shevet Miyehudah*. Jerusalem: Mosad Harav Kook, 1955.

Weiss, I. H., and Schlossberg, T., eds. *Sifra*. Vienna: Jacob Schlossburg, 1862.

Wertheim, S., ed. *Savfika Abudraham*. Jerusalem: Usha Press, 1963.

Zimmels, H. J. *Askhenazim and Sephardim*. London: Oxford University Press, 1958.

_____ . *Magicians, Theologians and Doctors*. London: Edward Goldstone, 1952.

Zlotnick, D. *The Tractate "Mourning."* New Haven: Yale University Press, 1966.

Index